Faith and Choice in
the Works of Joss Whedon

Faith and Choice in the Works of Joss Whedon

K. Dale Koontz

McFarland & Company, Inc., Publishers
Jefferson, North Carolina, and London

LIBRARY OF CONGRESS CATALOGUING-IN-PUBLICATION DATA

Koontz, K. Dale, 1968–
　　Faith and choice in the works of Joss Whedon /
K. Dale Koontz.
　　　　p.　　cm.
　　Includes bibliographical references and index.

　　ISBN 978-0-7864-3476-3
　　softcover : 50# alkaline paper ∞

　　1. Whedon, Joss, 1964– — Criticism and interpretation.
2. Television broadcasting — Religious aspects.　I. Title.
PN1992.4.W49K66　　2008
791.4302'33092 — dc22　　　　　　　　　　2008003188

British Library cataloguing data are available

©2008 K. Dale Koontz. All rights reserved

*No part of this book may be reproduced or transmitted in any form
or by any means, electronic or mechanical, including photocopying
or recording, or by any information storage and retrieval system,
without permission in writing from the publisher.*

On the cover: James Marsters and Nathan Fillion in a 2003 episode of *Buffy the Vampire Slayer* (UPN/Photofest). Front cover by TG Design.

Manufactured in the United States of America

*McFarland & Company, Inc., Publishers
　Box 611, Jefferson, North Carolina 28640
　　www.mcfarlandpub.com*

For BJ and Emily.
It was my labor, but you
were the midwives.

I had some things go on in my life that made me say: "I really want to get this message out, that it's not about blood."

— Joss Whedon

"When I talk about belief, why do you always assume I'm talking about God?"

— Shepherd Book, *Serenity*

Author's Note

In the summer of 1998, I was spending my days preparing to take the examination that would (hopefully) authorize me to practice law. Three difficult, rigorous, expensive years of study would all boil down to a merciless two-day tour of Hell that was designed to test my legal knowledge, ability to write under ridiculous deadline pressure, and overall endurance.

It was not a season of fun and sun.

No sensible person walks alone through the Valley of the Shadow of Death, so I had a study partner — the idea was that we would keep each other on track, drilling each other relentlessly on obscure points of law (as if there's another kind) to better prepare for the examination.

We went at it hammer and tongs until we could smoothly parrot the required elements of a negligence action, the finer points of obtaining personal jurisdiction over an out-of-state defendant, the dreaded Rule Against Perpetuities, and easily fifty other things that sane persons do not fret over.[1]

My study partner was a fan of a television show with the improbable title of *Buffy the Vampire Slayer*. When she tried to explain it to me, I thought she had been studying too hard. I recall that I listened politely, nodded my head a few times, and promptly dismissed the whole thing as the result of academically induced insanity. I hoped it was a temporary condition, as I quite liked her and found her to be a logical person, aside from this odd quirk.

Despite this touch of the weird, I couldn't deny that she was smart and funny, with an ability to make me laugh even when I was worried that I wouldn't work out as well as I hoped. In the kind, patient way of friends who are trying to point out the rubies on the breakfast table that others persist in not seeing, she kept asking me to give the show a try.

So really, this is all her fault.[2]

Hope she likes it.

Table of Contents

Author's Note   vii
Introduction   1

Part 1. Purpose: The Road to Damascus

1. What's a Key Without a Lock?: Dawn and the Promise of Purpose   13
2. Growing After Death: Angel, Spike and the Evolution of the Soul   27

Part 2. Family: A Place at the Table

3. Coming Apart, but Moving Forward: Magic Twins and Older Sisters in *Fray*   49
4. A Family of Believers, Just Not in the Same Thing: Faith in the *Firefly* Family   65

Part 3. Redemption: The Past Is Not a Prison

5. The One That Almost Got Away: Doyle and the Fish Story   85
6. "I Got No Rudder": Navigating the Sea of Faith with Malcolm Reynolds   98

7. The Depth of Shadows: Redemption and Doubt in
   Shepherd Book   119
8. Prodigal Daughter: Faith and Homecoming   132

Part 4. Zealotry: Blood and Fire

9. Burning River: Witchcraft and the "Other" in *Firefly*   149
10. No Girls Allowed: Caleb and the Evils of Misogyny   164

Conclusion: Buffy Goes (Back) to School   185
Chapter Notes   191
Primary Sources — Buffy the Vampire Slayer   205
Primary Sources — Angel   211
Primary Sources — Firefly   216
Primary Sources — Other   217
Bibliography   219
Index   227

Introduction

In the beginning were the names. Buffy. Xander. Willow. Angel. Cordelia. Doyle. Mal. River. Inara. Names that were exotic to me, living in a land populated by Davids and Lauras and Mikes. And I was tickled by what Joss Whedon was doing.

Then came the stories. High school as concentric circles of hell. Darkness desperately searching for light. Proud folks just trying to get along without being pushed and prodded by Those Who Know Best. And I was smitten by what Joss Whedon was doing.

Then Whedon took my expectations and turned them upside down. No, not just turned them upside down, but gutted them and showed me complex people dealing with responsibility and regret and loss and shame and redemption for past wrongs. Always, above all, redemption. Television series that were ostensibly fluffy, throwaway, slang-filled eye candy were instead populated with characters who were grappling with issues of sin and grace — and grappling with these issues far too often to dismiss the themes as simply being a plot device for a "very special episode." There was something much more going on here, something that was well worth exploring in depth. And I was entranced by what Whedon was doing.

The material in this book encompasses the characters, circumstances, and rules of the worlds of the television series *Buffy the Vampire Slayer*, *Angel*, and *Firefly*; the eight-issue comic book miniseries *Fray*; the three-issue comic book miniseries which bridges the events of *Firefly* to those in the feature film *Serenity*, and the feature film itself, all of which were created by Joss Whedon, third generation television writer and self-proclaimed nonbeliever.[1] When asked about his beliefs, Whedon has described himself as being "a very hard-line, angry atheist. Yet I am fascinated by the concept of devotion" (Nussbaum).

Huh-what?

There is a certain tension between Whedon the atheist creator and his work, which often crackles with hope for a better tomorrow. After all, what's an atheist doing giving the masses stories about redemption and grace in the first place?

Whedon's willingness to break out of accepted standards and blaze a new narrative trail was one of the first aspects of his work to attract my notice. After all, it would seem to be far more usual for a man who grew up digesting story structure and demographic appeal along with his mashed potatoes to stick to the tried-and-true. In network television, this often means shows about sexy blonde girls who haven't the common sense of a half-grown pup. With his creation of Buffy, a blonde cheerleader who discovers that it's her responsibility to save the world from the things that go bump in the night, Whedon negated the damaging stereotype of young girls who serve merely as bouncy victims. Instead, Whedon created something fresh in the world of televisual narrative. He's continued to mix genres and twist conventions to tell compelling stories ever since.

While his various shows contain no single unifying image—*Firefly* doesn't have vampires, *Buffy* doesn't have spaceships, and *Angel* and *Fray* don't have high school—there are *themes* that crop up again and again. These themes are Whedon's through-line; his ABCs, if you will. Chief among those themes are Whedon's literal ABCs—*acceptance, belief,* and *choice.* The vampires and the spaceships are really only window dressing, for Whedon is far more concerned with relationships, writing eloquently about what draws people together. Quite often, that tie is based on acceptance of others far more than mere biological blood ties. His stories instruct viewers in the ways of "big tent" belief and the consequences of choices.

The late cinematic master Ingmar Bergman lamented what he saw as increased isolationism in art, stating that "we finally gather in one large pen, where we stand and bleat about our loneliness without listening to each other.... The individualists stare into each other's eyes and yet deny the existence of each other" (xxii). Bergman longed to work collectively with others to create an artistic cathedral of great beauty, regardless of his own personal agnostic beliefs (xxii). While Bergman may have been a doleful agnostic and Whedon declares himself to be an ornery atheist, the work of both reflects a similar desire to build a cathedral in which all are welcome and in which meaningful relationships are honored. This is not a stone-and-mortar cathedral, but rather is one crafted of stories. Stories that, hopefully, serve to connect people with one another rather than leaving us bleating obliviously in our pens. For stories can be a haven of belief, as surely as a cathedral can be.

Stories, especially those spun by skilled tellers of tales, provide us with effective tools to thrive in the world. Beginning with *Buffy the Vampire Slayer* in 1997, Whedon has given viewers a vast array of morally complex characters who may not be traditionally heroic (Spike and Jayne leap to mind), but who are nevertheless compelling and even likable. Whedon has created hundreds of environments in which his characters can move and breathe; fantasy worlds rich in detail and nuance which fully embody G. K. Chesterton's sly observation that "Fairy tales are more than true: not because they tell us that dragons exist, but because they tell us that dragons can be beaten" (qtd. in Gaiman, *Coraline*). Whedon has demonstrated over and over again how dragons can be beaten — and while the dragons of Whedon's stories are sometimes literal, usually they are of the metaphoric sort, which often are much more difficult to vanquish.

Regardless of how technologically advanced a culture may become, there is no escaping the truth that stories are important. Stories serve as reminders that all of humankind, including the rich and powerful, are afflicted with problems. In fact, supermarket checkouts would be bare indeed without the celebrity tabloids that exist to remind us of this fact. Moreover, stories provide practical advice for everyday living, giving us hints and clues regarding the road ahead. However, there seems to be a lingering fallacy that dry nonfiction is the vehicle best suited to educate readers about serious topics. This view unfairly discounts literature as a whole, especially the genre of fictional fantasy, of which Terri Windling has eloquently written, "The fantasy story or novel differs from novels of social realism in that it is free to portray the world in bright, primary colors, a dream-world half remembered from the stories of childhood when all the world was bright and strange, a fiction unembarrassed to tackle the large themes of Good and Evil, Honor and Betrayal, Love and Hate."

Often, viewers dislike the inclusion of prominent "large themes" in popular entertainment — modern life just seems too uncertain to expend precious time and energy in considering our own conscription into the eternal battle of Good versus Evil. This egocentric line of reasoning stakes its position as *C'mon — why bother to expand my circle of care beyond my personal concerns and my particular moments? Everyone knows we live in dark and uncertain times; the stakes are higher now than ever. Let's have more car chases and less introspection.*

While such cynical viewers may consider themselves to be rational creatures who are skeptical of supernatural explanations, most people continue to engage in rituals that are not so very far removed from pure superstition as they may like to think. Such rituals include keeping a lucky coin, wishing on the first star at twilight, playing one's "lucky numbers" on a weekly lottery ticket, or making a birthday wish before blowing out the candles on the cake. When these demonstrations of belief in the supernatural are pointed out, the response is often, *Well, maybe. But that's a long way from believing in something as ridiculous as vampires! That's just silly!*

Yet the older part of our brains — the more primitive, lizard part of our consciousness that screams at us to fight or flee, but always to survive — still causes our vestigial hackles to rise and makes us shiver with fear when a vampire asks to come in. And they do ask to come in. Oh, maybe not actual blood-sucking fiends of the night, intent on battening on our hemoglobin, but there are vampires among us — people who delight in dragging us down out of the light we should rightfully walk in with our shoulders squared and our backs straight. In much the same way, there are demons in our lives — maybe not literal hell-born creatures with too many teeth and curved claws, but we are faced daily with temptations to leave the sunlit path, to live for ourselves only, disdain our fellow man, and curse the needs and concerns of others. To Whedon, the surest way to fight these vampires and demons is to band with others. We must draw our strength from our ties and relationships, for we're all in this fight together and it is far too big for any of us to successfully handle it alone.

There would seem to be a challenge, perhaps even a paradox, involved in writing about concepts of faith in characters created by an avowed atheist. It is true that Whedon's personal atheism is a fascinating element (and one which is given thoughtful consideration) in the examination of the role various aspects of faith play in the lives of his intricately imagined characters. However, Whedon's religious views (or lack thereof) need not pose an insurmountable stumbling block. There is no need that the discussion be forced to fit a particular Procrustean bed and "faith" need not be limited to mean "faith in the Divine." Whedon is an artist, which means by definition that he has the ability to imagine and create beyond that which he can perceive with the five senses. He then presents his creations to a wider audience to ponder and enjoy. We need artists to help us experience that which is beyond our personal knowledge — just imagine how boring life would be if only Russian Jews could truly appreciate the magnificent works of Marc Chagall or if only residents of the American Southwest could fully enjoy the lonely vistas of Georgia O'Keefe.

Also, since one of Whedon's primary strengths is his nearly uncanny ability to create fully realized characters, very little about any single character is neatly squared off, which gives rise to lively debates among fans and scholars alike regarding a character's motivations and thought processes.

Therefore, any attempt to jam these vibrant, three-dimensional characters into a rigid form would be to ignore one of the principal delights of Whedon's work, which is the appeal of watching messy, complex characters interact and develop. Viewers often do not quite "get" these characters, who seem pathological, puzzling, and pitiable in turns; however, viewers feel compelled to keep watching in order to continue trying to figure them out. These perpetual mysteries, which in the hands of a lesser talent would just be a grinding annoyance, are actually one of the crowning glories of Whedon's work.

Whedon's stories boldly challenge viewers to become deeply involved and emotionally invested in the parameters of the stories and characters presented; certainly to a degree beyond that usually asked by contemporary popular entertainment. Of course, this requires more active engagement on the part of the viewer than many shows require. In order to gain insight and discover the treasures beneath the surface allusions and references, viewers must be willing to dig deeper into the content of the frame and, consequently, into themselves as well. Matthew Pateman has commented on the Catch-22 nature of seriously critiquing Whedon, writing that the paradox is that "*Buffy* criticism cannot be 'real' because it is too influenced by fandom; or else it is so lacking in the required celebratory gestures of fandom that it is not 'true' to the show" (208). Hopefully, this book will successfully navigate the Scylla and Charybdis of fans and scholars, with each gleaning useful information from the text.

In some ways, Whedon has simply repackaged (albeit in a fresh and creative manner) ideas that have been lurking about for centuries. It is certainly not a contemporary idea to use faith to inform and affect popular culture. Throughout the history of Western civilization, no organization has wielded more power in this area than the Catholic Church and, indeed, the mythos of Western Christianity is the primary template held up to Whedon's work throughout this book. The Church quickly grasped the power of the visual arts to instruct and inform a primarily illiterate public and sought to tightly control the content of artistic portrayals in order to protect the public from unwholesome, even blasphemous, art that might lead down the dark path of sin. For example, during the Second Council of Nicea in the eighth century, church leaders compiled an extensive laundry list of what body parts of saints and religious figures could and could not be portrayed in paintings.[2] This stranglehold continued for centuries and was reiterated at the Council of Trent in 1563 when the Church decreed that the accurate depiction of Catholic dogma was to be strictly followed in all painting and sculpture (Heins 170).

However, artists have always found ways around the restrictive fence of rules. As an example, the Renaissance artist Paolo Veronese was questioned by Church authorities about his painting *The Last Supper* which contained such "vulgar" elements as a dog, jesters, and dwarfs. Veronese bravely defended his choices in the name of artistic inspiration, but the inquisitors were satisfied only when he changed the title to the "less sanctified" *Feast in the House of Levi* (Heins 170).[3] In a similar fashion, Whedon's blending of the sacred and the secular has often been viewed as irreverent and even profane. For example, his creation of the misogynistic ex-priest Caleb created a great deal of outrage among certain fundamentalist Christians, who viewed the character as a mockery of their beliefs.

Of course, the Catholic Church has never been the sole force attempting to regulate the "suitability" of subject matter reaching the masses, as society as a whole has performed that function for centuries. Again, artists are smart enough to wriggle under the fence, regardless of who erects it. Masterworks of the Enlightenment such as *The Toilet of Venus* and *The Death of Socrates* contain elements that have been deemed pornographic.[4] Also, the works of the Victorian artist Gustave Doré most likely would not have been welcomed so enthusiastically into the parlors of social leaders had they not been tastefully entitled *The Deluge* and *Jehu's Companions Finding the Remains of Jezebel*.[5] Nowadays, graphic depictions of violence are much more commonplace and Whedon's work certainly does not shy away from the portrayal of the consequences of violent actions.

Today, elements of faith continue to crop up in popular culture, often to the discomfiture of the established cultural gatekeepers.[6] Examples abound, but a brief examination of three should suffice to illustrate the point. First, in the 1980s, a singer with the religiously laden name "Madonna" shot to the forefront of the pop music scene with her canny use of religious icons as fashion accessories. This created an uproar of near–Biblical proportions as her legions of young, female fans rushed to emulate the look by decking themselves with crosses. Whedon's body of work includes many instances of Christian iconography, especially the Christian cross, which is used more as a powerful vampire repellent than as a simple fashion accessory. The vampire itself can be read as an inverse of basic Christian belief and is discussed in that context in the next section.

Second, in 1999, Lions Gate Films released the Kevin Smith film *Dogma* which treated the Catholic faith as simultaneously something to be reverenced and something to be poked at with a sharp, often vulgarly worded, stick.[7] While the Catholic League denounced the film as blasphemous, viewers apparently disagreed and the film turned a tidy profit. In a similar fashion, Whedon's works continue to tickle and engage the imaginations and intellects of fans and scholars alike.

Third, from 1995 to 2000, Garth Ennis produced the highly original comic series *Preacher* for DC/Vertigo. *Preacher* tells the tale of Jesse Custer, a disillusioned man of the cloth who has been blessed (or cursed, depending on your particular viewpoint) with the ability to speak with the literal voice of God. This God is a Creator who has abandoned His creations and Jesse searches relentlessly for Him, obsessed with forcing God to account for all the misery and pain draping the world. Ennis has been roundly praised for his work on this series.[8] The influence of *Preacher* on Whedon's work cannot be denied. As just one example, *Angel*'s half-demon Doyle has echoes of *Preacher*'s Cassidy, a likable, yet cowardly, Irish vampire.

Of course, not all depictions of faith in the arena of popular culture have been so preoccupied with depicting the dark underbelly of faith as *Preacher*, or with violating as many points of the outdated Hays Code as *Dogma*. Sales of Christian music are growing exponentially from modest beginnings in the 1960s to sales approaching 50 million units in 2004 (Peacock). Christian music groups are beginning to enjoy crossover success into the mainstream marketplace. These successful acts include artists such as Amy Grant, who recently starred in a television show called *3 Wishes*, in which miracles of hard work and faith transform people's lives in small towns across America. Whedon's works also amply demonstrate the positive side of spirituality, albeit in a wider form than strictly a contemporary Christian reading of faith. One example of this is Buffy's boyfriend Riley, who is depicted as being a regular churchgoer.

Also, no discussion about the role of faith in popular culture would be complete without a mention of Mel Gibson's 2004 film *The Passion of the Christ*. The film is controversial on many levels and was bombarded by charges including anti–Semitism and relentless violence.[9] However, it was also an uncontested blockbuster at the box office and sparked innumerable conversations about the nature of sacrifice and the role of the Divine in the everyday lives of ordinary, contemporary people. Judging from activity on Internet message boards, chat rooms, and academic conferences such as the biennial *Slayage*, Whedon's work also continues to incite similar discussions among fans and scholars alike.

While Whedon's infusion of faith-based concepts into the arena of popular culture is not unprecedented, he certainly does offer a fresh way of examining the intersection of faith, horror, and comedy. One method that Whedon employs is through the carefully chosen names he gives his characters. In this, Whedon is following the lead of one of his favorite authors, Charles Dickens, who was also a master of the serialized form of storytelling (Havens 41). Dickens scholar Elliot Engel has pointed out that Dickens built in clues to his characters through their names, using as an example "Mr. Choakumchild," the "wretched school principal" of *Hard Times* (Engel 37). That Whedon should choose names to reflect the inner nature of the character is perhaps not so surprising. After all, Whedon was born "Joseph," but decided in early adulthood to change his name to "Joss," which means "lucky" in Chinese (Havens 17). Clearly, this is a creator who understands the teaching of the *Tao Te Ching* that "naming is the origin of all particular things" (1). Since Whedon uses names as a key to unlock his characters, the meaning of names will be examined in every chapter.

Many of Whedon's characters have deliberate links to Western Christianity. Discussion will often center on these archetypal characters and how they reflect Whedon's own familiarity with the particular mythos of Western Christianity. It is crucial to note that "familiarity with" is different from "agreement with." As stated earlier, Whedon is an avowed atheist and, while many of his characters' names have clear links to faith-based traits, these names are often used in unexpected ways. This is one example of how elements of Whedon's stories can be read as reflections on the aspirations and anxieties of the western Christian mythos.

Of course, my approach is not the sole prism through which to view Whedon's work, as any successful work of art is open to multiple interpretations. Whedon, ever the trickster, wholeheartedly embraced this view when he famously challenged viewers to "bring your own subtext." This is easy to accomplish with a body of work as multilayered as Whedon's, where each layer can be read and studied for meaning and that meaning will naturally shift with the frame of reference of the individual viewer. This is as it should be. After all, there's more than one way to open a stepladder and if such a simple task can have multiple methods, surely the same is true for examining the intersection of popular culture such as the works of Joss Whedon and a concept as elusive as faith.

However, once you begin to look for Truth, there is a tendency to find it in the oddest of places. On the surface, yes, it seems odd that Whedon's work, concerned as it first appears to be with vampires and demons and gun-totin' rebels, should have anything contained within it to instruct the viewer in the ways of faith. Then again, great masters — ranging from spiritual masters such as Jesus to artistic masters such as Veronese — have often relied on parables to give their followers the Truth in manageable-sized chunks. St. Jerome is credited with saying that "The marrow of a parable is different from the promise of its surface." This holds true for Whedon's work, for what may appear at first blush to be silly stories of vampires, prom queens, futuristic thieves and Chinese-speaking renegades are so very much more beneath the surface.

It should be noted here at the outset that these lessons deal primarily with elements of spiritual *faith*, rather than with the dogma of a specific *religion*. The primary religious mythos that is discussed herein is that of Western Christianity; however, many other beliefs are discussed as well. In the context of this book, narrowly limiting the discussion to the tenets of a particular organized religion seems an unnatural and uncomfortable fit. Often, organized religion seems to overly concern itself with rules and restrictions, serving as a type of celestial "no," while spirituality remains a much broader concept, permitting the forest to be seen as well as the trees, serving as a Divine "yes" instead. Whedon's work has much to say about the transformative power of love, the importance of family, the possibility of redemption for past actions, and the dangers posed by fundamentalism and zealotry — all of which are concerns and concepts that people of good will, regardless of their individual faith, can gain from thoughtfully exploring. It is my hope that this text provides a springboard for those discussions and also advances the examination of Whedon's contributions to popular culture.

Consummate storyteller Neil Gaiman has said that "stories are, in one way or another, mirrors. We use them to explain to ourselves how the world works or how it doesn't work. Like mirrors, stories prepare us for the day to come" (*Smoke & Mirrors* 2). From walking in the hall of mirrors created by Joss Whedon's magnificent imagination, I have met many characters who reflect light back into the world. In the following chapters, I will discuss some of Whedon's complex characters and the lessons they can teach. For purposes of clarity, individual episodes are identified by title of the episode, followed by number of the season and episode; for example ("The Gift" 5.22). The title of the series is given only when it differs from the series that is the central focus of the chapter. So a reference to an *Angel* episode in a *Buffy*-centered chapter would be identified as follows: ("City Of" *Angel* 1.01). A primary source guide follows the chapter notes and provides information about the writer, director, and air date of each episode, along with publication information about Whedon's work in print media, such as the ongoing "Season 8" comic books for *Buffy*. The book is divided into four distinct sections and each section has a particular thematic focus. However, all of the chapters are unified in pointing to the ABCs of acceptance, belief, and choice that serve as the underpinning of Whedon's work.

In the first section, the focus is on *purpose*. This section focuses on Dawn from *Buffy* and the characters of Spike and Angel in *Buffy* and its spinoff, *Angel*. Dawn, who begins life as "the Key," finds that her life is not what she thought it was and must seek meaning in the life she finds herself living. Spike and Angel are both "vampires with souls" and these characters develop along some very interesting lines that allow for the exploration of what it means to have a soul in the first place.

In the second section, the focus is on *family*. Whedon creates large, unconventional families and this section specifically explores the families of

Fray and *Firefly*. In *Fray*, the roles of siblings and twins are discussed as Fray makes the decision to walk the path of the narrative hero. The *Firefly* family is discussed in terms of the roles played by each character within this atypical family and the strengths that can be derived from permitting individuals to go beyond traditional roles.

In the third section, the focus is on *redemption.* Whedon's characters are often faced with questions regarding past actions, doubt, and whether they can ever again walk in the light. This section uses the characters of Doyle from *Angel*, Malcolm Reynolds and Shepherd Book from *Firefly*, and Faith from *Buffy* and *Angel* to examine these issues. Doyle, like the Biblical Jonah, is given a dangerous mission and he searches his own conscience to decide if he is worthy, instead of simply trusting that he is fit for the task. Mal has suffered losses that have left him hostile to God and fiercely determined to protect his chosen family, yet without the necessary tools to successfully do so. He must find faith in something outside himself in order to connect with those around him and that "something" will not be his previous God. Book is a holy man who believes fervently in a kind and forgiving God, yet fears his own past is too darkened by shadows to permit him the grace to walk in the light he so willingly extends to others. Lastly, Faith illustrates the path walked by the Prodigal. She squanders her gifts and must be broken by her own actions before she is even willing to search for redemption.

In the final section, the focus is on *zealotry.* To Whedon, doubt is a strength and this section explores the negative aspects of dead-certain belief through the characters of River from *Firefly* and Caleb from *Buffy*. River's psychic abilities cause others to fear and shun her as otherworldly and somehow wrong, a view that is at odds with Whedon's message of inclusion. Whedon uses River to illustrate the desirability of expanding the view of others to draw a wider circle of acceptance. Caleb's deliberate choices to serve the cause of evil are discussed in the context of his misogynistic worldview. This is a view that Whedon clearly depicts as crippling to all genders of the human race, as it denies the potential and the very humanity of people.

Whedon's characters are not stopped by death, damnation, or even their own selfish, petty, and very human concerns. Yet they are not stainless, always virtuous folk who are incapable of making mistakes. In fact, they are beguiling mixtures of the best and the worst humanity has to offer, which makes Whedon's work so interesting to explore.

So come on in. Yes, it's a little dark in places and sometimes familiar things look different when they are shrouded in murky shadows, but don't worry. Joss Whedon was kind enough to leave lights for us. We just need to switch them on.

PART 1
PURPOSE: THE ROAD TO DAMASCUS

*You're hardly a part of the community,
let alone a respected one. People will not listen.
But you will make yourself heard.*
— Urkonn, *Fray #6*

1

What's a Key Without a Lock?

DAWN AND THE PROMISE OF PURPOSE

Joss Whedon's skill at throwing curveballs to his audience is amply illustrated by watching the last few minutes of the opening episode of Season Five of *Buffy*. In the straightforwardly titled "Buffy vs. Dracula" (5.01), Buffy has once again saved her friends and her town, as well as learning some hard truths about herself in the process. In this particular case, she has defeated the most famous vampire of them all, Count Dracula.[1] Her victory has put her in a celebratory frame of mind and Buffy announces to her mother her intention to go out to the movies with her boyfriend, Riley. Buffy then steps into her room and discovers a fresh-faced teenage girl standing there. Buffy indignantly asks the girl what she is doing there (a question the viewer also very much wants answered), but before the mystery girl can answer, Buffy's mother calls up to her, suggesting that "If you're going out, why don't you take your sister?" Buffy and the heretofore unknown girl simultaneously reply to this suggestion with familiar sibling exasperation, "Mom!" as the episode ends.

Thus the viewers' applecart is upset by Whedon, who believes that in order to keep the audience interested, a writer has to be willing to give the audience what it needs, rather than what it wants (Robinson). After four seasons, viewers who had become accustomed to Buffy being an only child are suddenly faced with the revelation that she has had a younger sister all along.

As more than one viewer put it, "What?" However, it is a mistake to think that Whedon throws the character of Buffy's sister into the mix of the show for no reason other than to test the theory of whether sibling rivalry is more pronounced on the Hellmouth. Instead, Whedon uses the character of Dawn to explore some very profound questions about purpose — specifically, discovering what our mission is in life as well as our ability to shift direction and change the current path we may be on in order to find it.

The startling introduction of Buffy's sister Dawn into the Summers family makes one point abundantly clear — things are going to change in some very unanticipated ways as Sunnydale begins to face a new day; one that begins with a Dawn. Although she was not introduced until Season Five, Dawn's arrival had been cryptically foretold earlier in the series. It has been established that among the many attributes of the Slayer is the gift of prophetic dreams ("Surprise" 2.13). Buffy is depicted at least twice in Season Four as having dreams which contain puzzling references that can be read as foreshadowing Dawn's appearance in Sunnydale. In "This Year's Girl" (4.15), Buffy has a dream in which she is making a bed with the second Slayer, Faith, who comments that "Little sis coming, I know" to which the dream-Buffy replies, "So much to do before she gets here." Later, in the Season Four finale "Restless" (4.22), the Scoobies all experience odd, unsettling dreams. In Buffy's, she is warned by Tara to "be back before dawn."[2] Based on these references and the benefit of hindsight, perhaps viewers should not have been all that surprised at the abrupt appearance of a "kid sister" for Buffy as the show moved into a new direction. Names are very important to the study of Whedon's work and it should not be considered a mere coincidence that the show's new day begins with a Dawn.

To the ancient Greeks, the goddess of the dawn was Eos. Her arrival announced the ending of her sister Selene's nightly reign and the coming of her brother Helios, the sun (Kravitz 89). While Whedon's Dawn does not have a brother who rules the day, it can be argued that her older sister certainly does rule the night, given Buffy's responsibilities as the Slayer. As the Chosen One, Buffy has a calling that requires a good deal of nocturnal activity to find and dispatch vampires and their ilk.

While the Greek goddess of the dawn is not featured in many of the myths of that culture, there is one telling story that emphasizes the featherheaded qualities of Eos, as well as the general fickleness of these gods. It seems that the goddess fell in love with a mortal named Tithonus. Stricken by the thought that, as a mere mortal, her love was fated to wither and die, she begged Zeus to make Tithonus immortal. Her wish was granted and the remainder of the tale illustrates the adage of being careful what you wish for. Eos never thought to ask that Tithonus be granted eternal *youth* in addition to eternal *life* and the poor man grew old and feeble in mind but was denied the natural release of death. In an act of pity, the gods finally turned the miserable wretch into a cicada (Carlyon 165). This desire to have what one wants, without fully thinking through the consequences, is also a hallmark of the immaturity of adolescents. Similar to Eos, Whedon's Dawn takes rash actions which cause turmoil and disturbance, although she seldom consciously intends the outcomes of her actions.[3]

For the Romans, dawn was the province of the goddess Aurora (Kravitz 42). Aurora is also the name given to the slumbering princess in some versions of the *Sleeping Beauty* tale, including the 1959 animated Disney film.[4] Sleeping Beauty is an apt comparison for Whedon's Dawn in a number of ways, including the fact that they both have their destinies mapped out for them by faraway forces who never bother to consult either Aurora or Dawn regarding their opinions on the matter. While Whedon's Dawn does not prick her finger and sleep for a century, she does live in a form of twilight existence similar to a deep slumber, for she begins her existence in Sunnydale as a teenage girl who lacks any inkling of knowledge of her own worth, abilities, and purpose in life. While a certain amount of existential confusion can be viewed as simply part of the price we all pay for being human, Dawn is more perplexed than most due to her unusual origins, which are discussed further in this chapter.

Like all of us, and from Buddha on down, Dawn will have to be awakened to self-knowledge and that awakening will demand that some hard choices be made. Nevertheless, one simply can't deny knowledge successfully for very long and the awakening, even if it is difficult, is inevitable if we are to achieve our full potential. Unlike the Disney tale, Dawn's self-knowledge will not come in the form of a gentle kiss from a handsome prince since only in fairy tales can a caterpillar emerge from a chrysalis unscathed by the journey.

It is a common theme in myth for knowledge, as well as the wisdom to wield that knowledge usefully, to demand a high price. Sometimes these prices are paid willingly; witness Odin the All-Father's exchange of an eye for permission to drink the water of wisdom from Mimir's Well (Davidson 112). At other times, the price is extracted unwillingly, such as Actaeon's loss of his humanity (and life) as the cost of accidentally seeing the goddess Artemis bathing. As a punishment, the furious goddess turns the hapless hunter into a stag who was then killed by his own hounds (Hamilton 374). In Dawn's case, in order to come into her own as a person, she will have to surrender the safety of thinking that she doesn't matter much, so not much is to be expected of her. While on the surface, Dawn faces a much less devastating sacrifice than that of Odin (or indeed, of Xander, the "heart" of the Scooby

Gang of Buffy's friends, who will also lose an eye), giving up our own illusions and preconceptions is often the most difficult thing humans are asked to do in life. And Dawn isn't even completely human, as we will see.

Dawn appears throughout the last three seasons of Buffy and her character undergoes a number of transformations during that time. However, she first appears to exist simply to serve as the "McGuffin" of the show. This is a term that was coined by Alfred Hitchcock to mean an object around which a plot is built. Examples of McGuffins include the "letters of transit" in *Casablanca* or the bejeweled statue in *The Maltese Falcon*. Dawn serves as the Season Five McGuffin in her role as the mysterious Key that the hellgod Glorificus is seeking with a bloody vengeance.

Without getting too bogged down in details, Glorificus (aka "Glory") was once part of a trio of deities who ruled a hell dimension. The other two unnamed gods became fearful that Glory would unseat them, so they banded together to banish her. Literally hell-bent on returning home, Glory relentlessly seeks a mystical "Key" that will dissolve the walls between dimensions, thus permitting her to return home. The downside of Glory's use of the Key will be the merging of all dimensions, which will inexorably lead to the utter destruction of this world, a niggling detail that does not trouble the unbalanced hellgod in the least.[5]

In its natural state, the Key appears to be a glowing sphere of energy. For centuries, it has been in the custody of an order of monks who are sworn to its protection. However, seeing that Glory will not be deterred, the desperate monks use magic and, quite significantly, Buffy's blood and memories to transform the Key into a fourteen-year-old human girl — Dawn Summers. To add an extra dash of realism to their masquerade, the monks magically implant memories so everyone sincerely believes that Dawn has always been a part of the Summers family.[6]

To return to the earlier *Sleeping Beauty* motif, the girl known as "Dawn" is not in her true state, which is that of an immensely powerful ball of pure energy. However, while the Aurora of the *Sleeping Beauty* tale has a hand in causing her slumbering state by invoking a curse when she pricks her finger on a spindle, it can be argued that it is Buffy's finger which is pricked in Whedon's world. Dawn, through no fault of her own, has been removed from her natural powerful state to that of being a pitiable human girl with no idea of her true identity and purpose in the world.[7] It is as if she is caught in a deep sleep and Dawn will only return to a consciousness of who, or what, she truly is in slow stages.

When Glory was exiled from her world and forced to fit into this one, she lost a fair amount of her power, although she is still abnormally strong and nearly impervious to harm. However, she must feed in order to maintain her strength and power. She does this by jamming her fingers into a human's head and sucking out all brain energy, a process that leaves the unfortunate victim little more than an insane husk.[8] Since people who are "outside reality" can perceive Dawn as she is rather than as she appears to be, Glory's periodic picnics have two unforeseen side effects: first, the sudden uptick of mental patients in Sunnydale provides a few clues for the Scooby Gang and second, Dawn begins to wonder why crazy people seem to think she's not herself.

It will take Dawn quite a while to unravel this tangled skein and find her way to the heart of the maze of her identity. Even though Buffy and her friends discover the truth, they try mightily to protect Dawn from that knowledge, reasoning that she's too young to be faced with the reality that she is not simply a teenager. Thanks to the monks' magic, this protective stance is understandable since everyone has memories of Dawn that seem to go back years. However, it is also ironic, as Dawn is supposed to be (and thinks she is) fourteen. This is only a year younger than Buffy was when she was first called to be the Slayer and had her state of blissful ignorance regarding the existence of all things that go bump in the night abruptly ended. Buffy aches to have the one thing her status as the Slayer forever denies her — a so-called "normal" existence in which she can focus her energies on everyday concerns. Perhaps it is because no one tried to preserve her own childhood that Buffy is so adamant that Dawn will have her shot at a typical teenage life, but it is not to be, for Dawn is as curious as a cat.

Upset at the evasive tactics of her family and friends, Dawn resolves to discover the truth. In "Blood Ties" (5.13), she and Spike break into the Magic Box, which serves as headquarters for the Scooby Gang, and she reads the journals kept so meticulously by Giles. Thus Dawn discovers the truth of her existence through stealth, with the news being delivered by a vampire. Imagine the shock of her awakening: her feelings of alienation and insecurity have not been the result of typical teenage angst, nor have they been a bad dream. Dawn is not, and has never been, fully human. All of her memories and emotions that she has been keeping in a series of diaries since the age of seven — all are false. She has not spent fourteen years as a Summers, but a scant six months. The remainder of her long existence has been spent as the Key, a glowing sphere of energy. She owes her human existence to the machinations of the ancient order of monks whose sole purpose is to prevent the Key from being used to crumble the walls between worlds.

The enormity of discovering that she is the Key to the Kingdom of Hell is entirely too much for Dawn to handle. Dazed and stunned by the reality her curiosity has forced her to face, Dawn slashes her arm with a sharp knife, marveling at her own ability to bleed, so like a human would. Shylock's cry for an acknowledgement of commonality in *The Merchant of Venice* echoes poor Dawn's confusion, although Shylock is battling societal misconception and Dawn's feeling of not belonging is rooted in harsh reality:

> Hath not a Jew eyes? hath not a Jew hands, organs, dimensions, senses, affectations, passions? fed with the same food, hurt with the same weapons, subject to the same diseases, healed by the same means, warmed and cooled by the same winter and summer, as a Christian is? If you prick us, do we not bleed? If you tickle us, do we not laugh? If you poison us, do we not die? [46].

Dawn is likewise crying out for sympathy and understanding. She is not human, yet it is all she knows.

Because of her origins, Dawn is not entirely human. Yet she has the same senses, circulatory system, and emotions as the humans she was made to resemble.[9] At the moment she cuts herself, Whedon shows viewers that Dawn is, in every meaningful way, a frightened and confused teenage girl. She has wanted to know who and what she is; she obtained that knowledge and now she has to live with what she has discovered. The secret she has uncovered about herself is far more terrible than she could have imagined, even with the unusual perspective given to her by growing up with a sister whose purpose is to save the world from the hordes of darkness on a regular basis. Here Whedon both sets up the coming confrontation with the triangle of Buffy, Dawn, and Glory as well as makes a statement about waking up to the truth about ourselves. Disney's Aurora gets off lightly, as the prince hacks his way through the enchanted brambles to find her and then gently awakens her to the reality of the world around her. In contrast, Whedon's Dawn will have to take a far more active role in creating a world in which she wants to live after waking up to the harsh knowledge of her identity, for engaged choice is far more valuable to Whedon than passive waiting.

Not that Glory expects Dawn to struggle with this thorny problem for long. In order for Glory to use the Key, certain time-specific rituals must be observed. The result of Glory's plan will be her return to the dimension of hell over which she once ruled at the cost of all existence. While Giles gently points out that it may be necessary for Dawn to die a human death in order to keep the Key from being used, Buffy vehemently rejects that notion as unacceptable. Dawn may not be human and the memories everyone has regarding her may be false, but Buffy knows enough to realize that family comes in a bewildering array of configurations. To Buffy, Dawn is her baby sister and there endeth the discussion. If Buffy's refusal to execute the being she thinks of as her sister is going to result in unbearable suffering for every creature in our world, the Slayer is determined that "the last thing she'll see is me protecting her" ("The Gift" 5.22).[10] In this way, Whedon emphasizes the importance of family and also of the consequences of the choices we make.

Knowing from past experience that it's always best to not fight an enemy this big solo, Buffy lines up her Scooby soldiers and attacks Glory with every weapon in her arsenal — magic spells, mystical artifacts, her mechanical twin (the "Buffybot"), and a wrecking ball all occupy Glory while the Slayer's friends serve as foot soldiers to attack Glory's sniveling minions. Despite this, one of Glory's acolytes, Doc, begins the blood ritual that will lower the dimensional walls.[11] Only Summers blood can close the rift and Buffy makes the sacrifice in a spectacular swan-dive, arms outstretched in the posture of Christ crucified as she hurls herself into the abyss.

By Buffy's actions, the entire world, along with Dawn, is saved. Usually, that would be the end of the story — the tender damsel, pale with terror and helpless in the face of her dastardly enemies, is saved by powerful outside forces and is now free to go about her business. But Whedon's worlds are very far from usual. In fact, he delights in taking standard character stereotypes and showing viewers that what they thought was one thing is actually, with a little bit of effort, something completely else. It is the narrative equivalent of seeing a simple sheet of brightly colored paper be transformed with a few flips and folds into an origami swan. It's not as odd a comparison as it may first appear, for Dawn will now begin the transformation from Key to human as she seeks her true purpose in a world that no longer has use for a Key. This chain of events is reminiscent of Siddhartha Gautama's awakening to the human condition by his witnessing what Buddhism terms the "four passing sights."

Many facts regarding the early years of Siddhartha Gautama (better known as "Buddha," a title meaning "Enlightened One" which was given to him by his followers) are cloaked in legend. In a similar fashion, the facts of the boyhood of Christ (likewise a title, rather than a name) and, for that matter, the Key's life before she became incarnated as Dawn Summers are also shrouded in mystery. While many facts cannot be ascertained with precision, according to Buddhist tradition, Siddhartha led a sheltered and prosperous life, shielded from all knowledge of life's rougher edges by an overprotective father who wished the boy to become politically powerful (Renard 306). This is similar to Buffy's desire to protect Dawn from the sharp edges and dangers of the world.[12] Siddhartha rarely left the protection of the family's luxurious residence and, on the rare occasions when Siddhartha's duties took him outside the confines of his father's stronghold, servants were under strict orders to clear the road of anything that might seem unpleasant to the young man.

Returning to the earlier comparison with *Sleeping Beauty*, the command of Siddhartha's father to his servants echoes with the fairy tale King's order to destroy all spinning wheels in the kingdom to thwart the curse laid on his daughter Aurora at her christening. Destiny does as it will, and eventually,

Aurora found one overlooked spinning wheel and the larger Wheel of Destiny began to spin. In the case of young Siddhartha, on one of his rare journeys in the outside world, the privileged young man came across the "four passing sights" as he encountered old age, sickness, death, and a peaceful monk (Renard 307). Traditional accounts of Buddhism hold that all four encounters were divinely ordained, with gods taking the roles of these suffering individuals so Siddhartha would be pricked into action by what he had seen and assume the mantle of his responsibilities in bringing enlightenment to all mankind (307). Dawn discovers the truth of her supernatural nature, despite the best efforts of her well-intentioned family and friends to shield her from the knowledge. However, knowledge is merely a tool; it's how we use that tool that shows the sort of being we are — or the sort of being we may become.

Shaken by the sights he had witnessed, Siddhartha renounced his life of luxury and mindless comfort and sought to understand the human condition. Dissatisfied with the spiritual approaches he encountered, he mediated alone under a tree, resisting the temptations of the clever demon Mara.[13] Buddhism teaches that following this time of mediation, Siddhartha arrived at a clear understanding of the most fundamental truths of life and dedicated the remainder of his life to teaching others what he had learned (Renard 308 – 309). Dawn's time of meditation on the nature of her existence is more abbreviated as she moves rapidly from being the McGuffin of Season Five to becoming her own person, with unique gifts and talents to contribute to the ongoing battle.

Buddhism is far from the only faith that contains examples of people transforming from one state of being to another and it would be futile to attempt to create a definitive list. Therefore, only one further example will be used to illustrate this point more fully. St. Paul, who became one of the chief pillars of the early Christian Church, was first an enthusiastic opponent of the fledging faith. Paul (then called "Saul") sought authority from the priests to hunt down Christians and return them to Jerusalem in chains. On a trip to the city of Damascus to capture Christians, he was struck blind by the power of God and told by a disembodied voice that only he could hear to proceed to Damascus, where further instructions would be given to him. Saul remained blind for three days, during which time he also fasted. A disciple of the new church, Ananias, was told in a vision to go to Saul and return his sight by the laying on of hands. Ananias protested this duty, since Saul was well-known as an enemy of the faith. Never mind, says God, I have plans. So Ananias goes to Paul's lodging in "the street called Straight"[14] where Saul (now referred to as "Paul") is restored to health and becomes a fervent believer (Acts 9:1–21).[15] In a similar vein, Dawn's horrible purpose has vanished and she has a new, larger challenge ahead of her as she seeks a reason to be here in this life. In short, she has chosen on which side of the ongoing battle of good versus evil she will stand, but how can she help? What gifts does she have, especially when compared to a super-strong sister who consorts with powerful witches who can actually stitch the fabric of reality to suit their wishes?

Paul had something to say on that very point. In Chapter 12 of his First Letter to the Corinthians, Paul addresses some concerns regarding different gifts and abilities of members of the faith. It is good, Paul writes, that there are many different talents, just as there are different parts to a human body that all work together for a common goal. There is strength is this diversity, for a body without ears could not hear and a body that was nothing but ears would lack the ability to see. Not everyone can heal the sick just as not everyone has the gift of languages; however, we all have something to contribute. This is the spot at which Dawn stands at the beginning of Season Six — she has gifts, but she must discover them for herself.

Self-examination is a necessary part of determining what one's purpose in life is to be. This belief is reflected in the statement attributed to Socrates that "the unexamined life is not worth living." A variation of this belief is at the core of the teachings of Chang Tsui, who was a founding figure of Neo-Confucianism in the eleventh century. This philosophy blended the traditional teachings of Confucianism with elements of other schools of thought such as Taoism and Buddhism. According to Chang Tsui, everything in life is worthy of deep investigation and the failure to do so causes humans to remain in a dream state, unable to awaken to become the true sages we are meant to be (Simpkins 40). In this context, sages are similar to buddhas— individuals who have been gifted with deep understanding and enlightenment (Simpkins 37). Simply put, we are intended to be more than mere sleepwalkers in our lives and we have a responsibility to sift through our experiences to find meaning there which we then must share with others.

Dawn has awoken to one purpose for her existence, that of being the Key; however, it is a purpose that Buffy's act of self-sacrifice has made superfluous. But rather than seek a new, and perhaps truer, purpose for her life, Whedon's Dawn would much prefer to roll over and go back to sleep and dream simple, human dreams that ignore the reality of monsters, evil, and whatever the plural of "apocalypse" might be. The path to self-understanding is a rocky one and Dawn is not eager to set foot upon it. While Dawn will ultimately be rewarded for walking the difficult path set before her, taking the journey must be her choice.

Buffy, who is resurrected from her grave through her friends' use of powerful magic, returns to a life of continual struggle — emotional, financial, and psychological. Prominent on Buffy's plate of troubles is the problem of how to properly raise Dawn, who has reacted to this unending parade of traumas by becoming incredibly self-absorbed. Rather than trying to find a way to fit into the world, Dawn is demanding that the world fit around her. Far from being the "rosy-fingered Dawn" of Homer's *Odyssey*, Whedon's creation has become "sticky-fingered Dawn," a teenager who pilfers from local shops in a bid for attention.

Dawn may have awoken to her existence through learning some unpleasant truths in the manner of Siddhartha Gautama's exposure to the four passing sights, but initially she is unwilling to move beyond feeling that the universe is being fundamentally unfair to her. She could benefit from learning about the Buddha's Four Noble Truths, which can be summed up as:

1. Life is suffering. Bad things will happen to all, regardless of whether they seem to "deserve" it. This is a constant in the human experience.
2. All suffering derives from either inappropriate attachments to physical objects or desire for physical things, including people.
3. Therefore, to avoid suffering, people must learn to avoid attachments and desire.
4. To avoid attachments and desire, follow the Eightfold Path. (Renard 316)

At this point, Dawn would definitely agree with the first of the Four Noble Truths, although she would probably use a more modern vernacular to express the sentiment. Further, Dawn most certainly does *not* follow the Buddhist Eightfold Path, which stresses moderation in all thoughts and actions.[16] On top of her other issues, Whedon's Dawn is a twenty-first century American adolescent, which means she is bombarded with continuous messages regarding sex and consumerism that run counter to the gentle introspection so prized by Buddhism. In Buddhist belief, a "bodhisattva" is one who has attained personal enlightenment, but who is "moved by compassionate zeal to aid his fellow men toward salvation" and therefore postpones his own entrance into Nirvana (Burtt 222). It is not easy for anyone to postpone such a reward.[17] Throughout the darkness that pervades Season Six, Dawn is portrayed as being self-centered, whiny, and oblivious to the very real possibility that her increasingly out-of-control behavior could have the effect of having her removed from Buffy's custody, thus completely severing her family ties. She must make a conscious decision to move beyond her present egotistical state and Dawn finds that very difficult to do.

Dawn, like most of us, longs to be "special" and special in a big, showy way. Surrounded by three commanding women such as Buffy, Willow, and Tara, it is not surprising that Dawn feels less than adequate. As far as male role models are concerned, Dawn is influenced by Spike who, as a vampire, has physical strength that can even give Buffy a run for her money. Moreover, he also has knowledge gained from an abnormally long lifespan (or perhaps that should be "deathspan") spent in the company of the occult and arcane. Giles, who serves as Buffy's Watcher, is intelligent and skilled in the ways of magic and the otherworldly. Only Xander seems to lack any larger-than-life abilities.

This is typical Whedon legerdemain, as Xander will be the one to save the world from a grief-crazed Willow at the end of Season Six. He will accomplish this through the use of his own gifts, which include the ability to love and connect with others. Far from being supernatural and otherworldly, Xander's gifts are ones that we can all share and ones on which Whedon places great value. Dawn will be the recipient of Xander's particular understanding of what it means to *not* be special; to be in the chorus, rather than the star. To use a sports analogy, Xander is the ultimate team player. His contributions are crucial, yet easily overshadowed by Buffy and Willow, who have flashier talents. To return to Paul's writings in First Corinthians, "And some of the parts that seem weakest and least important are really the most necessary" (1 Cor. 12:22). Xander is not the quarterback of Team Buffy, but he's quite a good defensive lineman. Due to his personal experience with life on the sidelines, he is the ideal person for Dawn to turn to for advice as she picks her way along this rocky path.

Guidance is crucial as we make our way through the dark woods of our lives. Ultimately, however, the path we journey on is ours to choose. Moreover, we can always change our direction. Mother Teresa provides an unexpected example of this.

One of the best-known modern day faces of benevolent Christian charity, Mother Teresa founded the Missionaries of Charity, an order devoted to providing care to the poorest of the poor throughout the world, including areas struck by natural disasters such as floods, war, and famine. She was the recipient of the 1979 Nobel Peace Prize for her unflagging dedication to the poor and dispossessed of Calcutta. Following her death, she was beatified, which is the final step prior to canonization, which confers Catholic sainthood (Hagerty). Her journey toward sainthood began when she was traveling to a retreat and heard what she claimed was the voice of Jesus Christ, who instructed her to form a new religious community that would directly serve the poor (Guntzelman). All of this makes for a lovely story of the results of straight-ahead action taken by one who had the assurance of her purpose in life. However, that is not the whole story, which is always more interesting, if less glossy.

Beginning with the train trip, Mother Teresa enjoyed an intense ecstatic relationship through direct dialogue with Jesus Christ for several months, which was the time it took for her initial request to be formally approved by Church authorities. However, with the start of this ministry, Mother Teresa's direct communications with the Divine abruptly ceased. She wrote of feeling "forsaken" and "thrown away" by God. In one letter to her superiors, she wrote, "I call, I cling, I want and there is no one to answer. The darkness is so dark and I am alone" (Hagerty). Throughout the remaining half-century of her life, Mother Teresa never again heard the voice she ached to hear and she never again had the assurance that she was, in fact, doing God's work. Nevertheless, even while questioning the very existence of God, she continued to do the hard work she believed God wanted her to do (Hagerty). Although an avowed atheist, Whedon may find common ground here, as many of his characters, including Dawn, also are tormented by self-doubt. In Whedon's world, the path of the hero is marked by action taken for the greater good despite the lack of absolute certainty.

In a world where even a now-beatified figure such as Mother Teresa is not exempt from doubting her faith and purpose, how can it be surprising that a troubled teenager such as Dawn Summers would be confused about her role in life? While Mother Teresa's work was not supported by ecstatic visions and holy dialogue with her God (in fact, Hagerty suggests that for much of her life, Mother Teresa was "running on empty"), she still continued the work she felt she was appointed to perform, guided by a spirit of fidelity and love (Hagerty). In other words, she acted "as if" she was in constant communication with God.

Whedon's Dawn does much the same — she wants to be a force for good, so she acts independently to gain skills that are useful to attaining that goal. Viewers don't see her accumulating these skills directly for, as Elizabeth Rambo has pointed out, much of Dawn's transformation in Season Seven takes place offstage (Rambo *Nobody Knows ... the Real Me*). In the final season of *Buffy*, Dawn takes great strides in moving from being a whiny teenager who only can trill "me, me, me" to becoming a strong, independent young woman who is confident in her own abilities and strengths.

Although many of Dawn's skills are attained offstage — viewers are happily spared a montage of her poring over Sumerian texts or practicing with weapons — she amasses quite an array of Slayer-friendly abilities over the course of Season Seven. Among these skills, Dawn is shown to possess talents with spellcasting in episodes such as "Conversations with Dead People" (7.07). She is able to perform tricky ancient rituals that have effects such as opening portals to the long-ago past for Buffy to pay a visit to the originators of the line of Slayers in "Get It Done" (7.15). She may be ignoring her usual homework assignments, but she's picked up enough ancient Turkish to read a spellbook in "Touched" (7.20). Moreover, while Dawn does not possess the heightened strength of a Slayer, she has acquired a taser and uses it with enough skill to indicate a certain level of familiarity with the device.[18] She's also learned to drive, a talent Buffy never really develops.[19]

Jes Battis states that Dawn can be read as a type of reflection of Buffy, a reminder of the carefree girl she once had been, as well as everything that Buffy fights so hard to preserve (76). This is true; however, over time, Dawn evolves into something beyond a mere construct for Buffy to protect and nurture.

Dawn is moving toward having faith and trust in her own inherent worth. This is, of course, an ongoing journey and one that is fraught with setbacks. In "Potential" (7.12), a spell seems to indicate that Dawn is a Potential Slayer — one of the girls who is in line to be chosen and marked out as "special." To be sure, this is a mixed blessing as the only way to ascend to the title of Slayer is for one of the previous titleholders (currently only Buffy and the reformed Faith qualify) to shuffle off her mortal coil. Dawn has no desire to have anything happen to her sister (or to the currently absent-from-Sunnydale Faith, for that matter), but she is understandably excited at the idea that it is finally her time in the sun. By the end of the episode, it is clear that Dawn was mistaken; that the Potential-seeking spell was not marking Dawn, but another girl. Rather than revert to her earlier, bratty behavior, Dawn accepts that, once again, it's not her who has been tapped as special, and she hits the books in hopes of tracking down answers that will assist the group.

But she's not alone in being not-quite-special in this group, as Xander, the heart of the Scooby Gang, sees.[20] He is able to offer Dawn understanding that no one else — no Slayer, no Potential, no witch, no Watcher, and no ex-demon — can provide. He knows that the Potentials are special but that none of them, not even Buffy, can ever understand life from his point of view, a perspective he now shares with Dawn:

> They'll never know how tough it is, Dawnie, to be the one who isn't chosen. To live so near to the spotlight and never step in it. But I know. I see more than anybody realizes because nobody's watching me. I saw you last night. I see you working here today. You're not special. You're extraordinary ["Potential" 7.12].

There's the point. Dawn may still be unsure of her exact purpose, which is continuing to unfold. Nevertheless, she is confident that she has a place on this team and that she has valuable contributions to make to the whole.

There is a reason for Dawn, as there is a reason for all of us. Some find in that reason evidence of a Divine hand, as the scientist and paleontologist Agassiz did when he wrote, "The eye of the trilobite tells us that the sun shone on the old beach where he lived; for there is nothing in nature without a purpose, and when so complicated an organ was made to receive the light, there must have been light to enter it" ("Great Poems"). Others would look at the evidence differently. For example, Buddhism is often referred to as a non-theistic religion, but that is not strictly accurate. At no time did the Buddha deny the existence of gods, but he insisted that solving the problems inherent in the human condition was the responsibility of the individual (Renard 319). This also fits with Dawn — whether or not her purpose was to dissolve dimensional walls, that is in the past. She has chosen another path and only she can walk it.[21]

As stated in the Book of Ecclesiastes, "To every thing there is a season, and a time to every purpose under the heaven" (Eccles. 3:1). However, like Dawn, it is up to us to seek and to find our purpose. What that may be is a wide-open field, as we all have gifts and talents that can be used to improve our world. Despite Dawn being initially coded as the Key, Whedon would argue that it is never a proper purpose to be a force for destruction and if that seems to be our purpose, we need to look harder. Dawn may have started life in Sunnydale enmeshed in mystical prophecy, but as Angel once reminded viewers, "Don't believe everything you're foretold" ("To Shanshu in L.A.," *Angel* 1.22). What we are is up to us. There's no guarantee that the road will not be rocky and the way hard, but it's a path we choose to walk, not a forced march. In Whedon's work, individuals are greatly defined by the choices they make as they pick their way along the route before them.

It's often a rough road and stumbles are going to occur, but that's okay, provided you stumble forward, toward something better than what you've left behind. In illustrating this, Whedon's Dawn truly lights the way toward a new day.

2

Growing After Death

ANGEL, SPIKE AND THE EVOLUTION OF THE SOUL

With his creation of Angel and Spike, Whedon creates not only two compelling, layered characters in their own right, but a pairing that seems to be eternally locked in a binary relationship, for much of what one character is can best be defined by what the other is not. This is a concept with which students of the visual arts are familiar — the idea of the "negative space" of compositions, which can be simply defined as the space between and around physical objects within the frame. The underlying notion of negative space is that what *isn't* in the picture can have as much weight in defining the composition as what *is* present.[1] An example of this is the famous black-and-white image that appears to be either a delicately curved vase in the middle of the picture or two profiles looking toward the center of the composition, depending on which color viewers focus their gaze. In a similar fashion, vampires in general, and Spike and Angel in particular, assist us in defining what it means to be human by their very lack of humanity.

Whedon's vampires borrow much from the version of the Undead first popularized by Bram Stoker in his novel *Dracula*. However, like Stoker, Whedon freely adapts prevailing conventions to suit his own purposes. One of Whedon's most extraordinary notions is that the Undead can regain the human soul that was lost when the victim was transformed into a vampire. In fact, Whedon gives viewers two "ensouled" vampires: Angel and Spike. He posits these two as foil-like oppositions; the "negative space" of one another, so to speak. As such, Angel and Spike provide a valuable opportunity to examine the evolution of the concept of the soul as well as Whedon's views regarding its value.

The many legends of the vampire draw on humankind's universal fear of death and the need to explain the seemingly unexplainable, particularly prior to the modern scientific era of microscopic examination of tissue samples and sophisticated embalming techniques. For example, traditional folk belief holds that human hair and nails continue to grow after death; an idea centered on the examination of exhumed remains. This belief is patently untrue and is based on an optical illusion. Rather than the hair and nails continuing to grow, the skin of the corpse dehydrates, shrinking away from the hair follicles and nail beds, thus making it appear that growth is continuing to occur (Macnair). Whedon raises a separate, yet related, question with Angel and Spike: can anything grow after death? A soul, for instance? Or is death the end of the line and a vampire's purpose to be merely a soulless killing machine, visiting terror and death on the living?

That a vampire was once a living human being is a common thread throughout the lore. However, determining who is "dead" can be a tricky proposition. Many of the common signs of death can be found in people who are not irretrievably "dead" — remember that Buffy herself is resurrected using cardiopulmonary resuscitation following her drowning at the hands of the Master in the first season of *Buffy*. Cessation of respiration, the lack of a detectable pulse, fixed pupils in the eyes, even rigor mortis — all of these indications of death can be found in individuals who are (to quote Monty Python) "not dead yet." Ethnobotanist Wade Davis recounts that the fear of premature burial had grown into such a public concern at the end of the nineteenth century (roughly at the same time Stoker was writing *Dracula*), that "prizes were offered for the discovery of a conclusive sign of death" (Davis 156). The obvious answer is sometimes the best answer, and in 1890, a Dr. Maze "was awarded the prestigious Prix Dusgate and twenty-five hundred francs simply for asserting that the only reliable sign of death was putrefaction" (156). In other words, the hallmark of life's "negative space" of death is decay.

That equation, however, is only true for most of us — for the vampire, physical death is merely the gateway to a new Unlife. This is one of the great appeals of the vampire — that there may be a way to cheat death; to remain young and vigorous beyond one's natural time. The bone-chilling fear that goes along with this is the price that is to be paid for unnaturally lengthening one's span of time. For Whedon's vampires, part of the process of "being turned" is the loss of the human soul which, in Whedon's world, contains the "spark" that sets a human apart from a vampire. The soul serves as a type of moral compass for humans and with that anchor removed, it becomes simple, even pleasurable, for the average vampire to wantonly indulge in the taking of human life.[2] The *physical* form may remain uncorrupted following the turning of a human into a vampire, but complete *moral* decay follows. Such ease in destruction is portrayed as the inverse (again, the "negative space") of the life-affirming message so often contained in Whedon's work.

While the specific characteristics of the vampire vary from culture to culture, a common factor in the global mythology of vampires is some form of bloodsucking. Matthew Bunson collected the specifics of many of these legends in his text *The Vampire Encyclopedia*, which details the habits of the Indian *bhuta* (133), the Javanese *sundal bolong* (138), and the German *nachzehrer* (106), among many others. Further, as Manuela Dunn Mascetti notes, "many of the original characteristics of traditional vampirism seem to have arisen from China (as well as Assyria), and coincidentally so also did the first bubonic plague" (203). While tales of the vampire far predate the advent of Christianity, Mascetti speculates that this disease with its unprecedented mortality rate may be a cornerstone of the Western European vampire myth. The plague, which swept into Europe from the Far East, "was the greatest fear of the ages, and no one seemed able to do anything much about it. In the fourteenth century it is said to have killed around one third of the world's population, and the people of the time believed that it would wipe out mankind altogether before it left" (203). No one was spared — the pious perished alongside the profane. The disease struck without warning and no effective defense against it was known. According to the legends, however, there are a variety of effective defenses against vampiric attacks.

While Whedon's vampires can be repelled by the Christian religious objects such as the Latin cross and holy water (more on that later), tales of vampires are found in many pre–Christian societies. As an example, the Roman poet Horace wrote of a *lamia* in his *Ars Poetica*. Traditionally, a *lamia* was a woman who sucked the blood of infants, although some stories state that the *lamiae* were a species of demon that lured grown men to their deaths (Bunson 150). The continuing fascination with vampires can also been seen in the multitude of vampire images that have found their way into a wide variety of artistic media. Representations of the vampire myth can be found in poetry such as Coleridge's 1797 "Christabel" as well as novels, chief among them Stoker's 1897 *Dracula*. Vampires also figure prominently in the visual arts and can be found in paintings such as Symbolist Edvard Munch's 1895 psychological portrait *Vampire* and in films as far back as F. W. Murnau's 1922 masterpiece *Nosferatu*. In twenty-first century American society a simple Google search for the term "vampire" instantaneously returns 32.8 *million* hits. Clearly, there is an ongoing allure to the character of the vampire that shows no sign of abating in our advanced, scientifically based culture.

In part, this continuing lure of the Undead is based in its very deviancy —

we are often fascinated by the very things that repel us and vampires revel in two things that humans are taught to hold in respectful awe at an early age: blood and darkness. While Stoker's Renfield may be known for reciting maniacally that "the blood is the life," the idea that blood is the source of sentient existence far predates Stoker's Victorian tale. Many societies throughout history have elaborate rituals and taboos regarding blood and in the Western world, this concept of blood as a sacred life force seems to be rooted in Jewish belief. This is first seen in the Book of Genesis in which Noah is told specifically to "never eat animals unless their life-blood has been drained off" (Gen. 9:4). The prohibition is more starkly given in the Book of Leviticus, in which the Lord of Israel tells Moses: "And I will turn my face against anyone, whether an Israelite or a foreigner living among you, who eats blood in any form.... for the blood is the life" (Lev. 17:10, 14). While a search of *Strong's Concordance* indicates that the specific term "vampire" is not mentioned in the Bible, it seems clear from these early prohibitions that the consumption of blood in any form was considered clearly repugnant to the Jewish faithful and a violation of God's covenant with His chosen people.[3] Even today, the consumption of blood is usually viewed with revulsion as an unnatural act, unless it is ritualized. Examples of ritualized blood drinking are found in the sacrament of Communion in the Christian faith and in the consumption of cows' blood by the Maasai tribe, whose society revolves around the herding of cattle (MacKenzie 220). It is fascinating to consider that both of these examples involve the blood being the life—eternal life in the case of the sacrament of Communion and physical life in the case of the Maasai—in a direct echo of the sentiment expressed in Leviticus.

As vampires, Spike and Angel both regularly consume blood. The two share other fundamental qualities, including the fact that both were brought into their respective Unlives by women and share some tangled vampire family bloodlines.[4] Also significant is the fact that, as mortal humans, both Angel and Spike bore the same name. During his life, London-raised Spike was known as "William" while the Irish Angel was known by that language's variation of "Liam." The popular name "William" is of Germanic origin and is a combination of "wil" (meaning "will" or "desire") with "helm" (meaning "defense"); therefore, the name can be translated into "protector" (Room 595). The name is used to ironic effect here since neither of Whedon's "Williams" are true to their given names, for they do not seek to be protectors. Liam seeks release from a life he views as boring and dull while William seeks revenge against those who scorn and mock him for his pretensions. As vampires, both surrender their given names, taking instead the names "Angel" and "Spike," and they both choose to spend more than a century slaughtering the defenseless and innocent.

Physically, the two characters are reflections of one another. William is pale as an English rose while Liam's coloration is dark in the "black Irish" style.⁵ The two men are also dramatic contrasts insofar as personality and background are concerned. In life, the Irish Liam was a drunken layabout, while thoroughly English William was an overly sensitive poet and a bit of a dandy. Some of this may well be due to their respective time periods — viewers learn in "Becoming, Part 1" (*Buffy* 2.21) that Liam was changed in 1753, a time which is smack in the middle of the Age of Enlightenment. The wastrel Liam is clearly unconcerned with contemplating the effect of God and Nature on mankind, preferring to drink and whore his way through life. In contrast, viewers learn in "Fool for Love" (*Buffy* 5.07) that William became a vampire in 1880, thus making him a product of the Victorian age, which prized rigid propriety as a way to maintain social stability in an industrial era that was causing rapid changes in every aspect of English life. Life around a vampire may continue and progress but, as a creature of extremes, the vampire seems to either get mired in the trappings and customs that were prevalent during his mortal life or turn completely away from them.⁶

Personalities also evolve once a person becomes a Whedon vampire. Following his turning, William/Spike trades his Victorian sensibilities and foppish manners for a reckless, "bad-boy" image, complete with bleached-blonde hair and black nail polish, while Liam/Angel retains his former wildness, although it is somewhat tempered by perverted family responsibilities towards "his women," as he refers to Darla and Drusilla. How the two vampires treat their human families also provides great insight into the two characters, for once Liam and William are transformed into vampires, the two not-men take very different initial actions. In "The Prodigal" (*Angel* 1.15), the newly resurrected Angel returns to his family home to slaughter his human bloodline, including the father to whom Liam was a perpetual disappointment. In marked contrast, in "Lies My Parents Told Me" (*Buffy* 7.17), Spike's first vampiric act is to return home to turn his mother, to whom William was deeply devoted, into a vampire to spare her a lingering death from the wasting illness from which she suffers. By retaining some of the feelings of their previous selves toward their families, both vampires are exhibiting a sort of dual consciousness — the human part is still present, in some fashion. The point of the dual consciousness of the vampire will be explored further in this chapter.

William may have fancied himself a poet, but Spike takes his prosaic name from the mocking of a privileged party guest who declares that he'd "rather have a railroad spike through my head" than listen to William's moonstruck odes to Cecily, a girl who is William's social better ("Fool for Love" *Buffy* 5.07). Indeed, Spike takes his new name to heart, as Giles mentions in

"School Hard" (*Buffy* 2.03) that Spike has a penchant for torturing his victims with railroad spikes.

Angel, on the other hand, has a name that is rife with religious meaning. Perhaps Whedon chose this name to underscore the fallen nature of the character or to emphasize the view that redemption is possible for all who sincerely seek it, despite the horror of past acts committed by the penitent. At any rate, Charles Panati states that the word "enters our language through the Greek word *angelos* which is equivalent to the Hebrew word *mal'akh*, meaning 'messenger'" (62). In his soulless state, Whedon's Angel is known as "Angelus," which is the name given to a devotional prayer composed of particular phrases from the New Testament that were selected by the fourteenth century Pope John XXII. The Angelus serves to honor Christ and Mary and is to be recited morning, noon, and night (Panati 35). Whedon's Angelus, however, honors nothing other than the extended kill, which he views as an art form. Indeed, Angelus stalks his targets with perverse enjoyment — a sadistic trait perhaps best seen in his seduction and transformation of Drusilla, who will later become Spike's vampiric "sire," or parent-figure.[7]

In "Becoming, Part 1" (*Buffy* 2.21), viewers see the lengthy process by which Angelus first drove the gentle Drusilla to the point of madness before turning her into a death-dealing vampire in 1860.[8] Drusilla is shown to be a girl with a degree of psychic ability, which her mother has told her is "an affront to the Lord," since only God is meant to know the future. Frightened, Drusilla seeks comfort at the local church, where she unknowingly confesses her supposed sins to Angelus, who realizes that a rare prize has just fallen into his bloody lap.[9] He derives heightened pleasure from the fact that Drusilla is an innocent, for destroying the already evil or downtrodden just doesn't have the same appeal to Angelus who, if nothing else, adores a challenge. As the ensouled Angel, he confesses his sins regarding Drusilla to Buffy, the woman he loves, revealing that in response to his relentless stalking and killing of her friends and family, Drusilla fled to a convent where he killed her on the very day she took her vows ("Lie to Me" *Buffy* 2.07). It is key to mention that *Angel* is the one confessing his sins. To help the viewer keep the players straight, "Angel" is the "good" vampire, the one with a soul who is trying mightily to find redemption for his past actions; while "Angelus" is the "bad" vampire, the one without a soul who drives sweet young women insane for pleasure. This character split is somewhat reminiscent of Robert Louis Stevenson's good Dr. Jekyll and his alter-ego, the violent Mr. Hyde. To Whedon, the good/evil split hinges not on a medical concoction as in the Stevenson tale, but rather on the presence of a soul and the choices a person makes.

Since the key difference between the two Whedon characters of Angel and Angelus (both played by the same actor; there is no noticeable physical difference between the good and evil halves of the former Liam) is the existence of the soul, two interesting questions are raised. First, how does a vampire lose his soul in the first place? Second, and perhaps more interesting, how does a vampire get it back? Whedon sets up strict parameters for his vampires regarding these matters.

Whedon uses some very strong Christian imagery with his portrayal of vampires. In doing so, he is keeping with what has become the standard Western image of the vampire, a creature that can be read as the very inverse of the ideals of Christianity. The highest sacrament in the Christian faith is the rite of Holy Communion, a ritual that involves the ingestion of the flesh and blood of Christ as a link to the eternal life promised by Christ to His believers based on His willing sacrifice for humankind.[10] Vampires turn this sacrament inside-out, violently rending flesh and drinking human blood from unwilling victims in order to sustain their Unlife. In an additional perversion of the life-affirming rite of communion, in Whedon's world, a victim can only be turned into by a vampire by partaking of the blood of the vampire following significant blood loss of the victim.

Christianity provides some protection from Whedon's vampires, who are repulsed by Christian crosses, although no other religious symbol seems to have this repellent effect.[11] It is likely that Whedon went down this path for a simple reason: he assumed his audience would be familiar with the vampire myth as addressed in Stoker, which has a heavy emphasis on Christianity as an effective means of vampire slaying. Further, Christianity is a faith that has a longstanding tradition of demonology, including detailed rites of exorcism.

At any rate, contact with a Christian cross will scorch and burn a Whedon vampire and in fact, both Angel and Spike are seen at different times with burns that have been inflicted by such contact. Moreover, while stories of the power of the stake to destroy vampires far predate Christianity, some critics have read into the stake an explicit connection with the Christian cross. For example, Berni Phillips states that "To the Christian, the connection is clear: only a piece of wood will kill the vampire because it points to the Cross and Jesus' sacrifice for us." Most would find this to be stretching the Christian connection to the point of snapping since, as previously stated, vampire myths can be found in multiple pre–Christian societies. However, regardless of the history, most viewers are familiar with the use of the stake to dispatch vampires.

In addition to the cross, holy water is also an effective weapon against Whedon's vampires. Buffy uses holy water to great effect in dispatching the mentally unbalanced vampire Zachary Kralick during the hellish "test" known as the Cruciamentum which the Watcher's Council forces her to undergo on her eighteenth birthday. She tricks Kralick into drinking holy water, which rather spectacularly consumes the vampire from the inside out. It is useful to note that, while Whedon clearly codes Christian objects and symbols as having power to repel vampires, nothing prohibits a vampire from freely entering a church *building*. However, most vampires steer clear of churches, believing the legends they have been told that such places are dangerous to their kind.[12]

Whedon does not slavishly copy either Stoker's traditional portrayal of vampires or the more modern incarnations of Stephen King or Anne Rice, all of whom have incorporated Christian belief into the worlds of their vampire creations. While many myths abound to explain the origin of vampires, Whedon's vampires are human corpses who have been hijacked by incorporeal demons.[13] As Giles explains, what we consider to be "our" world was first the realm of demonkind. As demons lost their hold on this world, they fled to other realities to wait for humans to die out. Vampires are the result of the blending of human and demon, for "the last demon to leave this reality fed off a human, mixed their blood. He was a human form possessed — infected — by the demon's soul" ("The Harvest" *Buffy* 1.02). Whedon has said that due to their half-breed heritage and the fact that vampires must have a human host, vampires are considered the dregs of demon society (Golden 93). While other types of demons may enter a living human, those demons may, barring a successful exorcism, leave and return to the human host at their own discretion, while the vampire is trapped within the body it has turned (Mascetti 192). Apparently, this lack of freedom to come and go marks the vampire as a sort of "lesser demon" in the hierarchy of the damned. Further, to return to the earlier idea of the "dual consciousness" of a vampire, a Whedon vampire is not a blank slate. Once the human soul is evicted, the demon continues to retain "the knowledge, memories, and some of the personality" of the human that the demon killed (Golden 99). This explains why Angelus sustains a hatred for Liam's father and why Spike retains a deep tenderness for William's mother.

Particularly noteworthy in Giles' explanation is that the "infection" of the human is caused by the presence of the *demon* soul. Therefore, souls in Whedon's world are not to be read as being limited merely to the human race — there are multiple types of souls.[14] However, it is the *removal* of the human soul through the death of the human "host" that permits the vampire to set up housekeeping.

If vampires provide "negative space" for humanity to see itself differently due to contrasting what we *are* with what we *aren't*, Angel takes the equation another step forward, for he is the "negative space" among vampires. Angel is rare among the countless vampires in Whedon's world in that he has regained the human soul that was taken from him when his Liam self died and Angelus was born. In fact, for a long, long time, Angel wasn't just "rare" in this — he was unique. But then came Spike, Angel's personal "negative space." Now that we have arrived at a "triple negative" (for Spike is Angel's negative, who is the vampire negative, who is humanity's negative), it is probably a good idea to stop and take a deep breath, for key to the discussion of the binary of Angel and Spike is the contrast in how these two regain human souls after so many years of slaughter.

In 1898, Angelus is gleefully living up to his billing as "the Scourge of Europe" when he kills a young Gypsy girl. In and of itself, that murder was nothing unusual; as Angel himself remarks, at this point in his history, he'd been "offer[ing] ugly death to everyone I met and I did it with a song in my heart" ("Angel" *Buffy* 1.07). However, this girl was different for, like Buffy, she had family who would not let such an outrage go unpunished. How do you torment a remorseless, immortal killer? Simple — the Gypsy clan called on magic to restore the vampire's human soul. With this accomplished, Angel now carries the full weight of his actions and was nearly crushed by the guilt, shame, and remorse for more than a century of bloodletting. As he explains to Buffy, "You have no idea what it's like to have done the things I've done — and to care" ("Angel" *Buffy* 1.07). Angel must now find a way to live with himself and his past actions. This will not be a simple task.

It is unlikely that Whedon chose to have Angel's soul restored by Gypsies by mere accident, for Gypsies (more properly called "Rom" or "Romany") have an important place in the history of the worldwide vampire myth. As a people, they date back to ancient India (Bunson 114). Most likely, the Rom brought the myths and legends of the vampire with them as they migrated westward and, over time, those stories and traditions merged with the ones of the communities in which they settled.[15] Common in the legends of the Rom is a "nearly universal terror of the dead ... and the return of a loved one was believed to bring about the most evil consequences. Swedish Gypsies held that their undead could transform into horses or birds, while Muslim Gypsies in Yugoslavia believed that both pumpkins and watermelons could turn into vampires if kept for too long" (Bunson 114). The Gypsies who restored Angel's soul were very careful. A fail-safe was built into the curse to guarantee that Angel would never relax his vigilance and lapse into complacency about his past misdeeds. For if Angel ever experienced a single moment of pure, unadulterated happiness, his soul would again be stripped from him. So Angel enters a twilight existence, for his vampire family is revolted by this new thing he has become, which is neither hunter nor prey as they understand it, and he cannot mix with humans, who he has considered as nothing more than game for more than a century. Despising himself and bewildered at this colossal crisis of conscience that has been foisted upon him, Angel keeps to the shadows, living off the blood of rats and skulking in alleys that must remind him of the one in Galway where he first died.

He finds his purpose when a good demon named Whistler seeks him out and challenges Angel to make a difference in the battle of good versus evil as opposed to wallowing in guilt and self-pity.[16] Angel rises to the challenge and becomes a champion for good. At least, he does until Buffy's seventeenth birthday, when the two make love, thereby causing Angel to experience that one moment of perfect happiness when he is with someone who knows exactly who and what he is, is knowledgeable of what he has done, and still loves him with her whole heart. What should be bliss turns into tragedy as Angel's soul is ripped away and Angelus is freed to wreak havoc on the world again.

Angel's soul is restored to him through a reversal of the powerful Gypsy spell, but the transformation happens too late and Buffy is forced to kill him in order to save the world.[17] Through mysterious (and quite possibly divine) intervention, Angel returns to the human world from hell, still with soul intact. He continues to struggle with his internal demon. Thomas Hibbs has commented that Angel's path to redemption comes with specific responsibilities, even with metaphorical markers (qtd. in Reiss 121). One of those markers is meteorological, for in the striking episode "Amends" (*Buffy* 3.10) Angel contemplates suicide by sunlight after being visited in Dickensian fashion by the ghosts of some of his past victims.[18] His death wish is thwarted by the timely arrival of a freak snowstorm that obscures the rays of the sun. Given the Christmas gift of a second chance, Angel reaches the decision to continue the fight, although he also reaches the painful realization that he and Buffy are sweet poison for one another. Ultimately, Angel leaves her to continue his quest for redemption in the ironically named City of Angels, Los Angeles. Angel thus takes another step toward being part of human society by choosing self-sacrifice over the more self-centered emotion of mindless passion.

Angel's departure creates a vampire-with-a-soul vacuum in Sunnydale, which will eventually be filled by the least likely of candidates — William the Bloody, aka "Spike," who proudly crows about the fact that he has already killed two Slayers. As plain old William, Spike's life was drab and ordinary, but as Spike, it pulsates with excitement. He can be the forceful, powerful man he could not be in his mortal life and he revels in the wearing of that persona. While he is no longer the ineffectual mooncalf he had been as a mortal, his vampire self retains portions of his previous personality. While he no longer simulates the tortured artistry of a Byronic figure, Spike continues to have ties to the mortal world; far more so than Angelus and quite arguably, far more so than Angel. Even without a soul, Spike is shown to be capable of love in his enduring, passionate relationship with Drusilla, whom he treats with tenderness and concern, possibly out of a twisted feeling of gratitude to her for turning him into a vampire in the first place. After all, Drusilla recognized in William something special, something worth nurturing. Further, Spike is content with the world as a whole, as well as his particular place in it. When Angelus seeks to destroy it all by freeing the demon Acathla, Spike takes the fantastic step of approaching his sworn enemy, Buffy, to stop the apocalypse, explaining, "The truth is, I like this world. You've got dog racing, Manchester United. And you've got people. Billions of people walking around like Happy Meals with legs. It's all right here" ("Becoming, Part 2" *Buffy* 2:22). Clearly, Spike is at home in the world, quite possibly more so that he ever was as a mortal human.

In addition, Spike has not completely lost the appreciation for poetry and loveliness he had as a mortal, although his aesthetic template shifted when he became a vampire. This shift is illustrated by contrasting his ode to the embarrassed Cecily in "Fool for Love" (*Buffy* 5.07) of "My heart expands/'tis grown a bulge in it/inspired by your beauty/effulgent" to reassuring Drusilla that he loves her totally "eyeballs to entrails" in "Halloween" (*Buffy* 2.06).

Meanwhile, the aesthetic abilities of Angelus seem to have developed upon becoming a vampire — both as Angelus and as Angel, he is shown to have a talent for sketching, something the ne'er-do-well Liam is never shown to possess.[19] Moreover, Angelus finds a certain perverse creativity in the thoughtful crafting of the most repulsive forms of torture and violence, as seen in his slowly driving the gentle Drusilla insane before killing her. Angelus is methodical, preferring to concentrate on one victim at a time and taking care to not arouse the suspicions of the community in which he is hunting. One doesn't rush the production of art, after all.

In contrast, Spike prefers to strike hard and fast, causing maximum carnage for its own sake. This may be why Spike has managed to kill two Slayers, while Angel has not. Spike kills not just to survive or to test his abilities, but because, like other psychopaths, he enjoys it. Writer Jane Espenson has commented on Spike's quality of "happy evil," saying that a character without remorse resonates with viewers because "if evil's having a good time, then it's much scarier. If evil is happy, that's creepy. It's aware of what it's doing and it likes it" (Golden 108). However, there is much more to Spike than his terrifying delight in causing mayhem.

Despite his palpable pleasure in causing pain and terror, the soulless Spike is able to be hurt emotionally. Following an experiment by a secret paramilitary group, Spike has a computer chip surgically implanted in his head that causes him great pain with even the slightest attempt to inflict hurt on a human.[20] Disgusted that "her boy" can no longer perform as a vampire should, Drusilla leaves Spike and finds comfort in the arms (presuming that there are arms) of a fungus demon.[21] Her infidelity causes Spike great emotional pain, which he attempts to work through with increased violence towards humans and the consumption of stupendous quantities of alcohol.

In addition to being subject to the very human pain of emotional hurt, Spike can also provide emotional support, as he does to Buffy as she is coming to terms with the severity of her mother's illness in Season Five. While he may have come to the house planning to kill her for her mocking of him as being "beneath her" (words that are an unwitting echo of Cecily's rejection of his fumbling advances), when he sees her sitting alone and sobbing her eyes out, his immediate reaction is to offer to help. He then moves to sit awkwardly beside her, providing her what silent comfort he can.

Despite these tender moments, it should never be forgotten that Spike continues to be evil, even with the inhibitor chip that frustrates his violent tendencies. After all, he took a shotgun to Buffy's house with the intention of murdering her and is himself bewildered by his rush of sympathy and desire to offer solace to her. Despite the chip, Spike willingly allies himself with the forces of darkness as personified by the man/monster amalgam Adam in Season Four and continues to take delight in causing mayhem even after that threat has been neutralized. Through this ever-evolving character, Whedon creates a complex portrait of the possibilities of change.

For example, Spike is shown to have a certain soft spot for Buffy's mother, Joyce. Following her death at the hands of a mundane illness rather than a vicious monster that the Slayer could vanquish, Spike comes to the Summers house bearing a bouquet of flowers as a sign of respect. When Buffy's friend and ally, Xander, accuses Spike of impure motives, the vampire snaps that "I liked the lady! Understand, monkey boy? She was decent. She didn't put on airs. She always had a nice cuppa for me. And she never treated me like a freak" ("Forever" *Buffy* 5.17). Further, when Buffy makes the ultimate sacrifice at the end of Season Five, hurling herself into an interdimensional abyss to save the world, it is Spike who is the first to physically break down at the sight of her lifeless body.

Following Buffy's death, Spike becomes more involved with the Scoobies. He acts as a protector towards Buffy's sister, Dawn, and mourns the loss of Buffy. A vampire who has killed two Slayers mourning the death of a Chosen One and babysitting her kid sister—truly Spike is an anomaly in the vampire world. Jana Reiss accurately refers to Spike as "a redemption in progress" (126). This progression continues after Buffy is returned to the world of the living through powerful magic exercised by her friends, who are convinced they are rescuing her from a demon dimension. In fact, far from suffering unending torment, Buffy confesses to Spike that she thinks she was in heaven and that this world is her hell. She is able to reveal this horrifying truth to Spike because his affection for her has clearly grown during her absence. For example, he is able to tell her that she has been "gone" exactly 147 days. He's been keeping track because, like the others, Spike has not been able to move beyond the moment of Buffy's death. As he explains to her, "But I want you to know I did save you. Not when it counted, of course, but — after that. Every night after that. I'd see it all again ... do something different. Faster or more clever, you know? Dozens of times, lots of different ways. Every night I save you" ("After Life" *Buffy* 6.03). Spike is growing more human, as shown by his willingness to love and to align himself with human concerns.

At the same time, the object of his affection is growing colder and more distant from the human world. Buffy takes advantage of Spike's infatuation to the point of repeatedly engaging in dangerous sex with him as a means to feel *something*— even if it's nothing more than disgust with herself— in this world which seems so harsh and alien to her. In many ways, throughout Season Six, Buffy and Spike have an unnatural swapping of positions, as if a cobra has fallen in love with a mongoose, although which character is best represented by which animal is up for debate.

When Buffy breaks off her tumultuous, malignant relationship with Spike, he reverts to his former violent ways. Spike has been rejected repeatedly— by Cecily, by Drusilla, and by Buffy — but this time, he's determined to "make her feel," convinced that she is in fact as deeply in love with him as he is with her. His attempts culminate in his attempted rape of Buffy in "Seeing Red," a sexual assault that is "attempted" and not "completed" only due to Buffy's Slayer strength (*Buffy* 6.19). The realization of what he has just tried to do horrifies him, even though he is a vampire who has rejoiced in the slaughter of innocents for well over a century.

He flees the house and is next seen somewhere in Africa, where he is engaged in a series of increasingly difficult trials. The prize for surviving these tests is a masterpiece of Whedon misdirection. Spike comments to the demon overseeing these ordeals that, once he wins, the demon will "give me what I want. Make me what I was so Buffy can get what she deserves" ("Grave" *Buffy* 6.22). Looked at in one light, a viewer can think that Spike has turned his back on all that was life in Sunnydale and willingly embraced his demonic nature. Faced with the harsh reality that he is a monster capable of trying to rape the woman he professes to love, Spike is undergoing these tests in order to receive the prize of having the inhibitor chip removed from his head, thereby unleashing his full demonic nature again.

Whedon enjoys making his audience yell at the television set. When Spike triumphs over the final test, the demon keeps his word, placing his clawed hand on Spike's chest and returning him to what he once was — by restoring his long-lost soul. Unlike Angel, whose soul is returned to him as the result of a vengeful curse, Spike has fought to regain his, whether or not he knew it at the time. Perhaps because the return of his soul is the result of choice, Spike is able to quickly come to some sort of peace with his past actions, rather than the century it took Angel.[22]

While the process may not have taken much time, Spike finds living with remorse painful, yet he seems to welcome the agony. This is perhaps best illustrated in the episode "Beneath You" (*Buffy* 7.02).[23] In a darkened church, Buffy learns that Spike's increasingly erratic behavior is due to his regaining his soul. Tired, bloody, and half-crazed, Spike haltingly explains to Buffy that he has regained "the spark," which Buffy deciphers to mean his human soul, in order to "be hers." The change is not going swimmingly well for Spike, however. With his back to Buffy, Spike walks up the nave to contemplate the cross, saying, "She shall look on him with forgiveness, and everybody will forgive and love. He will be loved." He drapes himself on the cross, his Undead flesh sizzling at the touch of the holy, sanctified object. As Jana Riess points out, "although the episode does not offer a clear-cut spoken expression of forgiveness, the visual image of the cross hints that such forgiveness is possible, and Buffy's tears make it complete" (88). In a series filled with heartbreaking moments, this image of Spike, stripped to the waist and slumped on a cross, is a standout. Oblivious to the burning of his own flesh and plaintively asking Buffy, "Can we rest?" this vampire with a soul is a pitiable figure.

At this juncture, Whedon has shattered traditional mythological constructs regarding vampires and given viewers two Undead creatures of the night who have had their human souls restored to them. The next question is: Which of the two souls is more valuable? In order to answer that question, the evolution of the concept of the soul should first be briefly examined.

Different religions and cultures have traditionally viewed the soul in a wide variety of ways. To the ancient Egyptians, the soul was the essential part of a human that carried a person's earthly deeds into the next world. After death, the jackal-headed god Anubis would weigh "the heart of each dead soul against a feather, the symbol of truth" (Carlyon 268). Charles Panati comments that apparently a "little virtue goes a long way in the [Egyptian] afterlife" (76). Panati also highlights the similarity of the Egyptian belief system and the belief contained in Proverbs 21:1–2 "that God weighs the goodness in each person's heart" (76). This may be mere coincidence or it may perhaps be a holdover from the time the Israelites spent in Egypt serving as slaves, according to the Biblical accounts in Exodus.

At any rate, the ancient Israelites had no belief in a soul that survived death and ascended to a heavenly afterlife. Rather, the "dead Israelite *descended* into the neutral underworld that was Sheol for a long, numbing sleep. For eternity" (Panati 450, emphasis in original). While Genesis speaks of man being created by God's "breath of life," this was a concept that was originally viewed as a simple "animating force," as opposed to an immortal part of the individual (450). Such beliefs have changed over the millennia. While contemporary Jews have a wide spectrum of beliefs regarding the afterlife, "it is fair to state that most Jews do not believe in a physical hereafter but share a belief that their souls, once released from their earthly remains, will ascend heavenward and join the infinite cosmos" (Gross 8). This is one example of the evolution of the concept of what the human soul can be.

The Greeks are the ones who first made the leap from viewing the soul as the "spark of life" that merely got humans up and walking to viewing the soul as something unique and eternal. Plato reasoned that "the soul contained the vital essence of a person, which, once released from its imprisonment in the body, grew strong, more powerful, more rarefied and refined — more godlike — and thus it floated upward" (Panati 451). In this view, the soul is the "embodiment of personality: desire, action, reason" although only reason survived eternally, while desire and action perished with the body (451–452). In Whedon's creations, shreds of the personality of the human host survive the death of that host and remain present in the new vampire incarnation of the victim. Consider again that both Angel and Spike retained their respective feelings towards their parents and further consider "vamp Willow's" wholehearted embrace of her sexuality in "The Wish"(*Buffy* 3.09).

It is sometimes said that the Age of Science has supplanted the Age of Religion and it is true that some contemporary scientists scoff at the idea of an immortal human soul, preferring to embrace a "reductionist" theory which posits that there is no "soul" as it is generally understood. Those who adhere to this theory believe that "consciousness — our sense of identity, our delights and sorrows, our loves and hates, our hopes and fears — is no more than a peculiar product of the machine that is the human brain" (Goldman 45–46). Dr. Francis Crick, who co-discovered the DNA double helix, is a proponent of this view, believing that eventually science will progress to the point that we will be able to "dismiss the idea of a mind or soul separate from the brain" (46). However, even Dr. Crick admits that "I myself find it difficult at times to avoid the idea of the homunculus — a little man in our head directing it all. One slips into it so easily" (qtd. in Goldman 46). Goldman also points out that the reductionist view is not the only one held by modern scientists, however. Many other scientists take a "dualist" view and believe in "the 'ghost in the machine' — some intangible spark that makes us more than just organic robots" (47). Mankind has always struggled with the meaning of life and this debate is just another round in the ongoing boxing match.

It is interesting to note that Dr. Crick's reference to the "homunculus" is rooted in a very ancient belief. Frazer mentions a nearly identical notion in his classic study of magic and religion *The Golden Bough* in which he describes the belief that "if a man lives and moves, it can only be because he has a little man or animal inside who moves him. The animal inside the animal, the man inside the man, is the soul" (207). Such a soul must be carefully protected against harm and acts of mischief since it is subject to malicious harm by outside forces.

Frazer notes that in many cultures, both the shadow and the reflection of a person are viewed as being manifestations of that person's soul and many elaborate taboos developed that were intended to protect the soul. Frazer speculates that these beliefs can be seen in the Greek myth of Narcissus, for "the Greeks regarded it as an omen of death if a man dreamed of seeing himself so reflected [in a pool of water.] They feared that the water-spirits would drag the person's reflection or soul under water, leaving him soulless to perish" (223). These beliefs regarding the power of a person's image may be the origin of one of the common myths regarding vampires — that since they have lost their human souls, they cannot cast a reflection. Whedon's vampires partially adhere to this convention and are unable to cast a reflection. However, they are able to cast shadows and their images also can be captured on film, as seen in the episode "Halloween" (*Buffy* 2.06) in which Spike studies a "game film" of Buffy killing several vampires in order to learn her fighting style. Interestingly, even with a soul, a Whedon vampire remains incapable of casting a reflection and many jokes are made about Angel's inability to see his own image. In a larger way, however, vampires are a dark reflection of the human experience. This foil provided by the vampire is merely a distorted reflection that only faintly resembles the true human form, similar to the way a photographic negative only hints at the true picture it contains.

In the final analysis, photographic negatives are about perception, which is notoriously easy to misrepresent. In Whedon's work, good demons can be found, such as the reformed (and highly capitalistic) Anya. Just as importantly to the Whedon mythos, human monsters abound, such as Warren from Season Six of *Buffy* and basically the entire workforce of Wolfram & Hart in *Angel*. Also, Angel's efforts to "help the hopeless" can backfire. For example, in "I've Got You Under My Skin" (*Angel* 1.14) Angel works relentlessly to save a possessed child, only to discover that the demon *wanted* out of the child because the child was far more evil than the demon ever thought of being.

Angel perceives the child and fills in the blanks to mistakenly code the child as a soul-filled innocent, when the reality is very different. In a particularly affecting scene, the child speaks to Angel in the voice of Angel's deceased guide, Doyle, to taunt Angel about his inability to protect those he cares about. Having had more than enough loss in his Unlife, the vampire wraps his hand in a cloth to protect it from burning and picks up a cross to perform an exorcism on the child. Since the child's evil stems from within rather than from without, the ritual fails — the demon may be gone, but the evil remains, along with the child's soul. To Whedon, merely having a soul is not a guarantee of saintly behavior, be the holder of the soul vampire or human, for there is always a choice.

Humans, even those fully equipped with souls, are capable of barbarous acts. In the eighteenth century, at about the time Liam was being turned into Angelus, a truly screwy movement was taking place in England, where "bored city dwellers became fascinated by sadism, sorcery, and a dungeons-and-skeletons sense of fun" (Ackerman 147). The bizarre notion arose among English cooks that an animal that had been tortured before slaughter resulted in healthier, better tasting meat. Cooks "chopped up live fish, which they claimed made the flesh firmer ... they tenderized pigs and calves by whipping them to death with knotted ropes; they hung poultry upside down and slowly bled them to death" all in the name of more appetizing meals (147). A variety of this sort of culinary sadism is referenced in "Unleashed" (*Angel* 5.03). In this episode, a very exclusive restaurant prizes itself on the rare game it is able to provide to its select, elite clientele — including a human girl who is a werewolf. To assure the customers that they are getting the "real deal," the girl is trussed up to be served alive, once the full moon has risen. The fact that they are going to consume a human being bothers the jaded customers not a bit; all that matters to them is the rarity of the experience. Therefore, they do not seem to be all that different from Angelus, who took great pleasure in torturing his victims. The primary difference seems to be that Angelus was soulless while the customers (presumably) still retained their souls while engaging in sadism and murder.

Also in this episode, Angel reveals that vampires have a choice whether or not to be evil. They "can control themselves if they want to." With this, Whedon is making a definite statement about the human soul: it may be easier to control your actions and conform to the side of good if you have a soul serving as your conscience, but it can be done without one. Further, having one is not a fail-safe that people will behave kindly and with compassion towards others.

The traditional Christian view is that grace holds the power of salvation; that divine aid is available to serve as a way to find meaning out of the confusion and suffering that are part of the human condition. However, two views of grace taken from the Hindu perspective can be quite instructive when looking at Whedon's creations. One is known as the "Cat School" and the other is known as the "Monkey School." John Renard explains:

> According to the Cat School, divine grace is all-sufficient and does not depend at all on human action. Mother cats carry their kittens around by picking them up with their teeth. According to the Monkey School, human beings must cooperate in the saving action of divine grace. Mother monkeys rescue their babies from danger, but the baby first climbs aboard and holds tight [262].

It is interesting to note that both schools of thought use mother imagery to articulate their positions, since Whedon so joyously celebrates the female. As an atheist, Whedon may disagree with the tenets of the Hindu religion (or any other), but he may be more at ease with a faith that reveres the feminine. At any rate, both Angel and Spike's actions seem to fit the Monkey School — a person (or a vampire) must *want* to be redeemed and then that person must be willing to work for it.

It is sometimes difficult to accept forgiveness, which is the cornerstone of grace, be that the human or the divine variety. As Christian philosopher C. S. Lewis has expressed, "Many promising reconciliations have broken down because while both parties come prepared to forgive, neither party comes prepared to be forgiven" (qtd. in Reiss 88–89). While Angel has had more time to adjust to his guilt and remorse than Spike, both characters occasionally exhibit a nagging need to be punished for their past misdeeds. In Spike's case, this happens dramatically when a potential Slayer named Dana, who has been driven mad by harrowing childhood trauma, confuses Spike with her tormentor. Overpowering the ensouled vampire, she proceeds to hack off his forearms. As Spike recovers from the operation to reattach his arms, Angel reminds him that what happened to Dana was not Spike's fault, a point of view Spike finds difficult to swallow. Spike confides to Angel that he doesn't feel justified in grousing about his present situation, remarking, "The lass thought I killed her family. And I'm supposed to what, complain 'cause hers wasn't one of the hundreds of families I did kill?" ("Damage" *Angel* 5.11) To Spike, the punishment is just, even if Dana was mistaken about exactly what sin he was paying for at the time. Spike is making a choice to take responsibility for his actions, which Whedon always portrays as a sign of moral growth.

Angel is made aware of a prophecy that promises that the "vampire with a soul" will be returned to human form once he fulfills his destiny. Like many prophecies, this one is coy about exactly what that destiny might be and with the appearance of the ensouled Spike during Season Five of *Angel*, there is much speculation as to *which* vampire with a soul this prophecy is intended to refer.[24] Stacey Abbott has pointed out that prophecy in Whedon's work is always fallible and is not to be trusted ("Walking the Fine Line"). To Whedon, people are defined far more by their own decisions and choices and are not ruled by scrolls and runes. Angel comes to the same conclusion, stating his philosophy of life: "If nothing we do matters—then all that matters is what we do, 'cause that's all there is.... All I wanna do is help. I wanna help because—I don't think people should suffer as they do. Because if there is no bigger meaning, then the smallest act of kindness is the greatest thing in the world" ("Epiphany" *Angel* 2.16). Ultimately, this is Angel and Spike's purpose—to teach those they encounter that, while the fight may seem to lack any real meaning, the meaning is in what you assign to your actions. Moreover, nothing is unimportant—what you choose to do will have a ripple effect on those touched by your actions.

Like Ibsen's Peer Gynt, Spike and Angel may occasionally fear that if they stare into their very cores, only blankness will greet them; but the mere fact that both vampires continue to fight for a better world should negate this fear. Love not only gives meaning to actions; love *is* the meaning and Angel and Spike both love humanity enough to fight to preserve it, even though they are not a part of it. Love is the answer, no matter what the question may be. And it's far easier to love with a soul.

It seems poetic that this lesson comes through an angel, although Whedon's Angel has often been an avenging angel and also has a bloody past as an angel of death. In many faith traditions, angels are classified into a number of categories, with those closest to the Divine afforded greater responsibility and respect. Annie Dillard explains that, in the Christian faith, "Seraphs are the highest; they are aflame with love for God, and stand closer to him than the others. Seraphs love God; cherubs, who are second, possess perfect knowledge of him. So love is greater than knowledge; how could I have forgotten?" (45). For it is love that enflames both Spike and Angel. Spike literally bursts into flame as he saves the world at the end of *Buffy*'s Season Seven; a sacrifice he willingly makes not merely out of love for Buffy, but out of a desire to ensure the Hellmouth is stopped for once and for all.[25] Angel finds enough love within himself to fight for humanity's survival every night, despite the fact that humanity is unlikely to ever even have an inkling of his existence, much less his battle record.

In the end, it is not enough to be forgiven for sins, nor is it enough to meekly accept the grace that is offered. As Reiss puts it, "The message ... is not simply 'Go then, and sin no more' but 'Go then, and devote your life to actively fighting evil in the world'" (121). Spike and Angel both fear that their sins are just too great for any sort of forgiveness or mercy to register; that their respective pasts are simply too horrible for the light and warmth of grace to reach them. While both vampires are willing to accept that their purpose may be to fight the good fight, they both occasionally despair that no reward will be forthcoming for their efforts.

Yet they continue to fight. As Whedon illustrates through the respective journeys of Angel and Spike, both souls are valuable—both Angel's cursed one and Spike's hard-won version have worth, but only because Angel and Spike treat them as precious. Having the conscience that goes along with the soul gives both vampires the necessary impetus to continue to fight against the ever-rising tide of evil. The fact that Angel and Spike engage in this ongoing battle even though no Divine brownie points or cosmic gold stars seem to accrue for their efforts is a lesson well worth paying attention to. In a world that often seems to celebrate shallow and self-absorbed actions, it's odd to think that two fictional vampires can teach viewers the finer points of what it means to be human. After all, these two characters are not just the "negative space" of humanity by being vampires; they dwell in a category of "double negatives" as they are neither humans with souls, nor vampires without souls, but are the extremely unlikely combination of vampires with souls who serve to reflect facets of humanity. Therein lies the true purpose of these characters for, like Spike and Angel, we shouldn't do the right things in life hoping for a payoff; we should do them because we should do them.

PART 2

FAMILY: A PLACE AT THE TABLE

Mr. Maclay: We are her blood kin!
Who the hell are you?
Buffy: We're family.
—"Family" *Buffy the Vampire Slayer* 5.06

3

Coming Apart, but Moving Forward

Magic Twins and Older Sisters in *Fray*

Even from a purely rational, scientific point of view, twins are creepy. Whedon uses twins in the eight-issue comic book *Fray* to explore the meaning of identity, the concept of what a person's purpose in life may be, and the impact that discovery can have on the person's family. Whedon's use of twins as a device to delve into issues of family and individuality draws on a very long-reaching human apprehension regarding the existence of twins. This stems from the biological basis of identical twins who come into being from the spontaneous splitting of a single fertilized egg in a form of asexual reproduction, causing the resulting children to be actual genetic clones of one another (Wright 12). In this fashion, identical twins cause us to question the comfortable concept of each person being a separate and unique individual, unlike any other who has ever walked the planet.

Throughout human history, the presence of twin children in a society has been an event viewed with varying degrees of wonder, suspicion, and outright fear. Moreover, these mixed feelings regarding twins are not limited to so-called "primitive" societies. For example, Nazi doctor Josef Mengele viewed twins as the perfect control group for a horrifying variety of sadistic studies. Today, twins continue to fascinate researchers, who routinely conduct far more benevolent studies on twins to probe the effects of various genetic and environmental factors in helping establish who we are as individuals. Twins are spellbinding to outsiders due to their peculiar nature. Even with the advent of fertility drugs which make multiple births more common, human twins are unusual and we often view the different with a degree of fearful eagerness.

Whedon works his way up to exploring twinship. He first delves into the duality of human nature with his use of doppelgängers for established characters. The clearest illustration of this is found in *Buffy*'s "The Wish" (3.09) storyline which introduces viewers to an alternate reality's "Evil Willow," who has been turned into a very enthusiastic vampire and the antithesis of the "real" Willow.[1] "Evil Willow" is a dark copy — a type of foil, really — for the Willow of the Sunnydale world.

This raises an important point about twins. A doppelgänger is merely a copy of an actual person and not a separate individual, as opposed to a twin, who has an independent life separate from, yet in many ways defined by, the other half of the equation. For someone as intent on exploring the large issues of good, evil, and personal choice as Whedon, twins are a subject that begs to be explored more deeply than he could by creating doppelgängers. The eight-issue comic *Fray* permits Whedon to more fully scrutinize the idea of twinship with the creation of Melaka and her twin brother, Harth.

Fray is a departure from the strictly visual text Whedon has traditionally employed. Therefore, the first part of this chapter will discuss the use of the comic book format as a literary form. The second part of this chapter will discuss how some societies have viewed twins, as well as the use of twins in both classical mythology and contemporary popular culture. The third and final part of this chapter will bring these two threads together to analyze the "hero's journey" undertaken by Whedon's Melaka Fray and what can be learned by readers who choose to follow her on that odyssey of self-exploration.

Comic books have been an important influence of Whedon's work. Indeed, in the foreword to *Fray*, he recounts his dismay at the age of twelve over the lack of interesting girls in comics and his delight at the introduction of Marvel's Kitty Pryde.[2] At this time, Whedon is currently immersed in writing the monthly Marvel title *Astonishing X-Men* and is also writing the "Season Eight" comic book version of *Buffy*, which was launched by Dark Horse in March of 2007.[3] As Whedon is a self-identified "comics geek" (Kaveney 60), one can only imagine his delight at being in the heart of comic creation in this fashion.

That said, comic books are seldom considered a true form of literature. Routinely, comics are denied serious consideration and are often unceremoniously condemned to sit at the children's table at the academic feast. This is somewhat strange, given that comics result from the marriage of two forms of artistic expression that have been studied deeply and analyzed critically for centuries: the written word and the visual representation of both the concrete and the abstract. Comics are gaining a level of respectability in academia through thoughtful work by scholars in the literary and popular culture arenas, as well as in texts such as McCloud's *Understanding Comics* (which is written in comic form) and Klock's *How to Read Superhero Comics and Why*. Moreover, events such as the granting of a Pulitzer Prize in 1992 to *Maus*, Art Spiegelman's creative and deeply moving Holocaust memoir in comic form, have increased interest in the comic book as literature.[4] Attitudes continue to shift in favor of the comic book, quite likely in response to the indisputable fact that modern popular culture itself is evolving and that evolution is bringing with it some new ideas of what is worth studying. In a world in which nearly everything seems to be mutable, it stands to reason that what was once dismissed as frivolous should be deemed worthy of at least another look.

In considering this blend of the visual and the written Sean Howe has concluded that this mixture does indeed contribute to what he refers to as the "ghettoization" of comics. This is because words are commonly considered to be "harder earned information than pictures" but that "images can invite the reader to reflect, to slow down, in a way that pure text never will" (Howe x).[5] Even the works of American master Roy Lichtenstein, who is best known for his creation of large-scale comic panels, were first dismissed by the art world as not being "true art," in great part due to his subject matter.

The disdain for the combination of language and pictures has a long history. Plato (who never met an Abstract Expressionist) notes in the *Cratylus* that "images resemble the objects they represent [while] words represent objects only by virtue of custom or convention" (Varnum and Gibbons xi). In the eighteenth century, Gotthold Lessing argued that painting and poetry belonged to separate and distinct spheres, as painting had to be arranged spatially while poetry had to be arranged temporally to have meaning. Lessing "disdained any effort to weaken the boundaries between these spheres, claiming that this might turn a painting 'into a speaking picture' or turn a text into 'a freakish kind of writing'" (Varnum and Gibbons xi). It can be argued that both Plato and Lessing came from more rigid worlds that were far more stratified than the one we currently occupy, which may provide an explanation for past critics desiring such fixed artistic spheres. However, contemporary American society is defined by a bewildering mixture of crossovers and blurred boundaries, both political and artistic. Visual images have undeniable power, an authority which is often derived from the symbolic meaning attached to the image itself. Varnum and Gibbons address this issue, stating that "All cultures possess a lexicon of images that, like its verbal lexicon, is built up through convention over time. In China, the characters of the written language itself are images. In the United States and many other western countries, both Superman and Mickey Mouse are instantly recognizable icons" (xii). It is worth noting that both of these undoubtedly American visual icons are male. This is hardly surprising, since comics have traditionally been a male sphere — as creators, characters, and as audience. With his creations of super-powered female fighters Buffy and Fray, Whedon continues to challenge the established male-dominated world of superhero comics. However, Whedon is not the first to do this. In fact, females have made their presence known in comics almost from the beginning, although female creators, artists, characters, and readers are often marginalized.[6]

The most successful early challenge to Superman's dominance in the superhero-comic genre came in 1942 with the introduction of William Moulton Marston's Wonder Woman, who was "designed specifically with girls in mind, and embodied feminist politics in a way that was unprecedented. Yet as the same time, the comic also managed to appeal to boys due to its undisguised eroticism" (Sabin 86).

For a time, the unabashedly feminist Whedon was associated with creating a live-action adaptation of *Wonder Woman* and undoubtedly, a meeting between Marston and Whedon would be an interesting one. Marston is credited with discovering the basic principles that would lead to the development of the lie-detector test. Moreover, according to Roger Sabin, Marston believed "that women were more honest than men, and he turned to writing comics as a way of expressing this and other ideas about the female mind. Wonder Woman would be the bearer of the message that women should realize their potential, should fight for equal rights and that a feminized society would be more caring than the prevailing patriarchy" (86). While Whedon may not believe that women are inherently more honest than men, his well-documented belief that women are beings worthy of admiration and respect is a guiding star illuminating his work. There is an inescapable irony that his powerful female fictional creations, including the character of Fray, are subject to being objectified by the male gaze — especially the gaze of adolescent boys. While many female comic book characters are portrayed with physiques that defy both gravity and common sense, Whedon stipulated to Dark Horse during the planning stages that Fray should be depicted as "a real girl, with real posture ... no cheesecake" (Whedon, *Fray* Foreword). With *Fray*, Whedon entertains his core audience without reinforcing negative stereotypes of women as mere objects of sexual desire.

While comics may be regarded by many as a disposable part of popular culture, Sabin wryly notes that it "is surprising how well 'disposable' pop culture can last" (7). After all, not only is the image of Superman instantly identifiable throughout the world, but his catchphrase of "truth, justice and the American way" is likewise well-known. In fact, it is this ability of comics to connect on such a visceral level with such a large audience that forms the very crux of their popularity. For instance, the public is generally more concerned about sex and violence contained in comic books than in the plays of William Shakespeare. The distinction seems to be based in the generally accepted split between "high art" (of which Shakespeare is accepted as an element) and "low art" such as comics.[7] Those who would declare themselves to be cultural arbiters often perceive a threat to their established authority in the popularity and easy availability of comics.[8] Therefore, from time to time, the content of comics is regarded as subversive enough to require careful monitoring. However, it is much more common for critics to simply dismiss comics as being beneath critical notice.

There are advantages to flying beneath the radar, however. Since comics rarely are reviewed with the same critical eye as other art forms, they remain a playground for writers and artists. As Sabin states, "There is a real sense in which [comics] are a site where 'nobody is looking,' and where it is possible to experiment and flex creative muscles" (9). While many comics are perhaps not yet worthy of serious academic consideration — certainly not every title has the artistic impact of a *Maus*— the same can be said for any form of art. To paraphrase Sabin, perhaps as much as ninety percent of all art is rubbish, whether the art in question is sculpture, narrative, or comics; however, it is the remaining ten percent that makes things interesting (9). Whedon's *Fray* certainly falls within that tantalizing ten percent. In *Fray*, Whedon uses the comic form to explore in depth serious issues of family, responsibility, and purpose, quite possibly with a freedom he could not have had in another medium that is more susceptible to immediate commercial pressures.

Perhaps it is the very "outsider" status of comics that serves as their chief draw in the first place. While analyzing his own attraction to comics, Sean Howe states that he is unable to determine "whether it was my deep, dark secret of [enjoying] comics that first made me feel apart, or the feeling of apartness that drew me further into comic books. It's perhaps a cruel irony that comic books simultaneously confer outsider status and offer supplication to the outsider" (vii — viii).

As a comics fan himself, Whedon must know something of this dichotomy. However, if it is true that comics are the refuge of the true outsider, what better medium exists for telling the continued tale of the Slayer, one of the ultimate outsiders? With the creation of Melaka Fray, Whedon advances the Slayer mythology in several completely new directions, including the fact that Fray is a twin.

Every human culture has had to confront the phenomenon of twins and the response to the presence of twins has varied wildly from society to society. As Lawrence Wright recounts, twins have frequently been viewed as a threat to the presumed order of a culture and the response has often been to kill the "unnatural" children as well as the mother (6). In other cultures, including societies in West Africa and Haiti, twins are exalted as "supernatural beings with a single soul, who are to be revered and feared" (6). This contrast — being objects of both veneration and dread — is a common response to twins, whose very existence calls into question our traditional sense of individuality. Wright goes so far as to use the term "divine prank" in reference to twins, as if twins were some form of cosmic joke (11). Since humans more commonly have single rather than multiple births, this term does seem particularly apt, especially in light of the fact that twins are often simultaneously prized as being something extraordinary while also considered to be something faintly otherworldly.

There is a long history of twins being perceived as having connections to powers beyond the ken of ordinary mortals. As an example, Frazer notes in his classic study of religion and magic, *The Golden Bough*, that control over the weather is an ability often attributed to twins, citing the culture of the Tsimshian tribe of British Columbia, who "believe that twins control the weather; therefore they pray to wind and rain, "Calm down, breath of the twins." Further, they think that the wishes of twins are always fulfilled; hence twins are feared, because they can harm the man they hate" (76). This widespread belief that twins have power over such uncontrollable events as the weather certainly makes a twin a natural subject to be the Slayer, although here again Whedon teases his reader. The Slayer is the one *girl* chosen in every generation to fight the powerful forces of Darkness that constantly threaten to overwhelm human society while most mythologicized twins are male.

Of course, Melaka Fray is not the first example of a twin being entrusted with the protection of humankind. For instance, a set of twins is credited with advancing human society by founding the city of Rome. Romulus and Remus managed to survive being cast in the River Tiber as infants and were suckled by a she-wolf — certainly not your average upbringing.

The constellation Gemini is the celestial representation of another set of twins with a supernatural history. As is the case with all myths, there are variations in the details of the narrative; however, Castor and Polydeuces (also known as "Pollux") are generally considered to be the twin sons of Leda and Zeus. The boys entered the world by hatching from a swan's egg. Another egg contained the boys' twin sisters, Helen and Clytemnestra, who also figure prominently in the epic tales of the ancient Greeks.[9] Castor and Pollux are often known as the "Dioscuri" or "Sons of Zeus" and when Castor is killed, their grief at being separated touches Zeus to the point that he hangs them both in the sky as the constellation Gemini, meaning "the twins" (Wolverton 75). Clearly, these twins are presented as being supremely dedicated to one another and their bond is presented as being, at least in part, based on their twin status.

In some versions of the story, Castor and Pollux are fraternal, rather than identical, twins and a distinction needs to be drawn between identical twins (such as Romulus and Remus) and fraternal twins (such as Whedon's Melaka and Harth in *Fray*). Identical twins are the result of a single fertilized egg that spontaneously splits into two beings while fraternal twins are the result of the fertilization of two separate eggs. Therefore, while identical twins are invariably of the same gender, fraternal twins may be of different genders, as are Melaka and Harth. Indeed, fraternal twins are theoretically no more genetically alike than any other pair of siblings.

Nevertheless, the genetic diversity of fraternal twins does not halt the proliferation of odd and often morbid beliefs regarding such children. As the Radfords point out in their collection of superstitions rooted in the British Isles, it was commonly believed in counties on the Scottish border "that if a woman bore a girl and a boy at one birth, she would never have another child" (345). This may be a simple coincidence, but it is clearly stated in *Fray* that Harth and Fray are the two youngest of their family, meaning that their mother (who is absent from the tale, as is their father) never again had a child after bearing the fraternal twins.

Perhaps the most famous fraternal twins are the immortal Apollo and his twin sister, Artemis. While Artemis owned the night and often was known to "accompany and protect travelers," she was also the only Olympian to whom human sacrifices were made (Wolverton 18).[10] Artemis would seem to possess Slayer-like qualities — as goddess of the moon, she is perfectly at home in the night, is familiar with weaponry and both enjoys and excels at traditionally male pursuits, such as hunting. Another similarity between Artemis and Whedon's Slayers is the use by both of a pointed instrument of death: Slayers often dispatch the Undead with a wooden stake, while Artemis usually killed her prey with arrows. However, unlike the painful death resulting from a stake, the arrows of Artemis were endowed with special powers to grant the victim "gentle death" (Wolverton 18). However, as mentioned above, human sacrifice was made to Artemis, so the "gentle death" notion should only be read as going so far.

Apollo, the twin brother of Artemis, was not originally the god of sunlight — that responsibility was transferred to him after his duties and those of Helios became confused over the years. However, it is interesting that these twins represent opposites in several ways. For example, Apollo is male and randy with ladies of both mortal and divine blood, while Artemis is female and sworn to virginity. Moreover, Apollo is the herald of day, while Artemis rules the night. While neither one is clearly the origin of the convention of the "evil twin" that is so often used in contemporary soap operas, Artemis and Apollo do beautifully illustrate the idea of dichotomy that makes twins such an object of fascination — if I have a twin, where do I leave off and my twin begins? Whedon uses the characters of Harth and Melaka to examine this very basic question of identity by having the abilities usually associated with the Slayer split between the twins.

Interestingly, among Apollo's many associations, he is also the Greek god most often connected with prophecy. His temple at Delphi was widely considered to be the holiest spot on earth (Wolverton 17). In *Fray*, it is the male twin, Harth, who receives the prophetic dreams that should have been his sister's signal to her calling as the Slayer. While it may not have been intentional on his part, Whedon's solid grounding in the classics is evident in this reflection of the duality the ancient Greeks associated with the twin gods Apollo and Artemis.

It is a common belief across cultures that twins have a stronger connection with one another than is usual between siblings. This belief is reflected in the story of the grief-stricken Pollux being granted the right to remain with Castor as part of the constellation Gemini. In contemporary pop culture, this connection between twins has been used for comic effect, such as in the 1961 film *The Parent Trap*, in which Haley Mills plays twins who meet at summer camp and switch places to get their divorced parents to reunite. The idea of an unusually deep connection between twins was also explored in a more unsettling way in the 1988 film *Dead Ringers* in which Jeremy Irons plays identical twin doctors who are pathologically dependent on one another, causing them to spiral into madness when one twin wants to sever the bond. In their research, the Radfords collected tales that indicated a belief that twins:

> are united by so strong a bond of sympathy that each knows when danger or misfortune threatens the other, even when they are separated. In the same mysterious way, any special state of happiness or well-being in one of the pair is reflected in the feelings of the other. It is often said that if one twin dies, the other will not live long thereafter...
> If, however, a twin does survive his fellow, the vitality of the latter passes to him, and he becomes stronger and more vigorous than heretofore [344–345].

The belief that a surviving twin may absorb the strength and abilities of the deceased twin would seem to reflect a belief that twins are indeed a "divine prank," to use Wright's phrase (11). In this view, twins seem to be a single being forced to live apart until death frees one of them to live with the full array of abilities and talents he or she should have always possessed, but for the existence of the twin. This is a parasitic view of twinship and a view that doubtless accounts for some of the apprehension many people feel regarding twins.

While Fray does not kill her twin, in order for her to triumph, she must fight him; in a literal sense, she must battle her other half. Popular culture has seen this before, perhaps most notably in George Lucas' first *Star Wars* trilogy, in which Luke must conquer his own fears in the tree on Dagobah as part of his training. When he slays the vision of Darth Vader within the tree, the concealing helmet melts away, revealing Luke's own face.

Lucas openly acknowledges that his work owes much to the writings of Joseph Campbell; indeed, the Bill Moyers/Joseph Campbell series "The Power of Myth" was first recorded at Lucas' Skywalker Ranch. Through his films, Lucas not only gave the world twin heroes in the form of the fraternal twins Luke and Leia, who were the offspring of good and evil, but he also walked the audience through Campbell's concept of the hero's journey. This is a trip Whedon also invites his readers to take with the story of Melaka Fray.

Even if readers do not know that Melaka Fray is a twin, her duality is immediately apparent in her surname. "Fray" has a double meaning, as it can be either a noun denoting a bloody battle or a verb denoting a falling apart. Fray will be engaged in both of these meanings throughout her hero's journey.

Joseph Campbell devoted his life to studying the myths and legends of many human cultures and his work has become a powerful influence on generations of journalists, writers, and scholars of all stripes. Whedon's Fray closely follows the path of the hero outlined in several of Campbell's writings, from the call to adventure through to the return. The return is paramount to Campbell who stated that, "the ultimate aim of the quest must be neither release nor ecstasy for oneself, but the wisdom and power to serve others" (Campbell and Moyers xv). While it can be argued that many of Whedon's characters follow this path, Fray accomplishes it in only eight issues of the comic, making this perhaps the most obvious example of Campbell's influence on Whedon.[11] According to Campbell, the hero's journey can be divided into three separate and distinct stages: the departure, the initiation and the return ("The Hero's Journey"). The application of each of these will be discussed in terms of Fray's development as the Slayer.

In the first stage, the departure, the hero is called to the quest that awaits her. As with many mythic heroes, Fray sees her life as an ordinary one. She is very nearly alone, as her family has unraveled (frayed, if you like) in the bloody world in which her story is set. Her parents are gone and presumably deceased. Her twenty-minutes-older twin brother, Harth, is dead, the victim of "lurks," the name given to vampires in her world. Her only remaining biological family is her older sister Erin, who has moved away from the crowded "warrens" where Fray ekes out a living as a thief. While her circumstances may seem pitiful to the outsider, Fray does not view her life as the stuff of tragedy — it's just life, and life is harsh.

As it always true with Whedon's work, the names of the players need to be examined, for nothing as important as a name is accidental to Whedon. "Harth" is a homophone of "hearth," a word that denotes home and safety. For Fray, her home (at least in the form of her twin) has been destroyed. As for her older sister, "Erin" is a name which has its origin in the Gaelic word for "peace" ("Etymology"). This is appropriate, given Erin's career choice to serve the city as a peace officer.[12] However, there is no current relationship between Fray and Erin, who holds Fray responsible for Harth's death. Further, the neighborhood in which Fray lives is referred to as "the warrens," the name given to the homes of rabbits, who are perhaps the perfect prey animal. The word choice is fitting, as the people who surround Fray are the downtrodden and forgotten and it appears that Fray will spend her life on the fringes of society as just another rabbit, albeit a spunky one.

Everything changes dramatically when a strange man appears and tells Fray that, while he is unworthy to come before her, she must know that she is the Chosen One who will "protect us. End the scourge... You will cleanse us all with fire" (*Fray* #1). He then touches a lit match to his gas-soaked clothing and immolates himself. Seeing the danger the flames present to the rickety homes of the warren, Fray literally dives into action, tackling the burning man and pushing them both into the foul waters of the harbor. The flames are extinguished, but Fray is left shaken and confused. After all, she's just a rabbit at this point. Then again, it's not at all uncommon for the hero to be reluctant to shoulder that title.

Fray attempts to walk away from this experience, to reject the call. This is part of the hero's departure, as well as being an entirely understandable reaction. Based on what she has just seen, it is far simpler for Fray to dismiss the self-immolation of this odd man as the act of someone driven insane by the casual cruelties of the city, rather than a call to some mystic destiny. However, despite her best efforts to reject what she has seen, she has in fact committed to this quest and it is at this point that her "guide" appears. Throughout the *Buffy* mythos, Slayers are shown to be guided in their duties by a Watcher, someone specifically trained to render assistance to the Slayer. In a departure from this carefully crafted mythos, the character of Urkonn is almost defiantly *not* a Watcher. In fact, Urkonn reveals to Fray that the burning man was actually a member of the remaining remnant of the Watchers' Council, who have descended into madness and inaction.

Urkonn needs to explain some history to his charge and armed with this new knowledge, Fray enters what has been termed "the belly of the whale." This image, which is taken from the Biblical book of Jonah, represents Fray's final separation from the world she has known as she contemplates the potential for a new world. Urkonn may be a demon, but Whedon has utilized demons as soldiers fighting on the side of good before.¹³ Urkonn explains the Slayer mythos to Fray, as well as to any readers who may be unfamiliar with the backstory. Fray is quite skeptical about the entire concept of Slayers, vampires, good and evil. She is a creature of the moment, living for excitement and thrills, but certainly not seeing any connection to past heroes who fought for the survival of humanity. Fray has no psychic link to past Slayers. Whedon establishes that she never had the prophetic dreams that single the Slayer out from other girls. Urkonn has difficulty believing this and becomes frustrated with his charge as Fray flippantly sums up the mythos of millennia by saying, "Okay. I'm supposed to fight the coming onslaught of lurks and I'm being taught by a sarcastic goat-thing whose idea of training is throwing scrap metal at me because the actual good guys all went crazy waiting for the monsters to come back" (*Fray* #3). No Slayers have been called since the "girl in the sunlit city" two hundred years earlier and "lurks" now freely roam the warrens of the lower portions of the city, where skyscrapers crowd out the sunlight, leaving the slums an ideal hunting ground for vampires.[14] In view of this, Fray's skepticism seems to be a practical response.

With Harth apparently dead and Erin a law-abiding citizen, Fray no longer has any connection to her biological family; but, in true Whedon fashion, she has created her own. She looks after a little one-armed girl named Loo who is in need of protection from the harsh world of the warrens. Harth's death hangs like a noxious cloud over Fray, who feels that his death is her fault. By taking responsibility for Loo, Whedon's Fray feels she is doing something right and good — something she was unable to do for her dead twin. While Harth was the older of the twins, he was physically weaker. His death was the direct result of his desire to tag along with Fray on one of her adventures in theft. During this adventure, the twins ran into a lurk named Icarus who threw Fray off a building and then slaughtered Harth. Understandably, this experience has made Fray frightened of vampires. This fear, coupled with her lack of dedication to her calling, causes Urkonn's masters to question the wisdom of continuing to use precious resources to train her. Fray's world is a harsh one. While Buffy's defiance of the Council's orders was cause for comment, Urkonn is baldly asked if Fray can be made ready to lead, since "to kill her and seek out the next Slayer would take time" (*Fray* #4). Whedon's future world is indeed a dark one.

This uncertainty about Fray's suitability as Slayer ratchets up further after Fray freezes when facing Icarus a second time, leading to her being badly injured by the gloating vampire. Leaving the hospital for the warrens, Fray makes the final commitment to the journey that awaits her. She has faced a frightening unknown and, while she has not triumphed over the darkness, she is willing to continue. With this dedication to her quest, Fray leaves behind her dangerous yet familiar world and fully enters the second stage of the hero's journey as laid out by Campbell: the initiation phase.

In the initiation phase, Fray continues to manifest her name by falling apart as she is tested and often found to be failing. However, success is not measure by how many times a person falls down, but rather by how many times she gets back up. Fray may fall, but she continues to fall forward, thus progressing on her journey toward becoming a hero.

As defined by Campbell, the initiation stage is characterized by a series of tests, training, and trials, often occurring in threes. Three is a number that has significance in many faith-based traditions, including the Christian trinity of Father, Son, and Holy Spirit and the more humanistic linkage of Mind, Body, and Spirit.

Campbell underscores the necessity in this phase for the hero to meet with "the goddess" who is often symbolized as the person who the hero most loves. Here, Whedon again turns the tables on his audience, as most hero tales involve a male hero and a female goddess, or loved one. In the case of Fray, our hero is a slightly built, sarcastic nineteen year old woman and the person she loves the most is her twin brother Harth, who is also her representation of home and safety. In a heart-wrenching twist, readers learn that Icarus did not merely kill Harth, but also converted him to vampirism. Indeed, it is Harth who is now pulling the strings of the elaborate plot to have the "lurks" overrun the warrens. While Fray never has an inkling of her destiny, Harth does — he is the one to receive the prophetic dreams that are the birthright of the Slayer and her link to her past sisters. Fray gets the strength, agility and healing abilities, but she never knows her purpose. Having his own purpose, the vampire Harth coldly uses his living twin to gain the necessary artifacts with which to open the gateway to hell and allow demons to return to earth.

This is the center point of Fray's journey and is often the precise moment at which the would-be hero is tempted to stray from the path and return to what was once known. According to archetypal tradition, the success of a hero is never guaranteed; if it were, continuing the journey would be little other than a hollow exercise.

Campbell emphasizes the magical nature of the number three in many heroic tales. In *Fray*, it takes three pieces of knowledge to bring Fray to her breaking point. The first piece of knowledge is her sickening discovery that her twin is the very evil she will have to defeat in order to protect others for whom she cares, such as Loo. Harth delights in taunting her with the unwitting part she has played in his plans.

The second piece of knowledge that tempts Fray to abandon her hero's path is provided by her sister Erin. Fray has taken refuge in Erin's apartment following the encounter with Harth. When Fray and Erin meet, Fray admits that Harth's death is her fault and tries to explain the unexplainable — Slayers, demons, vampires — to her logical, by-the-book sister, who understandably has trouble believing this seemingly wild tale. However, she can do one thing for her little sister: she tells Fray that it was Gunther, for whom Fray works for as a thief, who betrayed her to the police earlier. Erin's advice is for Fray to not trust him. That is not a problem for Fray, who replies to Erin that, "I don't trust anyone" (*Fray* #5). This statement is the last bit of bravado Fray has, for she does trust someone — Urkonn, her trainer and father-figure. As bizarre as the journey has been so far, Urkonn has been the individual who has been able to fill in the blanks for Fray and she is willing to believe what he tells her about her destiny.

The third and final piece of knowledge that could destroy Fray awaits her in her apartment, where she returns with Urkonn after her meeting with Erin. The apartment has been invaded and Fray's belongings have been thrown around by the interlopers. Sprawled obscenely on the filthy floor is the broken form of Loo, an innocent slaughtered simply to send the message to Fray that she can't protect anyone. Confronted with the tangible proof that death is coming for all she loves, Fray lowers her head, close to breaking. When she raises her head, her eyes are sad, yet filled with resolve. Far from driving her from her quest, Loo's death galvanizes Fray into action against what had once been her twin. She thinks she is ready for war; that this loss will be the final one for her.

Urkonn tries to explain that she is not yet ready, for "war is not just the business of death. It is the antithesis of life" and that war will require her to commit unspeakable acts (*Fray* #6). To this end, he provides her with a physical gift to serve as her "sword and scepter. Let it proclaim you the hero — and not the monster — that you will need to be" (*Fray* #6). With this, the mystical Scythe last seen in the final episode of *Buffy* re-appears in the mythos. Of course, the weapon is not Fray's only gift any more than it was Buffy's only gift. Her discovery of who she is in the world in which she lives is the true gift. Armed with this knowledge, Fray begins the last stage of her initiation into becoming a hero.

A person can't take something as large as a war to the streets without attracting attention. Erin worries that Fray has "lost it," meaning her grip on reality, while Harth muses that his twin has somehow "found it," meaning her purpose. Despite his desire to torture his twin further by having her actually witness the opening of the portal to hell, he acknowledges that she's killing enough foot soldiers to require removal. Therefore, he orders Icarus to "deal with her," but reminds his minion that he'll want the body (*Fray* #6). For what purpose, he does not say — perhaps just to make sure that she is actually dead. After all, Fray fled the scene without recovering Harth's body, assuming that Icarus had killed him and would seek to kill her as well.

Icarus may have killed Harth, but the roles of master and servant have been reversed. Icarus has flown far too close to the dark sun of Harth's charisma and now serves the one he sired. The battle between Icarus and Fray is swift and final. Facing the monster who killed her twin, Fray responds to his taunt of "What have you got besides a shiny new axe?" by dropping the Scythe to the pavement and responding with level eyes, "Faith." Well, that and a sister who drops a flying police car on Icarus as revenge for her brother's death.[15] While Erin thinks the death of Icarus ends the war, Fray knows better — the head minion's death only ends a battle; the war itself is far from over. It is this realization that marks Erin as a foot soldier, while Fray is coded as the hero-general.

Soon, everything is in readiness for the last stand. While some residents of the warrens are willing to join Fray in what is coming, many others are too scared or too wrapped up in the soft flannel of denial to assist. Urkonn tells Fray that those who will not fight should stay inside, since "lurks cannot enter a home uninvited," a bit of information Fray carefully files away for later consideration (*Fray #7*). The war is unlike anything Fray has ever imagined and it only gets worse. This is one of the lessons of becoming a hero — it can always get worse, because more responsibility is always expected of you. The counter of this depressing bit of information is that there is always more within the hero to bring to the fight, regardless of the size of the enemy.

Harth enters the battle riding on the back of a dragon-creature who consumes Fray. Harth thrills to think that his twin has been consigned to the literal belly of the beast and is further delighted to see Erin present to witness the end of the world, as well as Fray's death. However, heroes are notorious for their sense of self-preservation and Fray has been busy digging her way up out of the beast, exploding onto the scene like Athena emerging from the head of Zeus.[16] Fray pushes her way into the world through the eye of the beast, signifying her own vision of herself as the defender of this world. Harth's plans are destroyed, but he escapes to scheme anew, after giving his twin a kiss that could be a farewell, but is more likely a promise of hell to come.

At this point, the initiation phase of Fray's journey is complete, but there is still the return to make. One of the chief differences between heroes and gods, both of whom possess abilities far beyond those of mere mortals, is that heroes return with the knowledge they have so painfully gained, while gods just go. After all, it is Prometheus' gift of fire to mankind that makes him a hero, not merely having the knowledge of fire. And, as with Prometheus, Fray's knowledge comes with a high price, as vital knowledge is never received without a fee being paid.

Fray confronts her old boss, Gunther, who slithers and lies about his role in the tale. Fray, who has learned subtlety and finesse along her journey, has come with a very specific purpose in mind, which has nothing to do with Gunther. Rather, she reveals that she knows that Urkonn murdered the innocent Loo to goad Fray into action.[17] A price must be paid for that act but Fray is not without rough mercy. As she puts it, "He was a good teacher. Even a friend. For a friend, I make it quick" (*Fray* #8). And she does, killing her friend with a rapid thrust of the Scythe he gave her, for justice in Fray's world does not equal a second chance. Forgiveness for Urkonn is shown only in Fray's swiftness. Serving as a protector of the innocent means making hard decisions and Fray is now equipped to do that. She'll be no one's puppet, not even for those who possess great knowledge and believe they know best how to fight evil.

Those who walk the hero's as described by Campbell must achieve a certain balance between the spiritual and the material, which Whedon's Fray has succeeded in doing. While she continues to live with one foot in her old world of thieving, Fray has the other planted firmly in a better world, one in which humanity has a defender—a Slayer. By taking the hero's journey, Fray has achieved freedom from the fear of death which, for her, equals the freedom to live without either anticipating the future or regretting the past. She works to heal the breach with Erin, her remaining biological family, who does not possess the healing powers of a Slayer and is recovering from the battle in the hospital. Fray also works to defend her larger family of humanity and she is last seen crouched on the outcropping of a building, comfortably holding her Scythe. She watches "her" city with a smile, daring the forces of evil to try to take what she considers hers. Fray is a hero and she has the scars, both physical and psychic, to prove it.

As is typical in Whedon's works, there is no real resolution. The three siblings all live, yet Harth is a death-dealing vampire and Fray remains an incomplete Slayer, lacking even someone to train her. However, Fray has accepted her family and been accepted by the larger community in which she lives. On her journey, she has gained knowledge of both herself and the world that she did not have before. She is a complete person without being defined by her status as a twin; rather, her strength is derived from becoming a part of a community. With *Fray*, Whedon makes a very strong point about the ties that are formed by biological families and how strained those ties can become without actually breaking. These ties help determine who we are, as do the ties we form with other "families"—the ones who look after us and the ones who we look after. These connections serve to give us purpose in confusing and tumultuous times. However, while families can instruct us in what to do, it is still up to the individual to take action. Fray was always a hero, but the fact that she did not know that kept her from behaving like one. The journey to gain knowledge is necessary and, as Whedon so often illustrates, gaining knowledge is often a painful process, but it's a journey well worth taking.

4

A Family of Believers, Just Not in the Same Thing

FAITH IN THE *FIREFLY* FAMILY

Whedon's work quite often centers around families who do not fit the stereotypical model of breadwinner father/homemaker mother/children/picket fence. In fact, Whedon seems to be almost suspicious of that family structure, preferring the more flexible boundaries provided by a post-modern created family in his work.[1] Whedon addressed this issue in the commentary track of *Firefly*'s pilot episode, stating, "Every show I do is about created family, as opposed to actual family." In *Firefly* (as well as its big screen sister, *Serenity*), Whedon gave viewers a magnificent vision of the created family and the ways in which a family of one's choosing can be as strong and valid as any biological blood tie. Further, the created family in *Firefly* is composed of people who seem at first glance to be so mismatched as to defy attempts to bring them together. Therefore, this chapter seeks to answer a fundamental question: What are the common bonds that hold such disparate people together on a deep and abiding level — in other words, what makes them a "family" as opposed to a group of friends or co-workers? Specifically, this chapter will examine Whedon's use of the common dining table and the role played by both individual faith and food in forming those common bonds.

Human beings are social animals who seek out others for companionship and a sense of safety. In order to meet these needs, we form groups and establish rituals to distinguish our family group from others. One of the ways we mark ourselves and our family is through the fundamental need for food. At least since the beginning of recorded history, food has been used to create a type of circle, a sacred space delineating the protected family inside the circle from the unwashed heathen hordes who exist outside that boundary.

One obvious example of the use of food to serve as a boundary is seen in the use of bread and wine in the sacrament of Christian communion — churches often have very strict rules about who is privileged to partake in this rite and who is not. Less formal guidelines are used within most family groups — the undergraduate returns home to a celebratory dinner of ribs prepared by Uncle Roscoe with his special, secret dry rub. The new bride politely requests Nana's family recipe for borscht. Or, as is the custom among my people, grocery stores are stripped of black-eyed peas and collard greens as the New Year approaches.

While the cultures may be different and the ingredients of the dishes may vary, the function of the markers provided by family "comfort food" remains the same — these are meals that are used to mark the expansion of the family circle to include a new member or to commemorate a milestone in life's journey, such as a wedding or a funeral. These special meals do not have to be gourmet feasts in order to be special: in fact, comfort food is quite often the opposite of gourmet. Truly, family can be celebrated with chicken soup as thoroughly as with *foie gras*. Or, as in Whedon's *Firefly*, family can be confirmed with protein bars and rolls.

Much family bonding takes place around the homey plank table in *Firefly*, with the clearest illustration of this group of people as a family found in the last shot of the episode "Safe" (1.05). With the exception of Shepherd Book (who is recovering from a gunshot wound in his cabin), the entire family is gathered at the table for a meal following the crew's rescue of Simon and River. The table is anchored with Mal at the head and Inara seated at the foot in an homage to the traditional family structure with the "parents" firmly fixing the ends of the table as the "children" are scattered around the edges. As the *Firefly* crew is never shown as having anything as formal as assigned seats, this is the only time viewers see this particular configuration around the dining table and it should not be viewed as merely a happy coincidence. Whedon is making a very strong statement about the nature of family in this positioning as he clearly codes Mal as the "daddy" and Inara as the "mommy" of the family of the ship. Sure, *Firefly*'s Daddy is a wanted smuggler and Mommy is a high-paid whore, but (to paraphrase Eleanor of Aquitaine) what family doesn't have its quirks?

In fact, this dichotomy opens a very useful point of discussion, as none of *Firefly*'s characters are as simple as their initial coding would suggest. While they all fit into one type of standard trope or another, Whedon delights in creating characters who take stereotypes and fold, spindle, and/or mutilate those boundaries. Here, the result of Whedon's willingness to play the trickster is a host of characters who are dynamic, engaging, and almost aggressively three-dimensional. Simply put, Whedon creates people as opposed to mere ciphers. This is one of the reasons viewers so enjoy his work — the characters are complex, in much the same way that "real people" are. After all, most humans are more than the single line devoted to "occupation" on their tax forms. In real life, a person plays many parts — the mathematician might also enjoy restoring Ford Mustangs for instance, or the hairdresser may also translate French poetry. Whedon's characters have many layers, like fine Greek pastry.

This "baklava" approach to characterization is likely to be one reason why the crew does not have rigidly assigned places at the common table; they also do not have rigidly assigned roles within the family. Rather, the roles they play (especially within the structure of the created family) are fluid and changeable, depending on the situation and circumstances. While each of the *Firefly* characters deserves a much more in-depth analysis than can be given here, each will be discussed in turn as we make our way around the table, starting with the "Daddy" of this decidedly non-traditional family.

At the head of the table is Malcolm Reynolds, the captain of this ship and the head of this family. As with all Whedon's characters, it is illuminating to spend a moment decoding the name Whedon gave him. The captain is usually addressed by the nickname "Mal," which River points out is rooted in the Latin for "bad." Mal lives his life without sparing much thought regarding legality of cargo and propriety of conduct. He has made a deliberate decision to turn his back on the "civilized" life offered by toeing the line, seeking instead a life lived on his own terms.[2] Yet while he may want very much to be *left* alone, he has no desire to *be* alone, telling Zoe, his comrade-in-arms and trusted confidant in "Out of Gas" (1.08) that "There's nothing like real people"— provided, of course, they live life on his terms.[3]

In the usual construction of the archetype of a captain of a ship, the captain is portrayed as a decisive male, level-headed and diplomatic, who utilizes the more primal techniques of force only as a last resort, but then is able to use violence very effectively.[4] But Whedon prefers people to prototypes. Therefore, in a sticky situation, Mal has no problem seeking options and solutions from other members of his crew, for he realizes his own limitations. Moreover, he is rarely level-headed, almost never diplomatic, and he sees violence as a very useful tool that a sensible man does not hesitate to wield, especially in defense of his crew.

This is one element of the archetype that Mal does personify — a heightened sense of duty and protectiveness toward those under his command. While in many other permutations of the "captain-father," the crew is protected from harm through the wisdom of the captain, on the ship *Serenity*, bullets are much more likely to be used than what Mal would no doubt refer to as "jabber."

In another notable difference, Mal is only loosely coded as the "father" of this created family — his role is usually much closer to that of the oldest sibling, who acts with responsibility toward the younger, less-experienced-in-the-ways-of-the-world members of the family. Like many an older brother, he often maintains discipline and order with harsh words and harsher actions. Mal does not live in an orderly, tidy 'verse where food and replacement machinery can be conjured effortlessly through technology. He is a veteran of a lost war and rather than being concerned with snappy salutes and sharply creased dress uniforms, Mal's thoughts are often disorganized scrambles as he seeks with increasing urgency to keep his crew flying, fed, and (above all else) free. Mal's faith is a casualty of the war and in his current worldview, there is no God-as-parent to care for him and his so, as the captain of this band, he serves as the father-surrogate of this family. Therefore, the burden to keep the family intact falls squarely on his shoulders. All of his energies are devoted to carrying this cross and he returns to rescue Simon and River although it goes against the grain of his own self-interest to do so. After all, they're family, as we will see.

Sitting at Mal's right hand is Wash, the pilot of the ship and husband of war-hardened Zoe. Although his given name is "Hoban Washburne," he is only called that on his tombstone. He is always simply "Wash," a given name that is also a verb denoting cleanliness and purity. While he cannot be counted as the most innocent of the residents of the ship,[5] Wash's voice is often heard in opposition to those who would seek first to resolve their problems through violence. He is a type of brother figure to most of the *Firefly* family and he plays the role of peacekeeper whenever possible. He also provides comic relief to defuse tense situations when necessary.

As the pilot, Wash comes from an archetype that is often coded as being somewhat otherworldly and quirky. After all, prior to the twentieth century, flight was viewed by most as being the exclusive province of birds and angels. Even following the discovery and practical implementation of the principles of aviation, pilots were viewed as being people who were slightly "off," although the profession was also greatly romanticized, especially during the first days of aerial combat.[6] Whedon's Wash certainly has his quirks, as the plastic dinosaurs scattered atop the navigation console attest. Wash also has a sharp sense of humor, which is a useful tool among this family who skates the edge of lawful respectability. However, when flying, his attention never wavers — his concentration is complete and his calm is nearly uncanny when compared to his usual mien of relaxed jester. Wash's faith is placed in two seemingly opposite places — the freedom of soaring flight and the grounding provided by his marriage to Zoe. Normally, a pilot would hate being grounded; here Whedon furnishes another example of his willingness to play havoc with audience expectations.

One of the attributes that must be considered when discussing Wash is his ability to give and receive love as embodied in his relationship with his wife, Zoe. In many ways, this marriage is an inverse of the traditional husband/wife relationship, for Zoe can be read as exhibiting the more male qualities, making Wash more of the wife, despite his gender. Zoe is an army buddy of Mal's and she is definitely a warrior.[7] Wash isn't a soldier and apparently sat the war out entirely, but Whedon does not allow us to read Wash as a weak-willed coward. Wash's core strengths lie elsewhere — in his gentleness, in his humor, in his ability to love — and Whedon gives those strengths their just due.

Next to Wash is River Tam. Any person who has ever navigated a river is familiar with the adage that "still waters run deep," a phrase that is often used in a metaphoric sense, but one that has a literal side to it as well. The areas of a river that appear the calmest are often where the water is deepest, the current is strongest, and the trip is the most dangerous due to that deceptive calm. This is a particularly apt name for this teenage girl who first appears to be present on the ship to fill the role of the broken victim who must be saved. In River, Whedon drowns the stereotype of damaged damsel, for while River is undoubtedly unstable, she is also easily the most capable fighter onboard.

River has survived horrific physical and psychological trauma inflicted on her by the Alliance government. This was done in an attempt to transform River into a deadly weapon by sacrificing her humanity and consequently, River is not thought of by the Alliance as a teenage girl; nor really as a person at all. Rather, to the Alliance, the experiment was a qualified success, for River has combat skills honed to a fine edge and she also has demonstrated psychic abilities. Unfortunately, side effects of crafting River's undeniable talents include her multiple symptoms of paranoid schizophrenia and her utter inability to filter out or ignore unpleasant or inconvenient emotions.

After her rescue by her brother, River becomes quite literally a loose cannon, a weapon with the potential to do immense damage. The Alliance will stop at nothing to bring her back under their control, to be sure that theirs is the only finger on the button, so to speak. It would have been simple for Whedon to leave it at that and make River a traumatized victim of forces beyond her control who could be used to show the kind and compassionate side of the crew as they coax the broken girl back to sanity. This Whedon refuses to do.

Instead of being a one-scream pony, Whedon's River keeps faith with her name and becomes a girl-woman of unplumbed depths and wildly shifting currents. While her faith is placed squarely in her brother, she is painfully aware that she is not normal.[8] River can be fanciful, confused, frightened, and frightening in turns. These changing moods cause the crew to react to River with both a desire to protect her and misgivings about her, for while River has a nature-based name, the girl herself is decidedly unnatural. The crew must deal with the tension between the desire to provide River with a safe place to heal from what was done to her and the fear she engenders because of the results of what was done to her.[9] By having the crew wrestle with these conflicting emotions, Whedon uses River to further cement the ship's family together. On the commentary track to the pilot episode of *Firefly*, Whedon said of River that "A person who is broken becomes whole partially because the people around her decide that she is and, you know, that's the creation of family." In the end, the statement that Whedon is making with River is that family is who we say it is. Damaged as she may be, she belongs where she is because these people have extended the protection of the family to her.[10]

In typical annoying little sister behavior, River snatches the roll from the plate of the family member next to her. In this case, that person would be Jayne Cobb, the person most likely to sell out River and her brother Simon to the Alliance just to get rid of the vexation her presence causes, although the prospect of a hard cash reward causes his mouth to water as well. The hulking mercenary, who has enough of an intimate relationship with his guns to give them female names, has a girl's name himself. This is a direct inversion of the standard reading of a gun-wielding thug. Often, characters such as this are so undifferentiated that they aren't even given names. In opposition to that, Whedon gives viewers Jayne, a sneaky lummox who has unexpected glimmers of decency. Among the *Firefly* family, Jayne most closely fits the role of grown brother, the sort who pays little attention to the opinions of others within the family, believing that he knows the best and most direct route to take. This is an attitude that often can lead to friction within the family structure and Jayne certainly causes a great deal of *sturm und drang* on a ship that already has far too much of that particular commodity. Jayne's headstrong nature leads to confrontations and, on one notable occasion, Mal's serious consideration of removing Jayne from the family permanently.

Jayne's primary motivation is money; in fact, he comes aboard the ship after switching allegiances in response to Mal's offer to raise Jayne's pay scale.

However, he is also the only character shown to maintain ties with his biological family, to whom he sends a portion of his pay. In return for these tokens of filial devotion, his mother sends him gifts, including a hand-knitted hat. Jayne is the only crew member seen wearing a hat as part of his everyday apparel, as he wears both the knitted hat and a practical flat-brimmed hat from time to time. This is worth mentioning since in *Firefly*, people of ill intent (such as Badger and Patience) are the ones seen wearing hats, which seem to be used as a physical tag to mark untrustworthy types.[11] In this manner, Jayne is coded as an unknown quantity, a man who is morally ambiguous.

Interestingly enough, Jayne is shown as having a certain degree of religious faith, or at least some familiarity with the concepts embodied by Shepherd Book. Jayne removes his hat and bows his head at funerals and blessings said over meals and in "The Message" (1.12), he talks with the Shepherd about the possibility of Book saying kind words at Jayne's funeral. Despite this, it is safe to say that Jayne primarily places his faith in firearms and his quick use of violence.

Jayne's attitudes toward women are also different from the other men on the ship, all of whom are shown to have a respect for women as mechanics, soldiers, and businesswomen. While Jayne shares this attitude to a degree, he also offers to trade his gun "Vera" for Mal's unwanted bride Saffron ("Our Mrs. Reynolds" 1.06). Further, while the rest of the crew has other motivations, only Jayne is prompted by the offer of free loving to sign on to defend the residents of a whorehouse ("Heart of Gold" 1.13). In Jayne's defense, it is interesting to note that the trade involves his "very favorite gun" and he promises to treat Saffron "okay." Moreover, he takes some care in his appearance, even going so far as to don a collared shirt in place of his usual T-shirt to go to the whorehouse.[12] In his own roughneck way, Jayne has an idea of manners, although he can often be crude and socially inappropriate, which can give rise to comedic moments.

One woman Jayne does not address in crude sexual terms is the very person the casual viewer would expect him to treat as a lesser being — Inara Serra, the licensed Companion seated at the foot of the table. As a Companion, Inara earns her comfortable living exchanging sexual favors for money, a profession viewed with respect among the civilized worlds of the Core and one viewed with contempt by the man seated at the other end of the table. Traditionally, parents anchor the dinner table, which makes Inara the mother in this configuration. It is an apt title, for Inara is the definite maternal figure in this family, providing needed kindness and compassion to all onboard.

Inara's name is doubly interesting. Research indicates that the name is Arabic in origin, meaning "one who shines with light" (Bolton 247). This suits Inara, whom one client refers to as having "the smile made of sunlight" ("Shindig" 1.04). She is also the representation of the light of Alliance civilization, being portrayed as the most educated and refined woman onboard, having been in training since the age of twelve (*Firefly Visual Companion* 1:107). However, additional research reveals another, slyer reference.

"Inari" was a Japanese deity who, among other responsibilities, was the protector of both geishas and prostitutes (Barnhart 2112). Whedon has said that Companions work in a similar manner to geishas (*Firefly Visual Companion* 1:13). The term "geisha" is one that is often misunderstood in the West: a true geisha (a word that translates into "art-person" or "artist") was not a prostitute, but rather a highly skilled entertainer, well versed in the classical arts of dance and music, as well as being a clever conversationalist (Prasso 204–219). Geishas train for years before becoming "full" geishas and their fees are quite expensive. Whedon's Companions are far closer to the role of the cultured and refined geisha than to a mere streetcorner prostitute.

Since Whedon refuses to give viewers an easy way out by making the Alliance some sort of monolithic horror, Inara is far from being an oppressed whore. Rather, she is the very embodiment of all that is good about the Alliance, which is simply a government made up of separate individuals. Whedon states in *Serenity: The Official Visual Companion* that Inara serves to represent the positive features of the Alliance, including "enlightenment, education, self-possession, feminism" (11). Whedon has put a great deal of thought into creating the world of the Companion, which is a feminist world ruled exclusively by women. Companions select their own clients and no man is permitted to run a Companion house. Further, this is a highly respected and well-paid profession and upon retirement, many Companions rise to political or social prominence (*Firefly Visual Companion* 1:13). For reasons that are never fully explained, Inara has left the comfortable world of Sihnon where she trained and had shown immense promise as a Companion to travel with the *Firefly* crew, ostensibly to expand her client base. This is a decision that has cut her off from her plush, opulent world of luxury and affluence, but one that she apparently feels is worth making.

The primary religion on the Core planets, which includes Sihnon, the world on which Inara lived before joining the ship, is Buddhism (*Firefly Visual Companion* 1:12). Inara is shown to be a follower of this faith, which can be described as a non-theistic religion that has as its central purpose the personal enlightenment of the believer. As a follower of a faith that stresses the use of individual experience as a reliable tool to verify the truth of the religion's precepts, Inara has a *laissez-faire* attitude toward the faith of others and remains quiet about her own. Whedon has an appreciation for Inara's reserved beliefs, which add another layer to an already mysterious woman. In

Inara, Whedon shows viewers a sophisticated, sensual woman who has faith so engrained into her life that it need not elicit comment.

Seated at Inara's right is perhaps the quietest, yet toughest person aboard: Zoe Washburn, neé Alleyne. Her husband, Wash, is seated diagonally at the opposite end of the table, but theirs is a marriage that does not require them to be next to each other every moment. In fact, as Mal's right hand and second in command, it is Zoe who most often accompanies Mal on dangerous missions while Wash remains at the navigation console, for these are people who know to work to their strengths.

Zoe would seem to fit the traditional role of "warrior woman," for she is a sure shot, unswervingly loyal, and battle-hardened to the point of wearing a bootlace from the war as a necklace.[13] However, this is too simple a reading for Zoe, whose very name means "life" (Room 610). Unlike Mal, who is in many ways still traumatized into personal inaction by the events of the war, Zoe has been able to move forward with her life. She has found passion and commitment beyond that of simply being the hard-as-nails second in command. While many "warrior women" characters are endowed by their creators with a heavy-handed, gotta-be-tougher-than-the-guys personality, this is mercifully absent in Zoe. Instead, she is gifted with a dry sense of humor as well as "an innate understanding of right and wrong," according to Gina Torres, who plays Zoe (*Visual Companion* 1:77). This strict morality helps viewers see Mal as an honorable man deserving of respect, for if this woman is willing to follow him into some admittedly hare-brained situations, he has to be worth something.

Within the family structure, Zoe is a big sister figure, one who shoulders responsibility for the everyday workings of the family. Her desires are more adult than those of the younger siblings in the family: for example, when Kaylee expresses a longing for a frothy wedding cake of a hoopskirted dress, Zoe's response is that she'd prefer something with "more slink."[14]

In another of Whedon's details in constructing this 'verse, the fact that the ship's second-in-command is a woman is never remarked upon, nor is the fact that she is a married woman and/or a woman of color.[15] She's very good at her job and that's what matters. It's an interesting paradox that Whedon's strongest statements are often the ones he makes by withholding comment. In his view, a society that has embraced the basic principles of feminism would find Zoe's gender unremarkable when discussing her career choice.

Zoe's faith is placed in the here and now. She is not shown as having any sort of religious faith, although she is respectful of others' beliefs, such as the Shepherd's. But on a personal level, she believes in two men: her husband and her captain. This division has the potential to cause conflict, but somehow Zoe manages (for the most part) to walk that tightrope with the grace of a trained acrobat.

Next to Zoe is the character who feels the least at home at this table. Simon Tam is seated across from his sister, River, and has been the last to take a seat at the table, as he paused to hold a chair for Kaylee. Simon takes this action not only because he has a soft spot for Kaylee (as does any right-minded person who meets her), but because proper Alliance manners dictate that he hold a lady's chair. The Tam siblings were raised in a world of Alliance wealth and privilege, all of which carry absolutely no weight out "in the black." Within the *Firefly* family, Simon is a version of the geeky brother who has his useful qualities, but is a considered to be somewhat prissy. Indeed, Simon's refined manners and dandified clothing clearly tag him as an outsider among the crew and make him the butt of many a joke. Simon is generally seen dressed formally, in dark colors relieved with lushly patterned vests. The only other character who routinely wears such fine fabrics, as opposed to the crew's more practical work clothes of canvas, leather or denim, is Inara, who is also associated with the Alliance. Of course, it can be argued that Inara's silks, satins, and brocades are her version of "work clothes."

As a doctor, Simon would seem to fit the archetype of a "Bones" McCoy or, in a more traditional Western setting, a Dr. Quinn — characters who are often portrayed as bearing the civilizing lamp of medical knowledge and reason in often rugged situations. On *Firefly*, Whedon twists this trope, making Simon a slick misfit whose considerable medical skills cause him to be tolerated, but not held in awe. Whedon has commented that Simon is meant to represent the "anti–Mal" (*Firefly Visual Companion* 1:16). He does this by creating in Simon a character who fervently believed in the Alliance as a force for good and enlightenment but who has that belief stripped away with his discovery of what was being done to his beloved little sister, River. This treachery gives the polite, non-violent Simon common ground with Mal. The captain may have lost his belief during the war but Simon's loss was just as great; only the timing differs.

Simon's socially connected parents have abandoned their children, rather than acknowledge the horrific acts their government is capable of doing. In fact, they plead with Simon to stop searching for answers, telling him that everything is fine and that if he continues down this path, he will irreparably damage his career and his family. Unable to let go, Simon walks the only path he sees open to him. He has devoted the last two-plus years of his life to rescuing his injured sister and now that she is free from the Alliance Academy, his energies are focused on using his medical training to pinpoint exactly what was done to her and repair the damage. Whatever faith he may have once had in the Alliance as a civilizing, benevolent force has been irredeemably shattered and he clings desperately to his broken sister, seeing in her the only way possible to make everything he has endured worthwhile. Whedon codes him as a man betrayed — by his government, as well as by his original, biological family — who has been set adrift to find meaning in his life as best he can and to redefine his family.

Despite this bone-deep sense of betrayal, Simon continues to safeguard his polished manners, although he is well aware that this sets him apart from the others. This is Simon's central conflict — possessing the knowledge that he has means that he knows he cannot return to the life he once lived, yet he is understandably reluctant to cast off that life. So he holds tightly to scraps of it, despite the ridicule that is heaped upon him. Simon's name can be translated into "one who hears" (Austin 309). Circumstances have caused Whedon's Simon to reconsider his attitude toward what he is hearing these days and he listens much more critically than he may have done in the past. He certainly no longer listens to the reassuring crooning of the Alliance government, who convinced the Tam family that River was going to a special academy that would best develop her unique talents. Yet it is clear that he does not completely listen to Mal's commands either. While Simon seems to be almost pitifully naïve about the life he is living onboard the ship, this is a disguise, for the doctor is actually much more devious than he seems, as it becomes apparent that he has a very good idea of just how dangerous River may be, yet keeps his mouth firmly shut about that tidbit of knowledge.[16] The only part of Simon's life that matters to him is River, which is the reason why he and the woman seated on his right can't quite seem to figure out what to do with their obvious mutual attraction.

The last seat at the table is occupied by Kaywinnet Lee Frye, who came to the table carrying a basket of rolls. Miss Frye is known more usually by her nickname of "Kaylee," one meaning of which is "open" (Stafford 236). This is especially apt for *Firefly*'s resident mechanic, whose personality is all sunshine and trust. Moreover, it is interesting to note that an Irish "céilidh" is a gathering or party and that term is pronounced identically to Kaylee's name. This is also apropos for her, as Kaylee's affection is a gathering place of common ground for the crew. Whedon has commented that Kaylee was intended to serve as the soul and connection for the viewer to the crew, stating in the commentary to the episode "Objects in Space" that Kaylee "is so the person who just believes and has faith and gets hurt and is decent and you feel what she feels... Kaylee is an emotional 'in' for us" (1.14). Kaylee serves as the beloved little sister in the *Firefly* family. In fact, Mal occasionally refers to her as "mei-mei," which is Mandarin for "little sister." Kaylee is able to see (and therefore also allows viewers to see) Mal's good side, even when he is at his gruffest.

In the role of ship's mechanic, it would be usual for Kaylee to be more comfortable with machines than people; however, this is not the case with

Kaylee. Yes, she possesses nearly uncanny talents with machinery and she clearly has an engineer's love for the ship, which she refers to fondly as "her girl." Further, she bristles (well, as much as Kaylee can be said to bristle) when anyone refers to the ship with anything less than unadulterated adoration. But it is at this point that the traditional trope fails to fit Kaylee, who loves people easily as much as machinery.

Kaylee has faith in "her girl," but she also has faith in the inherent goodness of people. Like Anne Frank, Kaylee is convinced that people are basically good, despite evidence to the contrary. For example, in the pilot episode, Kaylee weakly attempts to tell Mal that he has to "have faith in people" as she is recovering from a near-fatal gunshot wound inflicted by a nervous Alliance agent. It is this heartbreaking sense of bruised innocence that makes Kaylee such a sympathetic character.

This is shown to great effect in the pilot episode (1.01). Viewers hurt along with Kaylee when Jayne crudely embarrasses her in front of Simon at the dinner table and viewers heartily approve of Mal's sending Jayne from the table as punishment for shaming her in this way. Yet, only a short while later, viewers find themselves siding with Jayne as he helplessly watches Simon operate on Kaylee following the aforementioned shooting. In this way, Whedon uses Kaylee to establish not only her role of cheerful optimist, but also to construct depth in other characters. In part, we like Mal because Kaylee likes Mal, even when he's being churlish. Moreover, we like Jayne because he cares about Kaylee, even though he's acted like the thoughtless older brother, tormenting her in front of a potential beau.[17]

Although we have now discussed the crew members seated at the table, there is one person absent from this homey gathering. Shepherd Book is not at the table in this scene, being indisposed due to a gunshot wound. Despite his physical absence, his presence is still felt. In fact, as Simon and River enter the dining area, Mal is overheard telling the punchline to a ribald joke involving a Shepherd, a Companion and a goat. While not a part of the crew in the strict sense of being employees of Mal's, it is to Book and Inara that Mal often turns for counsel, although he would vigorously deny that he does this. Regardless of whether Mal's stubbornness makes him the goat, the fact that the joke involves both a Shepherd and a Companion takes on added weight and significance. After all, the joke could just as easily have involved a mechanic and a mercenary.

As a Shepherd, Book serves as the preacher on this stagecoach in space. While he comes close to meeting the traditional wild west character mold of peaceful preacher, it is far from a tailor-made fit for him. Shepherd Book is far too conversant with worldly topics, such as the use of firearms and the identity of crime lords, to be seen as a purely spiritual person, despite his best efforts.[18] While Book may doubt his own effectiveness as a religious leader, he firmly believes in the possibility of redemption for all, including himself.

While the events of Book's past are not explicitly revealed, Book reminds Mal in the film *Serenity* that he "wasn't born a Shepherd." Whedon uses Book to ask the viewer to explore the expansion of the boundaries of faith: why *can't* a preacher know about guns and crime? What startling changes are possible for humans who are willing to change the path they are walking? While many of these questions are not fully answered, they are asked and Whedon trusts the viewer to arrive at his own answers.

Book no doubt wishes he was at the table. Whedon's Shepherd understands that commonly shared meals can be a very effective way of joining seemingly incompatible people together. In fact, one of Book's first acts upon joining the ship is to provide a veritable feast, heaping the table with food. Among the items are platters of fresh vegetables, which are scarce onboard. This stunning act of generosity cements the Shepherd's acceptance among the crew, with the exception of Mal, who just flat-out doesn't have much use for religious figures, although he tucks away his fair share of the food provided by Book.[19]

In the *Firefly* 'verse, fresh food is rare and expensive; therefore, it is often used as a status symbol.[20] Whedon heightens this point by having the crew's first heist involve the theft of cratefuls of bland food bars, which are loaded with nutrients and even contain medical supplements to shore up the health of the consumer. While this cargo hardly appears to be yummy treats, it is clear that the value of the foodstuffs is worth the risk they represent to the crew. In contrast, the wealthy citizens attending the ball in "Shindig" (1.04) are surrounded by luxury, represented not only by the frivolously beautiful floating chandelier, but also by heaps of fresh, sensuous strawberries that Kaylee immediately makes a beeline for, determined to gorge herself on this sumptuous treat while she can.

It is not that the crew never tastes fresh food. In addition to the Shepherd's home-grown feast, Jayne once buys a crate of apples to share with the crew. Jayne's generosity is so far out of character here to be the subject of speculation by Wash ("War Stories" 1.10). It can be argued that he purchases the apples as a way to make amends for past misdeeds, but there is a Biblical allusion here as well. By eating the apples, like Eve in the Genesis story, Wash sets into motion circumstances that cause him to achieve some very unpleasant knowledge — in his case, some specific knowledge of the dangers his wife faces when she leaves the ship on her second-in-command duties.

Since fresh food is expensive, it is more usual for the crew's meals to consist of prepackaged, dehydrated protein. In Whedon's 'verse, even flour is difficult to come by, so in "Out of Gas," the crew surprises Simon on his birthday with a lopsided cake made of chocolately tasting protein (1.08). Despite the unusual nature of the cake, this is still a significant event — strangers would not bother to celebrate the birthday of some random person in their midst; birthdays are events more commonly observed by friends and family. Even more so in this case, since Simon is probably the least popular of the residents of the ship, due to his ever-present air of privilege and his obvious discomfort at being among these people. The cake serves to symbolize the crew's growing acceptance of Simon as a real part of the family of the ship.

However, at the meal in "Safe" (1.05) that has been the focus here, Kaylee comes to the table carrying a basket of fresh, steaming hot rolls. At this meal, the assembled family actually breaks literal bread in an echo of communion.

It's worth keeping in mind who is *not* present at the table. While Shepherd Book's absence is completely understandable due to his injury, there are others who are never seen taking a meal at the *Firefly* table. These include people such as Patience, Badger, and Niska — all people who, given the opportunity and the proper profit margin, would rip this family apart. Even Saffron never sits at the table, although in her guise as Mal's naïve wife, she prepares a meal for him. Sitting at the table (especially to share a meal with others there) is reserved for members of this unusual created family. Whedon makes it clear that not everyone is worthy of the warmth and protection provided by this family. Therefore, the question is raised — in addition to the basic human need for the sustenance provided by food, what brings and keeps these disparate people together at this table? Their faith is scattered into many categories; they hail from different worlds, both literally and figuratively speaking; and they seem to have very little in common on any level. But, as Whedon reminds us, none of that really matters, for "family" in Whedon's worlds is not nearly as dependent on traditional ties of blood as it is on other bonds, which are forged in the fire of shared experiences.

In mainstream America, there is a lingering notion that "family" has a single, proper configuration; namely, that of breadwinner father, pearl-necklace-wearing mother, and two precocious children. If this family make-up sounds as if it is transmitted directly from 1950s television shows, it should. However, as family studies scholar Stephanie Coontz has commented, even during the 1950s,

> Everyone knew that shows such as *Donna Reed*,[21] *Ozzie and Harriet, Leave It to Beaver,* and *Father Knows Best* were not the way families really were. People didn't watch those shows to see their own lives reflected back at them. They watched them to see how families were *supposed* to live — and also to get a little reassurance that they were headed in the right direction [38].

Coontz also points out that, at the height of the male breadwinner/female homemaker model of "family" in the 1950s, still only sixty percent of American children grew up entirely in such a family ("The Way We Weren't" 19). Clearly, the American family has not followed this family model as much as is commonly thought.

In fact, the very idea of the male breadwinner and the stay at home, "nonworking" mother is a relatively new configuration for the structure of the American family, only emerging in the early nineteenth century. Prior to this time, women commonly worked outside the home, often in backbreaking, labor-intensive jobs such as agriculture or factory work. Coontz indicates that this "emergence of domesticity for middle-class women and children depended on its absence among the immigrant, working class, and African American" women who took on these roles (19). So as one group improved their social status and began to enjoy leisure time previously unknown to them, another group stepped in to fill the void left by the now upwardly mobile.

What all this shows is that family is complicated, regardless of how it may be portrayed. The liberal clergyman and peace activist William Sloane Coffin, Jr. addressed this when he eloquently stated his vision of the larger human family: "We all belong to one another, every one of us ... our sin is only and always that we put asunder what God has joined together. Human unity is not something we are called on to create, only to recognize and make manifest (6)." Reverend Coffin understood that, in discussing the true "family," love is the glue that holds it together, far outstripping the influence of biology. In the *Firefly* family, this is evident and it is a deliberate choice of Whedon's. Regarding the world he created for *Firefly*, Whedon has stated, "Life is hard out there... A world where, you know, things have to be made from scratch, including decisions, ethics" (Havens 147). It is also a world like ours, in which families sometimes have to be made from scratch. With the exception of Simon and River, these disparate people have no biological tie to one another and, as a married couple, only Wash and Zoe have a socially recognized tie. Nevertheless, shared experiences have forged these individuals into a family in every important meaning of the word.

This is in keeping with the concepts of a "faith family." Christ's chosen disciples were not taken from his "blood family," but rather from strangers. Further, Christ's ministry is strewn with stories of his interaction with the "less than" of his society, such as prostitutes (Luke 7:36–50), lepers (Luke 17:11–19), and tax collectors (Luke 19:1–10), to name but a few. Christ used the image of a lost and helpless lamb to illustrate his point that the helpless deserve help, not condemnation for their situations (Luke 15:1–10). To Whedon, a person's true family is not necessarily the one you are born into, for family bonds have a wider base of commonality than simple similarities in

DNA. Further, while all are worthy of being considered for inclusion within the family, that grouping is based on a person's actions toward the created family rather than hinging on an accident of birth.

When considering the family gathered around the dining table in Whedon's *Firefly*, it is especially apt to consider the Lord's Prayer. Also known as the "Our Father," this prayer was taught by Jesus to his followers and probably the best-known Christian prayer on Earth. In it, supplicants request *food* before *forgiveness*: "Give us this day our daily bread" comes before "Forgive us our trespasses." While the kingdom of God may be a heavenly, spiritual kingdom, the body has needs which require care on this plane; a fact Jesus clearly understood, as he made a habit of feeding the crowds before preaching to them.

Biblically, it should also be noted that the baptism of Jesus precedes his public ministry. Baptism is used as a method of claiming a person as a member of the church, which is simply a family of believers. It has already been discussed how the individuals gathered around the table in *Firefly* compose a true family of believers. While what they place their faith in varies, they all deeply value this family that shelters and cares for them. To a person of faith (regardless of whether the faith is placed in God or not), the obvious answer to Cain's whining question to God of "Am I my brother's keeper?" is a resounding "Yes!" for if we are worth looking after, we must also be willing to look after others in the family.

The basic idea of true family is so simple that we absorb the concept as small children. Unfortunately, many of us then spend a lifetime unlearning this lesson of love and acceptance. The Dr. Seuss classic *Horton Hatches the Egg* sums it up neatly, while rhyming to boot. When asked to take over egg-sitting responsibilities by the shiftless Mayzie, Horton sits faithfully on an egg for fifty-one weeks, enduring ridicule and torment all the while, since elephants aren't supposed to sit in treetops protecting eggs. Mayzie returns just in time for the egg to hatch and, since the hard work is done, she shrilly orders Horton away from "her" egg. Imagine the surprise of all present when the egg hatches to reveal an elephant bird, complete with wings and a trunk. The drive of DNA succumbed to the love and faith shown by Horton, who resolutely stuck by his promise to nurture, protect, and keep safe one who couldn't look after himself. As Dr. Seuss reminds us, "It SHOULD be like that!" And so it should, for true family are the ones who stick around, who keep faith with us by both celebrating the good times with protein-based birthday cakes and commiserating the tragic times with respectful silence at the gravesite. In this interpretation, chemical links such as blood and DNA have very little to do with the connections that we create which truly hold us to one another.

In the final analysis, true family does not rely upon conditions, whether biological or psychological. When membership is dependent on conjunctions as it is in the parental Tams' view — when we are "children until" or "sisters unless" — we don't really belong at all. The lesson Whedon teaches viewers here is profoundly simple; for his *Firefly* family knows that "You belong" is a full sentence, just as it is.

PART 3

REDEMPTION: THE PAST IS NOT A PRISON

Am I a thing worth saving? Am I a righteous man?
—Angel, "Amends" *Buffy* 3.10

5

The One That Almost Got Away

DOYLE AND THE FISH STORY

Whedon uses the half-demon Doyle, who serves as the soul-filled Angel's conduit to The Powers That Be, to illustrate that redemption is possible for everyone, even for those who seem paralyzed by self-hate and regret. Doyle is far from being a contemplative saint. In fact, he staggers beneath a nearly crushing burden of guilt and shame. While his wrongs do not put Doyle beyond the boundary of redemption, the penitential Whedon character must go beyond simply pleading for forgiveness. Only concrete deeds serve as atonement for past actions. Or, as in Doyle's case, past *inactions*.

For someone as fascinated by moral ambiguities as Whedon, it no doubt makes perfect sense to have his dark hero Angel be guided by a "good demon," the concept of which seems to be paradoxical. After all, aren't demons evil creatures bent on the absolute destruction of the human race? To Whedon, the answer is "no," for he never perceives the concepts of good and evil as being particularly clear-cut. Therefore, Whedon is able to utilize the device of such an apparently contradictory character to underscore the complexities of that position.[1] As another "good demon" explains in "Becoming, Part One": "But I'm not a bad guy — not all demons are dedicated to the destruction of all life. Someone has to maintain balance, you know. Good and evil can't exist without each other, blah, blah, blah. I'm not like a good fairy or anything. I'm just trying to make it all balance" (*Buffy* 2.21). Whedon's worldview is more intricate than a simple "demon bad, human good." Indeed, Whedon's view of demons borrows from H. P. Lovecraft's "Elder Gods" in that demons are a "variety of ancient, prehuman races who originally lived on earth" (Golden 2). As such, they can be terrifyingly evil, relatively benign,[2] or of uncharted depths. Such a one is Doyle, a half-Irish/half-demon who finds himself dragged into Angel's orbit by The Powers That Be.[3]

As is true with all of Whedon's creations, the name of the character serves as a type of map to the inner world of the character. "Doyle" is an Irish family name meaning "dark foreigner" (Doyle). This is a perfect moniker for this character, who fits the classic "black Irish" type of black hair and light eyes, and who is also very much a stranger in the strange land of Los Angeles. In addition to being a "foreigner" in the world of full humans, Doyle is also a stranger to the ways and means of redemption.[4]

When viewers first meet Doyle, it is quickly established that he carries his past with him as a burden. Angel is suspicious of Doyle's motives in offering to assist the vampire in his quest to "help the hopeless" and Doyle deflects the inquiry with a simple, "We all got something to atone for" ("City Of" 1.01). Angel doesn't press very hard for answers, being well acquainted with the notion of wanting to keep some sins private.

In the commentary for the first episode of *Angel*, executive producer David Greenwalt refers to Doyle as a type of "unconscious conscience" for Angel, while Whedon calls the half-demon a "mentor figure" for the vampire. Doyle's role is to provide Angel with information that helps the vampire actually connect with the humans in the world, rather than Angel's preferred "hands off" approach of merely saving the helpless and then melting into the darkness. This was a deliberate choice made by Whedon, who has said of *Angel* that the show is all about loneliness and fighting that loneliness with connections to other people (Commentary "City Of" 1.01). This is an admirable goal, but in the beginning, Doyle hardly provides a good example of connecting with others. Even in the midst of his impassioned plea to Angel to reach out to others and provide the lost with a bit of love and hope in a harsh, uncaring world, he brushes aside a begging woman without so much as a pause: "Get a job, you lazy sow. It's about letting them in your heart" ("City Of" 1.01). At this point, Doyle serving as a mentor to Angel just may be a fine example of the blind leading the blind. This is a carefully crafted choice on Whedon's part — after all, if Doyle had nowhere to grow, he wouldn't be nearly as interesting to watch.

Doyle also isn't particularly interested in being an active participant in the eternal battle of good versus evil. While he is never portrayed as wanting evil to triumph, Doyle is consistently shown to prefer the wings of the stage to the center spotlight. In Doyle's worldview, sticking your neck out for others is a really good way to get it broken. Although he has been selected by

The Powers That Be to actively assist Angel, taking such a visible stand grates on him, focused as he is on protecting his own interests, rather than those of the wider world. This is not meant to condemn Doyle, however. Most people would prefer to remain tortoise-like within their own shells of protection rather than venture forth to protect those weaker than themselves. This is the attitude political philosopher Edmund Burke had in mind when he stated that "all that is necessary for evil to triumph is for good men to do nothing." And always in the back of Doyle's mind is the memory of what happens when good men (or good half-demons, for that matter) do nothing, for Doyle's past is a dark country, scarred by betrayal and shame.

As a demon/human hybrid, Doyle is a character defined by boundaries. He is far from being at peace with his heritage and he is reluctant to share information about his past with others. Viewers learn in "The Bachelor Party" (1.07) that Doyle's Brachen demon side didn't present itself until he turned 21, by which time he was happily leading a life devoted to service to others — he taught third grade and he met his wife when they were both volunteering at a food bank, for example. The revelation that life had never been what he had thought was simply too much for him to accept — the sudden and total loss of his identity and certainty about his place in the world caused him to drive away his wife, who was willing to stand by him. Notably, he also changes his name at this point, casting off his given (and slightly prissy) name of "Francis," a name that calls up images of the gentle, kind St. Francis, in favor of being the one-name, more masculine-sounding "Doyle," the dark foreigner. Far from being an active, vibrant force for good in the world by teaching children and assisting the hungry, the now angry-at-the-world Doyle retreats from human companionship. He exists on the fringes of society in squalor and lives by doing a lengthy series of slightly illegal favors for other down-and-outs.

At this point, Doyle can be equated with the Biblical Job, only without the essential quality of faith. While Job was able to survive a crushingly unfair series of burdens and trials due to his unshakable faith in the inherent goodness of the Divine, Doyle flees, devoid of purpose, conflicted and full of self-loathing. His reasoning seems to be: *Half-demon. What good can come from that? All this time, I was just being played for a fool, so I might as well be what they say I am.* The fallacy in Doyle's reasoning is, of course, that "they" are seldom right and that, in Whedon's world, biological markers such as blood have far less to do with who we are than what we do. Doyle's failure to understand this principle will have lasting repercussions, both for him and for those around him.

On top of his self-hatred, Doyle is also mired in guilt. In "Hero" (1.09), viewers are shown in a flashback the source of much of Doyle's remorse. When

Lucas, another mixed-blood Brachen demon, comes to Doyle for help in escaping the Scourge (a band of pureblood demons who have a fiery hatred of "impure" half-breeds such as Doyle and Lucas), Doyle refuses to assist, claiming that he has his own troubles and cannot take on those of anyone else. Lucas pleads with him to help, explaining that the Scourge is determined to exterminate every mixed heritage demon being they can hunt down, a group that includes Doyle, despite his adamant refusal to see the connection.[5] Unable to convince Doyle that he's part of a family that is under attack, Lucas sadly leaves to fight as best he can for those he loves and wishes to protect.[6] Doyle then enters what St. John the Divine termed the "long dark night of the soul" as he resolutely stays put in his squalid apartment, unable to rest. It is at this point, with Doyle balanced precariously between angry self-interest and the desire to be part of something larger than himself, that he receives his first pain-filled vision from The Powers That Be as his mind's eye is flooded with images of a massacre.

Frightened into action, Doyle flees his bolt-hole to meet Lucas, but it is too late. Surrounded by the detritus of slaughter, including a hauntingly empty pair of child's shoes, Doyle is stunned into stillness. Maybe his presence would have made no difference at all, but Doyle is now forever branded by the results of his inaction. With this backstory, Whedon does something unusual in his work — he actually shows viewers the *why* of Doyle's guilt and remorse. Further, while most Whedon characters are attempting to atone for actions they have taken — Angel, for instance, massacred his way across Europe for a hundred years and bitterly remembers each instant of it — Doyle is unusual in that his desire to atone stems from *not* taking action; a sin of omission rather than commission. In short, the worst thing Doyle ever does is refuse to act and that refusal is itself coded as an evil act, rather than merely a cowardly one. For Whedon, evil comes not just from wreaking havoc on the lives of innocents, but also from failing to help those in need.

It is significant that Doyle characterizes his painful gift from The Powers That Be as "bone-crushin', head-wrenchin', mind-numbin' visions" ("I Will Remember You" 1.08). These disjointed visions are the tools that enable Doyle to assist Angel in his quest to help the hopeless, yet they cause tremendous physical anguish to the bearer of the visions. The timing of Doyle's receipt of the visions raises the question — are the visions sent as a punishment, to serve as a lash to drive Doyle from his cocoon of self-involvement into a more active role in making the world better for those who live in it? If so, it would appear that The Powers That Be are a vengeful lot who have cursed Doyle with a nasty sort of psychic hair shirt to serve as a constant reminder of his utter failure to help those who needed his assistance.

While The Powers That Be are deliberately never referred to as "God," there is a history of God talking to His creations with the experience usually described as a deeply frightening one for the human.[7] For example, in the third chapter of Exodus, God speaks to Moses through the form of a burning bush in order to issue his marching orders—a call Moses protests he is unsuitable to fulfill (3 Exod. 11). Later, the wandering Israelites are guided through the Red Sea wilderness "by a pillar of cloud during the daytime and a pillar of fire at night" (Exod. 13:21). Doyle's visions, which cause him to feel as if his skull is on fire, seem to fit within the images of flame that are so often used to describe a visit from the Divine.

Further, prophetic dreams (rather like Doyle's visions, minus the skull-shattering pain) are often mentioned as a means of Divine communication and the gift of interpreting dreams is a common one granted to prophets. For example, Joseph interprets the dreams of members of Pharaoh's household and Pharaoh himself in Genesis 40 and 41; Daniel has prophetic dreams in chapters 7 and 8 of that book (as well as interpreting the famed "writing on the wall" in chapter 5); and the Book of Revelation is all about visions and dreams.[8]

Yet, while these Biblical communications may have startled the recipient, none of them seems to have been accompanied by the pain of Doyle's visions. Even the conversion experience of Saul—a notorious persecutor of the newly formed Christian faith—implies psychic surprise rather than physical pain (Acts 9:1–9). All of which raises the question—is Doyle chosen as special, or is he cursed as unworthy?

Doyle is a conundrum. Clearly, he does not fit the mold of Angel's sidekick, a role that traditionally involves a younger and less experienced individual who requires guidance from an older and wiser mentor. While Doyle is younger than Angel (who clocks in at about 250 years of age to Doyle's mid-twenties), Doyle has his own knowledge of arcane, otherworldly items and beings. For instance, in the episode "In the Dark" (1.03), Doyle is shown to know the significance of a magical ring that renders a vampire invulnerable to stakes and sunlight. Further, Doyle's visions enable him to serve as a guide to Angel, giving him vital information about where Angel needs to be in order to assist worthy, yet helpless, humans. However, while Doyle is not Angel's sidekick, neither does he fit the inverse of that role, for he really does not serve as Angel's mentor. Traditionally, the role of mentor is filled by an older and wiser individual who is passing knowledge on to the younger generation and Doyle is neither a Yoda nor a Merlin. Even The Powers That Be seem to be dismissive of Doyle. In the episode "I Will Remember You" (1.08), Angel seeks out the Oracles, who act rather like gatekeepers for the unseen Powers That Be. Doyle has the knowledge to help Angel gain access to the Oracles, but he himself is not allowed in, being only a "messenger," whereas

Angel is a warrior and therefore deemed worthy to enter their presence. Doyle has a definite role to fulfill, yet he is made to stand on the wrong side of the mystical velvet rope. Whedon therefore codes Doyle as the perpetual outsider, relegated to hanging around the servants' entrance but expected to step quickly when called to serve.[9] Considering that the tug of the bell-pull calling him to serve is accompanied by intense physical pain, Doyle's initial reluctance to become a player in the game becomes understandable.

The role of pain in human existence is a topic that has fascinated philosophers for millennia. Medical doctors know that pain is an extremely useful phenomenon used by the body to indicate that something is wrong and that care should be sought. Pain, therefore, is not the natural state of being. The Christian philosopher and writer C. S. Lewis addressed this issue in his work *The Problem of Pain*, viewing pain as a means by which God communicates with people, stating that "God whispers to us in our pleasures, speaks in our conscience, but shouts in our pain: it is His megaphone to rouse a deaf world" (406). In the view of Lewis, pain is used to get our attention, to show us that our ways are not in accordance with God's plan for our lives. In this view, Doyle's painful visions have a dual purpose. First, they provide Doyle with a way to assist Angel in helping people in need and second, they remind Doyle that he is supposed to help people in need. Far from being unworthy of God's love and attention, Lewis would say that Doyle has been chosen to receive a very precious gift, one that not just anyone could carry, as the pain would be beyond what most could bear — a fact viewers see illustrated when the fully human Cordelia later attempts to carry the visions.[10] It is the physical strength granted to Doyle by his half-demon side that enables him to endure the pain and therefore, the very part of him that Doyle so despises becomes his greatest asset and strength.

To summarize, Doyle comes to seek redemption for his past cowardice and accepts the visions (and the accompanying pain) as an integral part of that process. In Whedon's work, redemption is always possible, but it requires action on the part of the penitent — a mere "I'm really sorry," no matter how sincere, accomplish nothing. Whedon's version of redemption requires the penitent to go into the world and work to make things right, rather than remaining isolated away from the hurt and sorrow of the larger world. In this way, Whedon echoes the admonition found in James 2:17 which states that "Faith without works is dead."

The Christian tradition is far from singular in the insistence that redemption requires action, in addition to sincere repentance. Christianity is rooted in the traditions of the Jewish faith, which has as one of its holiest days Yom Kippur, the Day of Atonement. Yom Kippur is the culmination of the High Holy Days and under Jewish tradition, prior to making peace with God and being cleansed of sin, individuals "must make our own peace with those against whom we have sinned, make our own turning to God" (Robinson 425). Simply put, it is offensive to assume that one can go before God seeking forgiveness if one has not first sought to put things right with one's fellows. A usual part of Yom Kippur services involves reading from the Book of Jonah, a story containing the theme of God's acceptance of man's repentance (Gross 78). Jonah's story has definite echoes with the character arc of Doyle and is worth a closer examination.

The first parallel that can be seen between Jonah and Doyle is the minor status of both. Just as Jonah is considered a minor prophet, with a book that spans only four chapters and a scant couple of pages in most texts, Doyle was present in less than ten percent of all *Angel* episodes. However, a person's worth is not measured merely by the length of the tale. Both Jonah and Doyle are worthy of exploration, since they cast very long shadows over the readers (or, as in Doyle's case, the viewer) of their stories.

Jonah is one of those people in the Old Testament who is the recipient of direct communication with God. He is to make a beeline for the city of Nineveh and preach that the end is well and truly nigh unless the city turns from its wicked ways. Jonah, however, is sore afraid — after all, Nineveh is the capital of Assyria, an empire distinctly unfriendly to the Jewish people. So he tries to escape God's call by fleeing on a boat bound for the foreign port of Tarshish, which is in the opposite direction (Buckeley). Having purchased his ticket, he "climbed down into the dark hold of the ship" to hide (Jon. 1:3). In a similar manner, Doyle also has direct communication with the god-like Powers That Be and is told to assist Angel, a task he initially tries to escape fulfilling.

God's plans for His reluctant prophet Jonah are not so easily thwarted and a storm springs up which threatens to capsize the vessel. Seeking to appease the spirits, the crew draws straws to determine who has offended the gods and Jonah the monotheist draws the short one. He admits that he is attempting to run away from God and volunteers to be thrown into the sea to end the storm, an action the sailors ultimately take. It is at this point that countless Sunday school lessons teach that Jonah is swallowed by a whale (actually, a "great fish"), in whose belly he remains for three days and three nights. As has already been discussed, Doyle refused help to those in need and suffered for his inaction, tossing and turning, unable to rest due to guilt and shame. Doyle needs no outside tormenting, for his conscience serves as the "belly of the whale" where he is forced to face his own shortcomings.

Humbled by the experience, Jonah prays with humility and gratitude for all God has done for him and he is delivered from the whale by being spit up on the beach. He now agrees to go to Nineveh without any further side excursions. Nineveh is a very large city — so large that it takes three days to completely circumnavigate the city and its suburbs. Jonah begins to preach and the Ninevite people, led by their king, begin to repent of their evil ways. For forty days, the citizens wear sackcloth and ashes and not even the animals eat or drink as the entire city beseeches God to spare them, which He does. Doyle, like Jonah, accepts the task that has been set for him and is delivered from his pit of despair. Doyle is shown as being a useful ally to Angel, both in providing guidance through the information contained within the visions and in his growing willingness to stick out his own neck to be an active part of the battle against evil in which Angel is engaged.

The entire Book of Jonah can be read as an extensive metaphor regarding obedience and forgiveness. However, many people get tangled up in the mechanics of whether or not a whale can swallow a human being, thus missing much of the point. At any rate, as Richard Shenkman explains, in Aramaic (the language in which the Bible was originally written), "anyone caught in a difficult situation was said to have been swallowed by a great fish" (205). Doyle has certainly found himself in a difficult situation from which there is seemingly no good way to extract himself; exactly the situation contemplated by the phrase.

Rather than getting bogged down in these details, the beauty of the story of Jonah is found between the lines. Only by engaging in a close reading does one discover that Jonah's reluctance is based in his knowledge of God's mercy. Jonah doesn't particularly *want* Nineveh to be saved: "For I knew you were a gracious God, merciful, slow to get angry, and full of kindness. I knew how easily you could cancel your plans for destroying these people" (Jon. 4:2). The Ninevites have been the enemy of Jonah's people who are supposedly God's chosen and Jonah has no desire to see anything happen to them aside from a good old-fashioned Divine smiting. In contrast, Doyle is an outsider who wishes to help those in need. As such, he echoes the overarching message of the Book of Jonah, which is one of acceptance: the love and grace of God is not reserved solely for one people but is freely available to all. God wants to construct a bigger tent, while Jonah would rather build a higher wall. In likewise fashion, Doyle has been chosen by The Powers That Be to "preach" to another type of heathen outsider; in this case, Angel, the vampire with a soul. Like Jonah, Doyle has tried mightily to escape this responsibility, although for different reasons than the narrow-minded point of view Jonah had. Lastly, like Jonah, Doyle is a very effective conduit for the higher beings, whether that is the Judeo-Christian God or The Powers That Be. This is a point about Jonah that is often lost — prophets of doom are notoriously ineffective. As one example, the Book of Nahum, which directly follows the Book of Jonah, is filled with prophecies of blood and fire for Nineveh, the same city Jonah is sent to save. In contrast to Nahum, Jonah's preaching actually has an effect — the city listens and turns away from its destructive ways, thereby saving itself. (Well, at least until the time of Nahum). Just as Jonah's testimony and subsequent sacrifice are enough to turn the sailors away from their pagan, polytheistic ways and begin worshipping Jonah's one God, Doyle's pain-wracked visions greatly assist Angel in furthering his mission to "help the hopeless." In this way, Whedon again makes a point about the need for inclusiveness: no one is beyond redemption and, at one time or another, we all need a champion to take our side, to feel that we're worthy even if we're not so sure. And that champion sometimes is not who we may think it is, for the world is a large and mysterious place.

The weak and outnumbered need champions far more so than the strong and numerous. This is true not only in Whedon's world, but in ours as well. For an example, one need look no further than Billings, Montana. In 1993, the residents of Billings had to face the ugly truth that hate-based crimes were increasing in their heretofore peaceful community. Racist fliers were placed on car windshields during a Martin Luther King, Jr. birthday celebration. Tombstones in the small Jewish cemetery were upended. The home of Dawn Fast Horses was covered in racist graffiti and spray-painted swastikas. The community reacted by holding candlelight vigils and helping to paint over the offensive slogans; however, the harassment continued to escalate. One night, cowards threw a chunk of cinder block through the bedroom window of Isaac Schnitzer, a Jewish boy who had placed a menorah in his window in celebration of Hanukkah. Isaac's parents, Tammie and Brian Schnitzer, asked *The Billings Gazette* to report the incident on the front page. The *Gazette* went further, printing a large picture of a menorah on the front page and urging citizens to place the paper symbol in the windows of their own homes and businesses as a gesture of solidarity with the minority citizens who were being harassed. Gary Svee, the editor of the *Gazette*, likened the response to the actions of the Danish king Christian X who, according to legend, donned the yellow star himself when the occupying Nazi forces ordered Danish Jews to identify themselves publicly with the wearing of the infamous yellow star.[11] Within a few weeks, over ten thousand residents of Billings had placed the paper menorahs in their windows in a visible symbol of support. This was not an action without risk, as there continued to be incidents of vandalism and crank telephone calls ("Not in Our Town"). However, thousands of people of good will found placing the menorah in their windows to be the right course of action. In one way, these actions serve as a direct contradiction to the lament of Pastor Martin Niemöller. While multiple versions of this quotation exist, the version included on the Website of the Holocaust Survivors' Network reads:

> They came first for the Communists,
>   And I didn't speak up because I wasn't a Communist.
> Then they came for the Jews,
>   And I didn't speak up because I wasn't a Jew.
> Then they came for the trade unionists,
>   And I didn't speak up because I wasn't a trade unionist.
> Then they came for the Catholics,
>   And I didn't speak up because I wasn't a Catholic.
> Then they came for me,
>   And by that time no one was left to speak up.

If we fail to act as our "brother's keeper," whom can we expect to "keep" us when we are the ones who require assistance? This is a question Doyle must ask of himself when faced again with the opportunity to help the weak and oppressed. He can no longer take refuge in bystander status, for through the visions, Doyle actually sees the terror of the fearful innocents. He rejects his previous philosophy of self-absorption, choosing instead to go actively into the world and assist others, doing what he can to alleviate their despair. Of course, his motivation is partly grounded in his previous guilt over his failure to help, but that in no way lessens the impact of his decision to render assistance at this point.[12] To Whedon, everything hinges on choice. If humans (or half-demons, for that matter) lack free will, there is no point in having intelligence and the ability to reason, for preordained actions have no more significance than the dancing of a marionette on strings.

Whedon would heartily approve of the actions of the more than eleven thousand "righteous gentiles" who are honored at the Yad Vashem Museum in Jerusalem. These were people who, at great personal risk to themselves, defied the hellish proclamations of the Nazi command against assisting their Jewish neighbors ("Righteous"). This is the same decision Doyle is faced with making — does he continue to play it safe and keep his head down, or does he step out into the light and risk everything, not knowing the outcome of his actions?

Throughout his association with Angel, Doyle becomes more engaged in the world. Doyle begins by merely slinking about on the sidelines and is even reluctant to drive Angel to his first battle, protesting, "I'm not combat-ready, man! I'm just the messenger!" ("City Of" 1.01) When Doyle hears the sharp crackle of gunfire as he waits for Angel, his first reaction is to throw the car into reverse and abandon the warrior. However, his cowardly impulses are tempered by an inherent core of decency that compels him to return and crash the car into the gate in an attempt to storm the castle.[13] This dichotomy is a hallmark of Whedon's work — the rough-edged Doyle is a rogue, but a very lovable one.[14] He is depicted as being altogether too fond of drinking and gambling. His fashion sense causes the ever-stylish Cordelia to regard him with undisguised contempt. Further, he spends much of his time searching for shortcuts that are intended to help him avoid the pitfalls of an honest living based on hard work, but often backfire and cause him additional trouble. For example, in "Rm w/a Vu" (1.05), Doyle uses his not-quite-legitimate connections to help Cordelia find an amazing rent-controlled apartment after her own attempts to find a suitable place fail. When she finally agrees to let him help, his reaction is one of relief mixed with exasperation: "Finally! What is it with you and Angel? You have to do everything the hard way" ("Rm w/a Vu" 1.05). Doyle's motivation here is not entirely altruistic, as Doyle has a crush on the unapproachable Cordelia and he fears her rejection of him. For that reason, he is careful to conceal his half-demon heritage from her. When the apartment turns out to be haunted by the malicious ghost of its previous occupant (who had walled her son up alive in the living room), Doyle uses his knowledge of magic and displays a willingness to help in cleansing the space. Later, in "The Bachelor Party" (1.07), Doyle single-handedly rescues Cordelia from a vampire attack after Cordelia's pretty-boy date has turned tail and fled. Beaten badly himself, his first question is to Cordelia — "Are you okay?" Clearly, he is closer to being the volunteering "Francis" of old than the wheeler-dealer "Doyle" of Los Angeles. He's learning from his previous mistakes and is making good use of his second chance. Whedon is willing to grant a true penitent a second chance, but rejecting that opportunity in no way guarantees that a third will be extended.

By the time of "Hero" (1.09), the final episode in which Doyle appears, he has made great strides in being an active member of the team. Even so, he is reluctant to take on the threat presented by the Scourge, knowing the bloody fate of the other half-demons who futilely tried to fight the Scourge's twisted ideas of racial purity. It is at this point that Angel learns from Doyle the source of his guilt and shame, the event for which Doyle is trying to atone.

The Lister half-demons who are trying to flee the Scourge are seeking the fulfillment of a prophecy that foretells the coming of a "Promised One" who will save them. The very next camera shot frames a nervous Doyle, although the assumption is that the heroic Angel must be the champion the frightened half-demons are so hopefully seeking. As previously discussed, prophecies are tricky things and in Whedon's work it is nearly always a mistake to confuse appearances with the actual article.

Throughout his time on the show, Doyle hides his demonic visage if at all possible and prefers to "pass" as human, although he is shown to be stronger (and therefore more effective in a fight) in demon form. Doyle is repeatedly shown to despise his demonic side, which he views as unnatural and therefore shameful and inferior. Similar to Buffy, Doyle longs to be "normal" and to fit in seamlessly with everybody else. Ironically, it is the very part of him he so despises that will grant Doyle the necessary physical strength to carry through with the heroic choices he will make, for choices are the defining characteristic in Whedon's work, not blood heritage. Therefore, half-demons have the same opportunity to be heroes as petite blonde cheerleaders.

Wishing to exterminate the "mixed-bloods" more quickly and efficiently, the Scourge have developed a new killing machine. This new weapon is a beacon that is very opposite of symbolizing the bright light of civilization and knowledge. Rather, this powerful weapon of mass destruction seeks out and annihilates anyone with human blood who is unfortunate enough to be within a quarter-mile of the scorching light.

Even though Doyle still would prefer to stay on the sidelines, remarking to Angel at the beginning of the episode, "Tell you what. You fight, and I'll keep score," he has accepted the fact that this path is no longer open to him. When the half-breed demons arrive seeking the help of their supposed Promised One, Doyle involves himself to a greater degree than viewers had ever before seen. When Rieff, one of the younger members of the tribe, runs away, convinced that the plan to escape the Scourge on a freighter is foolhardy and doomed to failure, Doyle seeks out the boy and provides counsel to him rooted in his own experience: "[Your family] put their faith in something, Rieff. You don't have to if you don't want to ... but the other option, losing yourself somewhere, hoping it all goes away — I *know* that never works" ("Hero" 1.09). Able to shore up Rieff's rocky faith, Doyle convinces the boy that his place is with his family and the two return to the docks. Cordelia, who has learned from the leader of the half-demons of Doyle's own mixed heritage, reveals that she can accept that and is actually a bit miffed that he thought otherwise. Well, well — things are looking up for Doyle. He's brought the lost lamb back to the fold and his crush has let him know that she can handle his heritage if he can. The path looks promising. However, when things look happy and bright in Whedon's world, it's best to buckle up — rough road is likely to be ahead.

The Scourge has also tracked the half-demons to the freighter and the beacon is deployed to kill anyone — human, vampire, or half-demon — who carries human blood in their veins. Angel, who has been cast as the hero from the beginning, is prepared to sacrifice himself in order to save the innocents. Doyle knows from his visions that Angel has a continuing purpose on Earth that will be thwarted by this action, even if it is calculated to save roughly two dozen people.

John 15:13 states that "greater love hath no man than this, that a man lay down his life for his friends." Doyle is about to disprove this — the greatest love comes not from throwing yourself on a hand grenade to save your friends, but from saving strangers to whom you have no tie other than those created by simply occupying the same planet at the same time. Seeing that the time has come for a decision to be made that no one else can make for him, Doyle takes decisive action. Perhaps at some point in his life, Doyle read John Donne and is familiar with Donne's observation that

> Reason is our Soules left hand, Faith her right, By these we reach divinity [149].

Having reached a balance between these two concepts, Doyle is no longer paralyzed into inaction and guilt. Shrugging off those burdens, he swings the "fist of faith" at Angel to knock him out of the way. With Angel unable to stop him (and thereby guaranteed a continued life to help others), Doyle changes into his stronger demon form and takes a literal "leap of faith" over the chasm to disconnect the beacon.[15] For once wearing his true face, he turns back to his friends who have given him the gifts of self-awareness and forgiveness and Doyle smiles, apparently at peace with his path of action. He disconnects the beacon, steadfastly maintaining his place even as the light painfully scorches away all that he is. If Doyle enters divinity as contemplated by Donne, he does it screaming.

Unlike Buffy, there is no bodily resurrection for Doyle. But while he loses his life, in the larger context, Doyle doesn't lose. Redemption is possible for Whedon's characters, but it takes hard work and there is no guarantee that the work won't hurt or that you'll come back from the journey. However, one of Whedon's main points is that, despite the risks, it's still worthwhile to set out on the journey.

As to how much atonement equals redemption, Whedon never answers that directly. That may be good, for if there were a definite answer, most seekers would probably stop looking. However, one answer can be found in the prayer of Thomas Merton, who reassured himself that "I believe the desire to please God does in fact please God" (qtd. in Jackowski 89). Whether or not Doyle's sacrifice balances the Divine scales is a question that cannot be answered with certainty. Regardless, Doyle leaves behind a worthy legacy, for he illustrates the idea that we all matter, even if we sometimes don't think that we do. Moreover, he reminds us that while we all deserve a second chance, it's up to us to make the most of that opportunity.

6

"I Got No Rudder"

Navigating the Sea of Faith with Malcolm Reynolds

Just as Whedon's Buffy is "not like other girls," his *Firefly* (and its big screen sister *Serenity*) is not like other science fiction. Set five centuries in the future, *Firefly* takes place in a universe (shortened down just to "'verse" in *Firefly* jargon) populated only by human beings. There are no other life forms out here — no fuzzy Ewoks or creepy Grays — and all we have is what we brought with us. Fortunately, that includes family, kindness, and faith. However, it also includes poverty, greed, and desperation. In short, the *Firefly* 'verse looks a lot like ours, only with spaceships. While technology has advanced in the world of *Firefly*, human nature is much as it ever has been, and that includes the very human search for meaning in one's life.

At the center of *Firefly* is one of Whedon's beautiful, loving, squabbling, non-traditional families, who has already been the subject of discussion in a previous section of this book. At the center of this family is Malcolm Reynolds, who represents Whedon's deepest plunge yet into the mysterious pool of faith. As Whedon has said, "Mal is a person who believes very little and thinks he believes nothing, and is conflicted ... but he's the only person who can save us from ourselves" (*Firefly Visual Companion* 1:23). Malcolm is a coldly furious ex-believer who has reacted to loss and betrayal by becoming a callous skeptic. However, skeptics always make the best seekers and Whedon uses Malcolm to explore man's search for something larger than himself in which to believe.

While Whedon uses Malcolm to scrutinize the redemptive qualities of faith, it would be a mistake to read *Firefly* and *Serenity* as focusing on the *per-*

fection of faith; indeed, Whedon's spotlight is always trained more on sinners than saints. The line between saints and sinners is often a very fine one and the wonderful thing about saints is that they are human, not superhuman, despite what many may believe. Phyllis McGinley comments in her book *Saint-Watching* that: "[Saints] lost their tempers, got hungry, scolded God, were egotistical, or testy or impatient in their turns, made mistakes and regretted them. Still they went on doggedly blundering toward heaven" (qtd. in Curry). What McGinley is reminding us of is that it is the journey that inspires and unchallenged faith is just not very interesting. The character of Malcolm Reynolds is fascinating to contemplate *because* of his flaws (faith-based and otherwise), rather than in spite of them. Malcolm often blunders, but like many of Whedon's characters (as well as traditional saints), he blunders *forward*.

That Whedon carefully selects the names of his characters as a means to understanding them is a point that has been previously discussed. The name of the captain of *Serenity* is a particular rich example of Whedon's attention to detail. "Reynolds" is a surname that means "powerful judgment" (Austin 285). Meanwhile, the name "Malcolm" derives from the word "dove" (Kolatch 183–184). A dove is, of course, a common Biblical symbol of peace dating back to the story of Noah and the Flood, as well as a symbol of the Spirit of God in the Gospel of St. Matthew. Taken together, the name would appear to indicate a man driven by a desire for peace, calm, and gentleness. In contrast, River reminds viewers that the captain's nickname of "Mal" is derived from the Latin for "bad" ("The Train Job" 1.02). Both names fit this complex character, who often calls the woman he loves a "whore" to her face, yet who doesn't hesitate to send anyone else sprawling who would presume to insult her in such a rude fashion. So which is he? And when? Fortunately, Malcolm's life as a Browncoat (those who fought against the idea of centralized governmental control of the 'verse and who were thoroughly defeated) provides viewers with a bright-line dividing mark: the Battle of Serenity Valley.

While viewers see battle footage in the opening credits of every episode of *Firefly*, there are two more extended battle scenes that depict Mal in battle; first, during the pilot episode where the end of the pivotal Battle of Serenity Valley is depicted and second, during "The Message" where the earlier Battle of Du-Khang is shown (1.12). In both, Sgt. Mal Reynolds is observed fighting with an almost fierce joy. Since the Battle of Du-Khang occurs first chronologically, it will be discussed first.

During the Battle of Du-Khang (ironically, this term translates into "temple" or "prayer hall"), viewers have an opportunity to observe the contrasting combat styles of Sgt. Mal Reynolds and Cpl. Zoe Alleyne. Mal provides a sharp contrast to the frosty cool of Zoe, who sternly lectures the inexperienced Pvt. Tracey on the virtues of stealth. Mal then enters the frame from the opposite side, screaming and shooting with exuberance, prompting Zoe to note dryly that "there are other schools of thought." With the only officer present a shell-shocked lieutenant who is unable to command, Mal unhesitatingly takes charge to get the remaining troops out of the Buddhist temple (the "du-khang") they have been using as a makeshift bunker and regroup with other Independent forces. There are two interesting details to note about this scene. The first is the use of a religious site as a combat zone; apparently in Whedon's world no faith provides protection from the carnage of war. The second is Mal's taking the time in the midst of a firefight to craft the illusion that the traumatized lieutenant is the one who orders the troops to retreat from their current position and regroup with the other soldiers. In this scene, Whedon clearly establishes both Mal's leadership abilities and his protective nature, as well as his expectations that his orders to those under his command will be followed.

In the Battle of Serenity Valley, Mal's joy in fighting is even more apparent. Although his comrades in arms are beginning to waver after weeks of combat, he is gloriously free of doubt, reminding them that the Alliance never expected the Independents to hold onto the valley for more than a day or two and that the Browncoats have "done the impossible and that makes us mighty. Just a little while longer, our angels are gonna be soaring overhead, raining fire" on the Alliance forces ("Serenity" 1.01). Having propped up the morale of his troops with the promise of Biblical apocalypse for the enemy, he prepares to fling himself back into the bloody fray. First, however, he pauses long enough to pull a silver cross out from beneath his uniform shirt. He reverently kisses the religious icon and briefly, yet fervently, prays. This, more than any other moment in the series, is the point at which viewers see evidence of the apparent strength of Sgt. Reynolds' religious faith. Viewers need to look quickly, for Reynolds' faith is about to melt away as completely as butter dropped onto a hot skillet.

Despite ever-present danger, Mal reassures his troops that "We can't die... We are just too pretty for God to let us die" ("Serenity" 1.01). At this point, the faithful Mal has no qualms, for the outcome in his mind is a certainty — Divine Providence is on the side of the Independents and all the rest is nothing more than simulated danger, much like a roller coaster. This is faith, but it is blind faith, and while it can be an undeniably powerful force, it often also leads straight to arrogance and zealotry, which are negative aspects of faith.

Regardless of Mal's faith, the Independent command has decided that surrender is warranted in the face of overwhelming odds. Mal and the few surviving troops are abandoned on a bleak, blasted battlefield, and a good man's faith in a just God is shattered. As Mal stands in the foxhole, staring in disbelief, Bendis, the young soldier Mal was revving up earlier with promises of God-sent hellfire for the enemy, is fatally shot while standing next to him and Mal's religious faith dissolves into the ether.[1] Mal had never considered that anything other than absolute victory was a possibility and his empty, rabbit's-foot faith leaves him with nothing to walk him through a world marked by this crushing defeat.

Following the aftermath of the war, Mal has a fierce determination to reject what he sees as a failed faith and instead construct a life built solely on self-reliance. It is well worth pointing out that he never quite manages to become a *dis*believer; rather, he is an extremely angry *ex*-believer.[2] He exhibits hostility towards displays of belief, as evidenced by his refusal to permit grace to be said at his ship's table as well as his disdain towards the very presence of Shepherd Book. Mal takes a perverse delight in springing the true nature of Inara's work as a Companion on the Shepherd, who has been led to believe that she is some sort of state official by Mal's mocking use of the title "Ambassador" to refer to her ("Serenity" 1.01). It is nigh-impossible to be that angry at God without believing in His existence on some level.

God has let him down and Mal adamantly refuses to give God another shot at disappointing him further, viewing total self-reliance as the safest path. In a way, Mal is following a perversion of the Golden Rule's proclamation that we are to "do unto others." God has ignored what Mal wanted, so Mal intends to ignore what he thinks God wants from him; namely, devotion and attention. In fact, Mal's hostility is so advanced that his references to the Divine post–Serenity Valley tend to be in the form of curses or exclamations of shock. Often, these references are made in Mandarin Chinese rather than English. By keeping Mal's references to God in a language which is foreign and undecipherable to most viewers, Whedon is emphasizing Mal's views of God as being nothing useful, benevolent, or even relevant.

While Mal has read his Coleridge,[3] he would have done well to study Annie Dillard as well, who reminds us that "We are most deeply asleep at the switch when we fancy we control any switches at all" (62). I can only imagine the eye rolling Mal would exhibit if anyone were foolish enough to quote Heb. 11:1 at him: "Faith is the substance of things hoped for, the evidence of things not seen." Following Serenity Valley, Mal believes solely in the tangible and the concrete and he is convinced to the marrow of his bones that *he* is in control of his life, not some abstract Deity. This self-centered philosophy is one Mal adheres to more and more tightly as the series progresses.

Mal's angry rejection of faith and his turning from it in the face of personal tragedy is an example of rabbit's-foot faith that is better suited to unsophisticated children than to mature adults. That said, it is still a comforting idea to many believers to think *So long as I observe the rituals and say the magic words, God won't let anything bad happen to me and I can live a peaceful life.* When Mal discovers that this is not true, that ritual doesn't guarantee a magic shield of protection to those who think themselves righteous, his watery faith evaporates, leaving him (he thinks) faith-less. However, faith comes in many forms, only some of which are found in religion. Whedon may be a self-proclaimed "angry atheist," but that certainly doesn't keep his creations from finding meaning in their existence. For Malcolm, this will be a long, arduous journey.

In 1941, Catholic Bishop Fulton John Sheen addressed the issue of faith involving active effort rather than empty ritual in his radio broadcast, challenging his listeners to remember that, "Peace is not a passive but an active virtue. Our Lord never said, 'Blessed are the peaceful,' but 'Blessed are the peacemakers.'[4] The Beatitude rests only on those who make [peace] out of trial, out of suffering, out of cruelty, even out of sin" (qtd. in Safire 504). Whedon uses all of these — trial, suffering, cruelty and sin — to begin the transformation of the character of Malcolm Reynolds from cold skeptic to renewed believer.

Faith is deeply ingrained in Mal and faith is difficult to completely cast off, although it can be buried and ignored, which Mal will expend considerable energy to do.[5] But similar to hope resting at the bottom of Pandora's Box, faith has a way of quietly surviving and patiently waiting to be rediscovered and, in Mal's case, redefined. And what is faith, if not hope's sister?[6] Regarding this point of "patient waiting," there are some rather striking parallels between Mal and Johnny Cash (making Mal the "Man in Brown" perhaps). Discussing Cash, Ken Garfield wrote, "Here was a Christian with scars inside and out, a complicated soul who rediscovered and ultimately embraced God, even if the journey was filled with a lifetime of wild detours.... a man whose life and death sends a message as powerful as any creed. Any one of us can find God, even after we've lost him." Despite the time and effort Mal spends tramping the dirt down on the grave of his faith, he will ultimately rediscover it. However, the journey will be a circuitous one and the final form his faith will take will be a far different one than the overtly religious, saucer-shallow type Mal carried into Serenity Valley during the war. Whedon uses Mal to illustrate that faith can take many forms and Mal's is a moving target.

At the time *Firefly* begins, six years have passed since Serenity Valley — six years in which Mal has carefully buried his faith in anyone and anything outside the small circle of his ship, his crew, and himself. In a scene that was cut from the pilot episode, Zoe explains Mal's post-war worldview to Simon in brutally simple terms: "Mercy, forgiveness, trust. Those are things he left back there. What he has now is the ship — the ship and us on it" ("Serenity" 1.01). Mal has spent the intervening years attempting to deliberately calcify himself into a dark, bitter husk of a man, unlikely to be touched or moved and therefore, unlikely to be disappointed or hurt. Mal's faith (such as it is at this point) is placed firmly in the here-and-now. Abstract notions such as trust and mercy have been cast off in preference to the solid bulk of the ship and the bone, muscle, and hearts of those who call her home.

Far from epitomizing the creed of the Golden Rule, the post-war Mal often reacts to the harsh, sharp-edged world in which he lives with acts of stunning ferocity and sudden violence. Three examples will illustrate this point. First, in the pilot episode, Mal shoots Agent Dobson without even breaking stride, much less indulging in the usual "let's be reasonable" speeches viewers have grown to expect from their Western-style heroes. Second, in "The Train Job" (1.02), Mal unhesitatingly kicks the bound Crow into a splattery death in *Serenity*'s engines. Third, in "Ariel" (1.09), Mal prepares to murder the traitorous Jayne in a 26th century version of keelhauling.[7] To Mal, these violent acts can all be easily justified as a way to protect (or avenge wrongs done to) his crew. Seemingly soft traits such as mercy and forgiveness are not traits Mal prizes, for his experiences have shown him the value of harsh reactions.

Mal's cruelty can also be seen in the words he chooses to employ. He is quite willing to refer to the gentle, cultured Inara as a "whore" on multiple occasions and often goes even further to insult her. An example of this is the cutting exchange in the episode "Objects in Space" (1.14) in which Mal responds to Inara's complaint that his work is preventing her from finding "decent clientele" by saying, "Well, I'm sorry if I'm cutting into your retirement fund, but would it kill you not to spread for a spell?" Whedon makes the point here that insulation is provided by insults — Mal shoves the gentler things in his life (such as tenderness and mercy) away to prevent the possibility of those concepts and the people who embody them getting close enough to hurt him again.

Two other examples illuminate Mal's willingness to be verbally cruel to those around him. In the pilot episode, Mal informs Simon that Kaylee (on whom Simon performed emergency surgery following her shooting by Dobson) has died, although he knows the opposite to be true. He later laughs about this with his assembled crew, saying as he guffaws, "I'm a bad man." Even more telling is his harsh rebuke of the sweetly naïve Kaylee in "Shindig" (1.04) when she expresses a desire for a fancy hoopskirted dress in a shop window by barking, "What are you going to do in that rig? Flounce around the engine room? Be like a sheep walking on its hind legs." Although he immediately regrets the hurt he sees he has caused the woman he often refers to affectionately as "mei-mei" ("little sister" in Mandarin), the damage is done and hurting Kaylee is as useless a thing to do as scalding a kitten.[8] Whedon understands that viewers must be able to relate to his anti-hero so, despite his willingness to be harsh in order to get by, Mal never descends to the level of being a completely heartless monster. However, his lack of faith in anything outside himself is burrowing a hole in his heart, making him more and more likely to use violent methods to achieve his goals.

By the time the film *Serenity* begins, Mal has descended deeper into darkness. The wolf is at the cargo bay door: money is beyond tight, the ship is falling apart and prospects are thin. Both Inara and Shepherd Book have left the ship, thus removing two of Mal's most stabilizing influences.[9] By the end of the film, Mal will be transformed, but he will also have, without hesitation, shot three unarmed men: The first is the man from the trading post who begs to be taken along to escape the Reaver attack, the second is the Operative at the Companion Training House and the third is a crew member of the crashed Alliance ship that attacked Haven. Of the three shootings, the incident involving the man at the trading post is the most upsetting. While Mal's actions here can be viewed as a sort of mercy killing (what the Reavers do to captives is sickening), and while the man would have survived if he'd followed Mal's orders to go into the vault in the first place, the trouble lies in Mal's use of violence as a *first* response.[10]

While there may be some justification for Mal's actions, they nevertheless directly contradict his statement to Simon in the pilot episode that "If I ever kill you, you'll be awake, you'll be facing me, and you'll be armed." Mal's code is becoming disturbingly flexible as he spirals inward toward what will prove to be a nearly empty center.

If the darkness is all that resided in Mal's soul, he might be a tortured character, but he would not be particularly compelling. After all, drama stems from contrast, not similarity; and it is the conflict between his desire to be an empty, unfeeling crook and his inherent, bone-deep decency that make Mal so intriguing. He has always had redeeming qualities and regardless of how hard he tries to be bad "Mal" who shoves away any who may sneak beneath his ever-present guard, the dove "Malcolm" keeps sticking his beak into events, causing unending complications.

Viewers see this dichotomy in the very first episode of *Firefly* when Mal reacts to Jayne's deliberately crude remarks to Kaylee by ordering him to leave the table. He later suggests that the Shepherd take dinner to Inara (who is staying clear of the new arrivals at this time) although he has earlier insulted them both. This leads Shepherd Book to comment to Inara that Mal isn't "wildly interested in ingratiating himself with anyone, yet he seems very protective of his crew" (1.01). Indeed, if Mal has a creed at this point, it is that he looks out for those on the ship and expects the rest of the crew to do the same. The crew has been hand-selected by Mal, providing him with an opportunity to set up his own world and establish his own rules. In this, Whedon shows us a man seeking what most of us seek—a family, redemption for regrets, and a safe place. It is Jayne's failure to adhere to this code of "family first" by attempting to betray the fugitives Simon and River that nearly leads him to be executed by Mal, an event discussed in greater depth later in this chapter.

Mal's lack of interest in "ingratiating himself with anyone" is underscored by his actions in "The Train Job" (1.02), where he incurs the near-lethal wrath of the sadistic crime boss Niska by returning the cargo his crew has been hired to steal. He feels that he has no other choice once he discovers that the cargo is medicine which is badly needed by the dirt-poor settlers. Stealing from the Alliance or those who support the Alliance is acceptable to him (in fact, he tells Zoe that he'd do that sort of job for free), but taking medicine from the sickly poor is quite another. While the Alliance doesn't care much about the fate of the settlers and the theft is only a minor annoyance, to Niska, who has employed the crew for this heist, Mal's high-minded actions are an affront to his honor and reputation; an affront that earns Mal everlasting enmity. In Niska, the adage of "the enemy of my enemy is my friend" falls dramatically apart. To Whedon, doing the right thing in returning the medicine to those who truly need it is a decision that will have long-lasting repercussions, for doing the right and moral thing is seldom an easy decision to make.

While Mal can act selflessly, his more noble actions are usually spiced with at least a dash of self-interest. As Simon states in *Serenity*, Mal's guiding star seems to be "what's of use" to him personally. Mal originally offers Simon (and by extension, Simon's sister River) a home onboard despite the added danger of transporting wanted fugitives due to his need for a skilled medic. However, when the siblings are kidnapped by settlers desperate for a doctor in "Safe," Mal returns to fetch them although he acknowledges that life would be easier without them on board (1.05). Here Mal has a perfect opportunity to cut and run, to "haul anchor" and have life run more smoothly—yet Whedon has Mal make the tough moral choice, electing to return for Simon and River, despite the near certainty that trouble will ensue.

Upon returning for Simon and River, Mal finds River tied to a stake and Simon ready to burn with her as the "hill folk" prepare to reenact the Inquisition. The powerful Patron of the town, whose deep secret has been accidentally read by the psychic River, admonishes Mal that "This is a holy cleansing. You cannot think to thwart God's will." Rather than enter a lengthy theological debate, Mal indicates the abundance of firepower being impressively displayed by Jayne, who is dangling above the woodpile, then calmly orders the crowd to release River.[11] The siblings may be two kinds of trouble that Mal does not need, but they are his crew and, for him, that ends the discussion. Whedon makes a key point regarding faith here. While the "faithful" of the village are willing to burn River alive for her difference, it is Mal the faithless who acts to save her. To Whedon, it is very possible to be moral without faith and be immoral with all the trappings of faith.

Loyalty is a fundamental quality to Mal. He gives it unstintingly to his crew and expects it in return, no matter how tense situations may become. Mal's loyalty to his crew is also amply demonstrated in "Ariel" (1.09) when he discovers that Jayne has attempted to sell out River and Simon. Although Jayne has proven himself to be greatly useful to Mal in the past and the siblings are trouble since their fugitive status puts a bull's-eye on his ship, Mal does not hesitate to dispatch Jayne for this betrayal of his crew.[12] Jayne, who naturally thinks that Mal's reaction is extreme to say the least, protests that his actions do not indicate any disloyalty to his captain. Mal disagrees with this perspective, claiming that there is no difference whether Jayne turns on Mal himself or on any of his crew, for they are ultimately the same. Although Mal would probably snort with derision if the parallels between his actions here and the admonition of Christ in Matt. 25:34–45 were remarked upon, he is nevertheless echoing the flavor of "When you refused to help the least of these my brothers, you were refusing help to me." Jayne's inability to perceive this commonality makes him a threat Mal feels he must remove to ensure the safety of the whole — Mal has worked very hard to create this family and he will protect it at all costs.

Jayne manages to save his life, despite Mal's obvious readiness to end it, by seeking redemption for his actions. He pleads with Mal, not for his life, but to not reveal that he was a Judas, imploring Mal to "Make something up. Don't tell 'em what I did" ("Ariel" 1.09). Mal relents, perhaps seeing in Jayne's desire for redemption something of himself. Here Jayne represents the end of the slippery slope for Mal, as Jayne is a man who is apparently motivated purely by profit and self-interest.

Usually, Mal's more noble actions (such as rescuing Simon and River) are partially motivated by his intense desire to be in control and to be the sole voice commanding the actions of his crew. Mal believes strongly in personal responsibility, a belief which he can take to near-rabid extremes. One of Whedon's keys to the character of Mal is that because Mal's in charge, he feels keenly responsible for the safety and well-being of his crew. Mal desperately wants to control circumstances in order to control the likely outcome. With no faith in anything larger than himself, that puts the entire burden squarely on his shoulders — a burden not even Atlas could successfully shoulder.

Despite Mal's rather pronounced tendencies toward control-freakism, he acknowledges that he does not actually "own" anyone onboard his ship and that humans are not meant to own other humans, who have free will to choose their own lives. As an example, Mal assumes that River is being transported in a cryogenic state to serve as a slave for either "some borderworld baron" or belongs to Simon himself (1.01). This misunderstanding does nothing to endear Simon to Mal, who feels protective towards River from his very first glimpse of her, despite lacking any biological tie to her.[13] Slavery, which Mal finds reprehensible, is presented as an accepted fact of life in the *Firefly* 'verse and it provides a useful prism through which to examine Mal's actions and motivations.

Although many other references exist to provide grist for the discussion mill, the episodes "Shindig" and "Our Mrs. Reynolds" will serve as the focus here. "Shindig" (1.04) begins with Mal and Jayne playing pool in a rundown bar, with Inara looking on. Their opponent, a man ironically named "Wright," is relating the tale of a recent smuggling job of his own, in which the cargo was human beings. Wright remarks on the huge profit margin of this enterprise since it is not even necessary to lay in additional rations. Mal registers his protest against this type of business by picking the man's pocket, which begins a rousing bar brawl.[14] Later, Mal will express his disapproval of Inara's consideration of Atherton Wing's offer to make her his personal Companion by saying, "You think following the rules will buy you a nice life—even if the rules make you a slave." One of the primary reasons Mal so despises her work as a Companion has to do with its involvement in the buying and selling of humans by one another. In Mal's worldview, it is irrelevant that Inara lives comfortably, is viewed as a respectable professional, and carefully selects her own clients—to him, it's nothing more than selling yourself on a plushly upholstered auction block to the highest bidder.

To Mal, any impediment to human beings living their lives freely is an abomination. Paradoxically, this philosophy means he must acknowledge that he has no right to interfere with Inara's decisions, including her decision to stay or leave, regardless of how distasteful he finds her profession. Those who elect to travel with him are expected to adhere to his rules, but they are also free to seek their fortune elsewhere. It should be noted at this point that religious faith also has rules and that Mal once followed those rules into the very hell of Serenity Valley, where his faith was repaid with abandonment. The rules of society or religion (or Mal's ship, as far as that goes) may be rooted in benevolent intentions, but to Mal, rebellion is the natural order of existence when the rules impinge on a sentient creature's free will. Mal's inner code is further complicated by the fact that his moral compass lacks the true north of a belief in anything larger than himself. In the film *Serenity*, he complains of being "rudderless," subject to being spun about by whatever wind is prevailing at any given moment, especially where Inara is concerned.

When the rules of the "civilized" society in "Shindig" conflict with Mal's Byzantine moral code regarding who can call Inara a "whore," he finds himself embroiled in a formal swordfight for which he is woefully unprepared.[15] Atherton Wing, Mal's opponent, is by far the superior swordsman and Mal's death during this duel of honor seems a foregone conclusion until Mal steps outside the ossified rules and relies on his bar-fighting skills, clubbing Wing with the broken sword hilt. The rules of this society dictate that Mal must now kill the downed and humiliated Wing; rules that he rejects with his own unique flair.

While Malcolm's code of conduct permits killing, especially in defense of himself (the man's not a Quaker), it emphatically does not permit murder, and slaying an unarmed and helpless opponent who has been removed as a threat would violate that code. This is emphasized in *Serenity* when Mal refuses to execute the Operative, choosing instead to "grant [his] greatest wish ... to show [him] a world without sin," despite the fact that the Operative has beaten him bloody and run him through with a sword.

The desire for personal freedom is a hallmark of Malcolm and this aspect of his personality is highlighted when he discovers he has apparently exchanged bachelorhood for wedded bliss. In "Our Mrs. Reynolds" (1.06), Mal acquires a wife named "Saffron," ostensibly as partial payment for a job.[16] Being unaware of the theology and customs of the settlers, Mal has no idea he has become a husband until he discovers Saffron as a stowaway on the ship following a celebratory evening of drinking, dancing, and flowered hats. Discovering that he is apparently married causes great consternation for him and great mirth for the rest of the crew, with the telling exception of Inara, who finds "the whole thing degrading."

Although eager to obtain a divorce, he tries mightily to convince Saffron that she has inherent worth beyond being currency for someone's debt, telling her, "Wife or no, you are no one's property to be tossed aside." When Jayne offers to trade his "very favorite gun" for Saffron, whom Mal obviously does not want, Mal lays down his law regarding humans as property: "She's not to be bought. Nor bartered, or borrowed, or lent. She's a human woman who doesn't know a damn thing about the world and needs our protection" (1.06). This protection extends to Mal's valiant efforts to resist taking sexual advantage of her, which she repeatedly encourages him to do, despite his protests that to do so would not be "morally right."[17] Eventually, he succumbs to his baser nature, lamenting that he's bound for the "special hell" Shepherd Book warned him about earlier. Whedon sets up an interesting (and comedic) contrast here between Mal's persona as the hardened criminal and his true nature as a protector by having Mal attempt to explain to Saffron why it would be wrong for him to "play house" with her. The fact that throughout this conversation he averts his eyes from Saffron, who is as blissfully naked as Eve in the Garden, underscores his desire to behave according to his own moral code, which doesn't permit the seduction of the innocent. However, as is characteristic of Whedon's work, the roles are reversed here — Saffron is the seducer, while Mal is the seduced. The duplicitous Saffron doesn't need Mal to give her rights; she's fully in control of the situation. In fact, the "special hell" Book warned Mal about turns out to be rooted firmly in this life, rather than in the next, as Saffron incapacitates the ship and flees, leaving the crew to die and the ship to be scrapped — events that happen because Mal let down his guard and trusted himself to handle the situation.

As seventeenth-century poet and clergyman John Donne could have reminded Mal, "no man is an island, entire of itself." However, for reasons which seem sound to him, Mal has carefully expended a tremendous amount of energy to limit his circle of trust and interaction to the point that he may be considered at least an isthmus. Nowhere is this more evident than in the brilliant episode "Out of Gas" (1.08), in which Mal sends off every other resident of the ship following a crippling accident that has left the ship without life support hundreds of thousands of miles from anywhere. Zoe, his second-in-command, has been rendered unconscious and Mal must rely on his own judgment. He decides to remain with his ship. Inara tries to convince him to come along in the shuttles, which are not realistically expected to reach a destination, but by sending them off, Mal at least is not having his created family wait helplessly to die either from freezing or asphyxiation. Her pleas fall on deaf ears, as Mal replies with conviction, "I'm not leaving *Serenity*."[18] Inara begs him to reconsider this death-wish since "This isn't the ancient sea, Mal ... you don't have to die alone." In response, Mal looks at her with incredulity and pity, then states the simple truth that "Everyone dies alone," which he prepares to do once the others have left, retrieving a blanket and curling up on the bridge to die. He survives through a most unlikely chain of circumstances involving a passing salvage ship with the correct missing part, a murderous captain, and his own loyal crew.[19] In fact, it is Zoe who steadfastly insists that they return for Mal, rather than leave a man behind. Whedon uses this foreshadowing to emphasize the growing divide between the two soldiers. Emotionally and spiritually, Mal remains in the utter hell of Serenity Valley, while Zoe has found a way to move beyond that point and forge a life that doesn't center solely on the war, although her code will not permit her to leave her captain behind to die alone.

Despite this instance of clearly needing others to survive, Mal does not ordinarily see himself as part of a larger society. Mal is aware of this, referring to his crew when he comments to Simon in the film, "So here is us, on the raggedy edge." It is interesting to note that Mal uses the plural "us," indicating that he may belong to a tiny tribe, but it is nevertheless a tribe, which is an important thing to have on the outer edge of space. A key theme of *Firefly* is found in its accurate depiction of the sheer size of space; the staggering hugeness of it. One little ship is not a lot to hang your faith and trust on amidst the incalculable vastness of space, yet Mal does just that.[20]

In his desire for independence bordering on isolation, Mal shares much with the literary character of Huckleberry Finn, particularly in terms of both being outcasts from so-called "respectable" society who give every impression of liking it just fine that way and creating unconventional families to meet their human need for the company of others. Due to what Mal sees as his betrayal by the Divine, he demands that relationships operate only on his terms. Intimacy (as well as faith) demands a willingness to be vulnerable, which for Mal is tantamount to begging for a bullet. His desire for limited human interaction does not go unnoticed. In the episode "War Stories" (1.10), Wash comments on Mal's "intimacy issues."[21] This is further explored in "Heart of Gold" (1.13), in which Mal shares one tender night of passion and need with Nandi, a friend of Inara's. Nandi is the madam of a whorehouse who the crew is assisting in their struggle against a wealthy man named Burgess who has impregnated one of the girls and who intends to forcibly claim the child once it is born. Nandi makes no demands on Mal and their encounter is not bought and paid for, but is rather the result of one human offering comfort to and receiving comfort from another.

It is instructive to examine the juxtaposition of the scenes of Mal and Nandi with Burgess's treatment of Chari, a prostitute who is in his employ as a spy. The scenes involving the societal outcasts of crook and whore are riddled with sly double entendres regarding religion. Moreover, these scenes are drenched with playfulness and a certain tenderness, as evidenced by Mal saying to the madam, a woman used to earning her living as the short-term property of men, "If I'm overstepping my bounds, you let me know." Meanwhile, the respectable pillar of society, Burgess, treats Chari with a casual viciousness, parading her in front of his assembled thugs and thundering, "Let us all remember, right here and now, what a woman is to a man!" His face a mask of brutality, he then orders her to "Get on your knees!" To Burgess, Chari and all the other residents of the Heart of Gold are nothing more than property to be purchased and used as the purchaser sees fit. To Whedon, who is *actually* moral and who is *presented* as moral can be tricky to determine. Hence, he gives us the violent pillar of society and the honest crook.

In the ensuing firefight, Nandi is killed, leaving Mal shaken. Inara later states that she is glad Nandi was with Mal on what turned out to be her last night, but Mal finds no comfort in this. With the weight of the world crashing down on him, he replies that he wishes he'd never even met her, for he failed her. At this point, viewers can easily see that Malcolm is a man who keenly feels the weight of his responsibilities toward other people, which is the primary reason he lets so few people within that sacred circle — he believes that if he fails them, they will die.

Exactly how will a man who takes his obligations this seriously react to losing people he has known, not for a mere few days, but for months or years — people who are members of his self-selected tribe who have been permitted to enter that sacred circle? Someone he has come to rely on to act as his conscience and remind him of what he might yet aspire to become? Someone who he trusts to fly the ship which is much more than simply his livelihood and safely bring her home? Dramatic events transpire in the film *Serenity* which will provide the catalyst for Malcolm to undergo an inner transformation in reaction to the dangerous force most feared by the Alliance — sincere, unselfish love. Love is the force that will galvanize Mal to take action, rather than continuing to mourn his losses by becoming increasingly brittle and bitter.

Love, especially spiritual love (also known as "agape"), as a force with the power to transform people is a theme that has been expounded upon by poets, writers and sages over the centuries.[22] However, it seems that this amorphous force can have little effect on a man who has retreated so deeply within himself to cause his chosen little sister Kaylee to mournfully predict that "He'll drive us all off, one by one" (*Serenity*). Throughout the time viewers know Mal, he has been paring his life down further and further, cutting his connections with other people until even he acknowledges his lack of "groundedness" to Inara. As has been demonstrated, Malcolm was once a man of apparently strong, yet essentially superficial, faith. He initially takes comfort in Christian ritual (such as prayer) and symbols (such as the cross) and is shown to be familiar with Christian scripture and references. Yet he is steadfastly ignoring the bedrock principle contained in 1 John 4:8: "He that loveth not, knoweth not God; for God is love." To love is not just a good and desirable thing; it is in fact the moral duty of a Christian and it is a duty that Mal believes he has cast off. Diane Ackerman reminds us that pre–Christian gods tended to be sadistic towards their creations, but "[i]n contrast, the Old Testament God, obsessed with love, commands his people first and foremost to 'love the lord your God with all your heart, and with all your soul, and with all your might'" (Ackerman 47). Love of others is the Great Commandment, trumping all other laws. Even at his most lost, Mal follows this law, although he would argue that he doesn't.

At this point, if Mal considers his behavior to be altruistic at all, he would argue that it is extremely limited in scope. It is likely that he would say that it may be true that he would move heaven and earth to protect his tiny tribe, but only because they fill certain needs of his — to care is only practical. After all, if he had to rely on his mechanical skills, the ship's going to fall right out of the sky within a week. So Kaylee is essential. The ship needs a pilot, so Wash gets to decorate the bridge console with plastic dinosaurs. Mal needs muscle, so Jayne's presence can be tolerated. He needs someone he can trust and for that, he has Zoe. Simon's skills as a doctor are quite useful and he is a package deal with River. Book and Inara are ostensibly paying passengers, so their presence fits into his economic worldview. But Mal, like Shakespeare's Queen Gertrude, is protesting too much. He is not seeing his behavior clearly, for he still wears the blinders he put on when he buried his faith back in Serenity Valley.

If Mal Reynolds would take the time to examine his own actions, he would see that he has always been motivated by love. He protects his *mei mei* by sending Jayne from the table for crudely insulting Kaylee in the pilot episode, yet he tries to help Jayne make sense of the events with the Mudders in "Jaynestown" (1.07). He permits Wash and Zoe time and space to build a relationship he can't quite fathom. He nearly gets himself killed in a swordfight when someone else implies Inara is a whore (1.04). He returns for the Tam siblings when they get themselves in a woodpile of trouble. He risks both his beloved ship and his freedom to get medical help for the injured Book (1.05). Moreover, in *Serenity*, Mal will go still further and reach out beyond himself at tremendous risk to be a part of a larger society, a step he has avoided taking for years. Whedon's point here is that love, like the people it affects, is a complicated proposition requiring action, not murmured ritual.

It appears obvious that love is to be construed within the Christian faith as an undeniably powerful force, a view which is shared by the spookily unnamed Operative in *Serenity*. The Operative understands the immense power that can be wielded by someone whose actions are motivated by love. After the Operative reviews the holographic recording of River's escape from the clutches of the Alliance with the assistance of her brother Simon, the doctor in charge of the project tells the viewer that Simon "[t]urned his back on his whole life. Madness." To which the Operative replies: "Madness, no. Something a good deal more dangerous. Have you looked at this scan carefully? At his face? It's love, in point of fact." The Operative sees himself as an agent of the forces of good; a type of peacemaker, although he admits that he is "a monster," capable of doing terrible, bloody acts in furtherance of his ultimate goal. In the *Official Visual Companion* to the film, Whedon stated that the Operative is a person "who wants a better world and will go to no end of horror to find it" (21). Whedon may have also be influenced by the writings of Thackeray, who could have had the Operative in mind when he wrote, "The wicked are wicked, no doubt, and they go astray and they fall, and they come by their deserts, but who can tell the mischief which the very virtuous do?" (qtd. in Matsuoka) The Operative is the purest sort of zealot — one who can readily admit that his actions cause suffering and pain, but who truly believes that these actions are regrettably necessary in furtherance of obtaining the prize shimmering on the horizon; in this case, the creation of a world without sin. While Mal and the Operative are on opposite sides, they also serve as dark mirrors of one another. The Operative has total devotion to a belief, he is polished and sophisticated, yet capable of committing heinous acts of violence upon the innocent. Mal lacks belief in anything outside himself and his crew, he's unpolished and rough, yet moral to a fault. The truly fascinating point is that both the Operative and Mal are convinced that they are doing the right thing — the Operative in stopping at nothing to kill River before the secret she knows can be told and Mal in stopping at nothing to be sure that secret reaches everyone in the known 'verse. It is clear that Whedon prefers the doubting ruffian over the confident zealot since Whedon's narratives without exception favor freedom of thought and expression over toeing the party line.

Obviously, Whedon has an interesting way of looking at the world and he has stated that one of the major themes in the film *Serenity* was to destroy the idea of simple moral absolutes; that "what some people consider 'sin,' I consider human characteristics" (*Visual Companion* 20). Whedon uses the smoothly polite Operative to advance this theme. A great deal of the Operative's thoughts are consumed with the concept of sin, which is often understood to be a transgression of divine law (Panati 179). The writer Harper Lee would agree with this view of sin serving to separate humans from the Divine. She wrote that "The most common barriers to love are greed, envy, pride and four other drives formerly known as sins" (Lee). While Whedon's belief is that "sin" is a natural (though undesirable) part of the human condition and Lee says these "sins" block the flow of love, the two statements agree that people do not have to be bound as slaves by these faults. There is love, which can overcome sin and which Whedon will use as the powerful catalyst to transform Mal.

Returning to the Operative, not only is his goal the creation of a world without sin, but he also enjoys asking his victims if they are aware of what their sin is before ritually running them through with a sword. He identifies the Alliance doctor's sin as pride, since he paraded the psychic River before key governmental officials who were privy to every secret in the 'verse. When the Operative later poses the same question to a badly wounded Mal, he refuses to choose, replying that he is "a fan of all seven," indicating his familiarity with the so-called seven deadly sins of wrath, lust, greed, envy, gluttony, sloth and pride.[23] Mal ultimately goes with "Wrath," an understandable choice for a man who is not Christ who has just had his side pierced with a sword. Mal certainly has a different point of view about who is acting "sinfully" at this juncture. The Operative clearly sees himself as committing sin for the greater good and that steadfastness of belief is what makes him such a dangerous foe. Mal is well aware of the danger posed by a zealot. He said of Burgess in "Heart of Gold" (1.13) that "There's nothing worse than a monster thinks he's right with God." The same can be said for the Operative — a man who not only has faith, but has absolutely no doubt about the rightness of his actions. To Whedon, the Operative's dogmatic beliefs pose an extreme danger, especially when coupled with his willingness to use ruthless methods against all those who disagree with his viewpoint. The juxtaposition of Mal's lack of faith with the Operative's dead-certain faith illustrates Whedon's view that, in some cases, no faith is far better than an excess of faith.

To triumph over the evil presented by the Alliance's Operative, Mal will have to go outside his own meager resources. This will require him to shift away from his most fundamental way of looking at the 'verse — his belief that he (and only he) is in control. This viewpoint has stopped working for him. Even the ever-loyal Zoe begins to question Mal's actions, pointing out after the trading station robbery in which Mal shot a man in an act of mercy killing that "in the time of war, we would never have left a man stranded." Rather than disagree, Mal flatly states, the light gone from his eyes, "Maybe that's why we lost" (*Serenity*). Mal has never placed his belief in anything as fickle as luck, choosing instead to channel all of his considerable former religious faith into belief in himself and, by extension, his crew. Mal's trouble is that his creed of self-reliance is no longer getting the job done and he sees nowhere else to turn. Mal has become disillusioned about his ability to provide for his family and his desperation is causing him to spin wildly out of the control he prizes so highly.

Following River's spectacularly violent "activation" via subliminal triggering in a rough-and-tumble backwater bar, Mal takes two actions that baffle him, but not the viewer. First, after Simon has used another "trigger" to cause her to fall asleep, Mal scoops up the sleeping River rather than leave her stranded and helpless, although only a moment ago, she was pointing a lethal firearm at his face with every intention of using it. It is interesting to ponder if it is at this point that Mal begins to return to his "old self"— the one who would never leave a man behind. Second, he seeks Shepherd Book.

The Shepherd has left the ship at this point, following the events depicted in the three-issue comic that links the stories of the television series and the film. As many viewers are unfamiliar with this important bridge between *Firefly* and *Serenity*, a brief summary is useful. Book is preaching to a small congregation when the crew's heist of a local bank goes terribly wrong, prompting the faithful in the church to scatter to safety. Book is apparently growing weary of his life among the increasingly desperate crew, pausing in his empty church to ask, "Oh, Lord, you clearly know I'm helping do your Work, so why do you find me trouble?"[24]

Book helps rescue the crew and then Mal takes on a riskier job to replace the botched one. When Book and Mal clash over the wisdom of this plan, words are exchanged and ultimately, Book is pushed too far and reacts violently. Although Mal later tells the Shepherd, "It don't matter that you hit me," a line has been crossed for Book that necessitates his leaving the ship. As Book puts it, "Which is exactly why I need to be away from you. Because sooner or later, it won't matter to me, either." Following this, Mal is seen sitting slumped on his bunk, alone and forlorn. Although he has been growing more desperate as his center begins to disintegrate, Mal's descent into darkness begins to proceed more rapidly once the Shepherd leaves his circle, fearing the possibility of backsliding into his once-violent ways. Even though he is not a believer, Mal has a respect for Book based on the Shepherd's ability to both resist proselytizing and his handiness with firearms. While he didn't want the Shepherd onboard initially and is often rude to him, Mal is lost without him.[25]

On Haven, Book is able to provide Mal with information that is both helpful and disturbing; namely, that the Alliance is most definitely coming for River. Book stresses that Mal is going to need belief to walk him through what's on its way, to which Mal idly chucks a rock towards the mining camp and explains that he isn't expecting Divine assistance. Faintly impatient, Book asks him why belief to Mal automatically means God. At this point, Mal is unready to answer, for he has never considered faith to be anything other than an element of religion. As discussed, Mal has roundly rejected that concept; however, Shepherd Book's notion of faith is quite a bit larger and he sees what Mal does not. Mal has *always* had faith — faith in love, faith in his created family, and faith in freedom. For Malcolm Reynolds, this faith — especially his faith in freedom and the inherent *rightness* of it — is the key that will release him from his self-imposed prison of empty, frantic desperation. However, at this point, Mal does not even realize he is in prison, much less that he is holding the key.

When the crew later returns to Haven, they find that the entire community has been massacred by the Alliance. Mal realizes with aching dread that his harboring of River is the root cause of this carnage and his responsibility crashes down upon him when he discovers the badly injured Shepherd Book. Although clearly dying, Book is unwilling to give up on Mal, entreating him that "it's on you now ... you have to find a course ... I don't care what you believe! Just believe it!" Whether Mal has a sincere belief in God, Buddha, or the Great Pumpkin matters not a whit to the Shepherd. All Book wants is for Mal to have a sincere belief in *something* that provides him with comfort and conviction and doesn't require him to slaughter the innocent. Whedon makes a powerful statement here — it is more important to have a sincere belief in a system of moral understanding than it is to profess belief in some popular faith that is devoid of real meaning to the individual.

Book's death signals the needle hitting "empty" on Mal's personal resources — absolutely nothing is left to sustain him. However, it is often at the seemingly worst and darkest moments that dawn begins to lighten the sky. Thomas Merton understood this, writing that, "Prayer and love are learned in the hour when prayer becomes impossible and your heart has turned to stone" (qtd. in "Reflections"). Mal must undergo his personal Gethsemane, retreating to the quiet darkness of one of the ship's shuttles to squarely face his own despair and isolation.[26] There is something vital and noble buried deep within this hardened skeptic that is struggling mightily to rise to the surface, something tough and holy — love.

As Paul Tillich has observed, "Something is holy to everyone, even to those who deny the holy" (qtd. in Schneider 126). Mal's holy touchstone has always been love; specifically, love of freedom. Love led him to fight as a Browncoat in the first place and to later cobble together the crew of *Serenity* in order to create a life outside of authoritarian governmental control.[27] Love is the holy touchstone that becomes Mal's rudder when he discovers "the truth that burned up River Tam's brain"— namely, that the Alliance, in a misguided attempt to create a "world without sin" actually caused the death of an entire worldful of people, except for the one-tenth of one percent who had the opposite reaction and were transformed into the roaming horror known as Reavers.[28] Love is the touchstone that prompts Mal to undergo a transformation and finally open his own personal Pandora's Box to release Hope and her straight-backed sister, Faith.

While viewers have seen Mal's more noble side before, this is something different. Mal takes a deliberate step towards being part of a larger society with his decision to risk life, limb, family, and ship to get a terrible truth broadwaved to the rest of the somnambulant 'verse and to serve as a voice for the forgotten dead. Mal will do this not out of self-interest, but rather because he sees the greater good that he has been called to serve, telling the Operative that it is not enough for Mal and his crew alone to know the truth, "the rest of the 'verse is gonna know it too. 'Cause they need to." Mal is able to reach this decision because he understands what the Alliance does not — that human beings are incapable of perfection and attempts to perfect them are doomed to failure. Sin is a natural part of the messy business of being human and is a part that the individual human certainly can decide to fight against, but it is not the role of the government to fight that battle for any person.[29]

What makes Mal's transformation so compelling to witness is the basic shift away from who he has become that it requires. Mal is now prepared to stop jackrabbiting and take a stand based on a new faith, even though he is fully aware of how much he has to lose and the likelihood that he will lose it — and no one ever makes a stand without believing in *something*. The fuzzy, warm, "rabbit's-foot faith" he possessed in Serenity Valley has been burned away in the crucible of experience and what he is left with is a stronger, tougher faith; the sort that allows the faithful to be convinced that, while the outcome of the path is unknown and uncertain, the journey is nevertheless worth making. He has a belief worth dying for (although he would be the first to tell you "that ain't exactly Plan A") and he is no longer demanding a guarantee regarding the end result. Indeed, he will suffer a great deal of pain and loss on the way to achieving his goal of broadwaving the truth regarding the Alliance's failed experiment in "making people better" on Miranda, including the killing of Book and the tragic death of Wash. But it is a fallacy to equate certainty with faith. As Mary Jean Irion says, "Faith is *not being sure*. It is *not being sure*, but betting with your last cent. Faith is not making religious sounding noises in the daytime. It is asking your inmost self questions at night — and then getting up and going to work" (qtd. in Bauer). Rather than losing himself in the darkness that has been threatening to overwhelm him, Mal gets up and goes to work. He becomes part of a larger society, leaving behind his isthmus of self-isolation.

By acting beyond his own selfish aims and by putting the well-being of others first at considerable risk to himself, he embodies Harper Lee's statement that "As one holds down a cork to the bottom of a stream, so may love be imprisoned by self: remove self, and love rises to the surface of man's being" (Lee). As a result of his willingness to remove himself from the equation and let love control his actions, he is transformed from the self-absorbed man he has been. The Operative sees his own false faith in the desirability of a world without sin shatter irreparably when he is shown in vivid, excruciating detail exactly what results from that desire to make people better as the message is sent and Malcolm's mission is concluded. Mal does not attempt to force people to accept the truth of what has been revealed; to do so would violate his basic belief in human independence and freedom of thought. However, now people are in possession of the proper information to reach their own decision about the benevolence of their government. Whedon prizes independent thought in decision-making, including decisions about faith. To have meaning, faith must be a private decision rather than being a glitzy bandwagon people unthinkingly jump to join.

At the conclusion of *Serenity*, viewers are left with a transformed Mal, one who intimately understands the nature and power of love and has reclaimed his faith, albeit in a different form than the overtly religious faith he had in Serenity Valley. The ship has been repaired at the orders of the humbled Operative and the crew prepares to depart in a raging rainstorm, with a much-saner-than-before River in the co-pilot's chair and Malcolm in the seat formerly occupied by Wash.[30] Comprehending the power of love, he proceeds to explain to the psychic River that love is the very first rule of flying. When River replies to this bit of philosophy that the "[s]torm's getting worse," Mal simply replies, "We'll pass through it soon enough," supremely confident in the ability of love to see him and his family through whatever the 'verse may throw at them.

Whedon has little use for organized religion and his overtly religious characters tend either to have nasty hidden agendas, such as the pyromaniacal Patron in "Safe," or their faith gets played for laughs, such as Riley being late for services at a local Sunnydale church, but being just in time for the battle with the vampires who have commandeered the sanctuary. In *Firefly*, Whedon takes his exploration of faith in a different direction. Viewers see Mal move from shallow faith in ritual to angry self-reliance to the acceptance of what can best be termed a "secular faith" which is one not rooted in religious ground. Mal's new-found faith is tougher and more resilient than that which he carried into Serenity Valley, for it is rooted in what he can see and experience. For a man so tied to the tangible, that has far more meaning and impact than incense and muttered prayers. His belief in love of freedom and every person's inherent right to live life according to the dictates of their own conscience has transformed him from the bitter man he had been to the faithfull man he has again become. While he probably will never again wear the cross as he once did, Mal's recovered faith in love may have finally equipped him to lay down the one he has been carrying since the war.

7

The Depth of Shadows

REDEMPTION AND DOUBT IN SHEPHERD BOOK

As one might expect from a creator with an atheistic point of view, Joss Whedon rarely presents formalized religion in a positive light in his work. For example, in "Anne," the opening episode of *Buffy*'s Season Three, viewers meet Ken, an apparently kind-hearted man who runs a faith-based shelter for the homeless of Los Angeles. However, the sanctuary he offers turns out to be a clever ruse designed to suck in the destitute and desperate to serve as slaves in a hell dimension where Ken reigns as a demon. To Whedon, religion is often a trap for the unwary.

Nevertheless, in *Firefly* and *Serenity*, Whedon creates a dynamic man of faith who is depicted as embodying positive qualities of faith such as kindness, compassion, and a willingness to defend the helpless.[1] Yet Shepherd Derrial Book is far from serene in his faith. He is often shown to be racked with doubt, burdened with worldly knowledge that seems incongruous for a man who has spent time living a life of contemplation within the walls of a secluded abbey. This conflict is hardly surprising, given Whedon's obvious fondness for creating nuanced characters who break archetypes.

In the commentary track accompanying the pilot episode of *Firefly*, Whedon notes that Shepherd Book is "a man *of* peace, but not a man *at* peace." Whedon uses this character to underscore two very clear points. First, redemption is possible for past acts, for while the past is always carried with us, it need not be a crushing burden; and second, doubt itself is not a sin. Before beginning the exploration of Whedon's use of the complex character of Shepherd Book to make these points, it is useful to first examine the views of religion within the 'verse of *Firefly* and *Serenity*.

Whedon has said that the "future is the past in a blender" (Said). In the future society of *Firefly* and *Serenity*, this puree is evident in the elaborate mixture of American and Chinese influences. The result is a lush cultural gumbo, giving viewers such sights as down-and-out ruffians with six shooters effortlessly speaking Mandarin. This rich mélange extends to the depiction of religious faiths in *Firefly* and *Serenity*, which was a goal of Whedon's from the beginning. In *Serenity: The Official Visual Companion*, he addresses the issue of faith in his created 'verse, stating: "When you have people that far out and you're dealing with culture as much as any science fiction does, faith becomes very important, the idea of religion and belief systems" (11). It is important to note Whedon's use of the plural here, as there is no single religion which is depicted as being dominant in the 'verse.

The mixture of faiths in *Firefly* and *Serenity* includes a multitude of Buddhist images, including a battle scene in a Buddhist temple. Women in the 'verse are occasionally seen draped in full *burqas*, a garment associated with fundamentalist strains of Islam. The Chinese custom of white mourning veils is shown at a funeral that also features a haunting *a cappella* version of the Christian hymn "Amazing Grace." Christianity in the 'verse has many forms, including the sect of the Triumph settlers who apparently follow a version of the Bible which includes verses regarding sexuality that would make the author of the "Song of Songs" blush.[2] Further, in *Serenity*, viewers see a clip of Mr. Universe's wedding to his Love-Bot; a ceremony which contains unmistakable Jewish elements, including the crushing of a glass and the wearing of a yarmulke. Clearly, people walking a variety of faith paths are welcome in the brave new worlds of *Firefly*.

Introduced into this mix is Derrial Book, a Shepherd re-entering the secular world from a life of seclusion in Southdown Abbey. Having decided that the time is right for him to return to the world, Book ambles through the docks of Persephone searching for a ship to take him somewhere; anywhere.[3] The specific destination of the ship is secondary for, like all seekers, Book knows that the journey is the important part.

Whedon swiftly establishes Book as a "Shepherd," a title given to religious leaders who follow a Christian path in the *Firefly* 'verse.[4] He accomplishes this coding in part through Book's costuming, including a vaguely Roman-style priest collar, which is apropos since Whedon's shepherds function much like priests in contemporary society. Book observes certain strictures regarding his personal life as dictated by his membership in a particular religious brotherhood. For example, viewers learn that Book's order dictates that his long hair be worn in a tidy ponytail (or, in *Serenity*, in neat cornrows) and that he subscribe to a life of celibacy.⁵ By joining the ship's family, it appears that Book has traded one monastic family of faith for another, albeit one with quite a different code.

The copacetic Kaylee has been charged with the task of barking for paying passengers and she marks the Shepherd as a likely customer. While Book has some money to pay for his passage, it is a small box of lush, ripe strawberries from the gardens of the Shepherd's abbey that entice her to accept him as a passenger, although she is aware of her captain's hostility towards all things religious. Despite risking Mal's irritation with this choice of passenger, when the audience sees Kaylee's visceral, sensual joy at eating the first strawberry, it is evident that she is content with her decision. Given that nothing in Whedon's work wanders into the frame by accident, it is fascinating to note that strawberries, which grow humbly on the ground without pit or thorns, have been used for centuries to symbolize Christ's sacrifice (Bruggman). The strawberry was also used to great effect in Ingmar Bergman's masterwork *Wild Strawberries*, in which the fruit represents the poignant moments and uncontrolled passions in our lives. As the Bergman film illustrates, strawberries can be an effective symbol of both purity and sensuality, which fits nicely with the sweetly innocent, yet earthily sexual, Kaylee.

Kaylee's decision to accept Shepherd Book onboard is enthusiastically received by the rest of the delighted crew, who are treated to a delicious home-cooked meal of actual, non-processed food prepared by Book on that first evening.⁶ However, Mal's hostility is immediately evident as he responds rudely to the Shepherd's request to say grace over the meal while simultaneously continuing to placidly eat the dinner provided by the man he has just insulted. The locking of horns between Mal and Book is due solely to Mal's own animosity; Book has no problem with the captain, nor any other onboard. The Shepherd is able to form warm, caring relationships with everyone from the tightly wound Simon to the sensual Inara to the crude mercenary Jayne. In large part, it is this ability of Book's to relate to people without judging their choices in life that precipitates his acceptance onboard *Serenity*, despite the captain's unconcealed bitterness towards all displays of faith. Thus, Whedon very swiftly establishes a tense dynamic between the captain of the ship and the captain of the soul.

While initially presented as a gentle, kindly man of God, it quickly becomes apparent that Shepherd Book has a high level of familiarity with worldly, violent things, although he has apparently rejected that life in favor of a contemplative one. In fact, Shepherd Book's very name is a riddle. He introduces himself to Kaylee by saying, "I'm *called* Book," which has a different meaning from saying, "I *am* Book." Aside from the implication that it is best to not judge any Book by its clever cover, it is an interesting name choice. The Christian Bible is routinely referred to as "the good Book" and, among followers of the Islamic faith, "people of the Book" include Jews, Christians and Muslims, since followers of all three faiths harken to portions of the Bible as a basic text of their faith (Panati 312). The Bible is a text that the Shepherd is often seen referring to for guidance and he is shown to be comfortable with the content and lessons of this "Good Book." However, while he may currently be a Shepherd who wishes only to tend gently to his found flock of misfits, Whedon makes it clear that this good Book contains a very unsettling prologue.

Tantalizing clues are often dangled regarding Book's past, which hint at dark and bloody deeds. For example, in the pilot episode of *Firefly*, Book is seen capably incapacitating a federal agent who has shot the innocent Kaylee in a panic. The Shepherd then thwarts the large and enraged Jayne in his desire to swiftly dispatch the agent, hoping to seek a less violent solution.[7] There are many instances of Book exhibiting a level of skill with combat that seem incongruous with his chosen vocation of Shepherd. For example, in "The Train Job" (1.02), Book knows the name and reputation of the psychotic crime lord Adlai Niska, prompting Jayne to comment on the oddity of a man of peace being aware of the identity of such a man. As is often the case, Book refuses to provide a clear answer, choosing to keep his own counsel regarding his past. Such secrets are a hallmark of Whedon's complex characters, always leaving mysteries to be explored.

This particular mystery is re-visited when Niska later reappears in "War Stories" (1.10). Niska captures Mal and Wash, gleefully planning to slowly torture them to death to repair the damage done to his reputation by the events in "The Train Job." While trying to piece together what happened at the scene, Book is able to immediately identify the type of specialized weapon used.[8] Book also unhesitatingly joins in the rescue operation, prompting icy-calm Zoe to ask with a trace of amusement if taking up arms won't violate certain Biblical precepts. Unruffled, Book replies that the Bible is quite clear about the undesirability of killing, but that there is some leeway "on the subject of kneecaps." During the daring rescue, Book shoots and shoots well — without always aiming for the kneecaps. While Book may abhor the use of violence to solve problems, Whedon's choice to make him a more-than-capable marksman raises teasing questions about how the compassionate Shepherd came by this particular skill set.

Book and the sadistic Niska also share a disconcerting familiarity with the works of the warrior-poet Shan Yu, who wrote extensive meditations on the effects of pain and anguish.[9] While Niska very well may own an autographed copy of these works, it seems an odd item of interest for a benevolent holy man. However, it should be noted that it is not without precedent for devoutly faithful persons to come to their faith through unusual paths.

For example, Saint Augustine, whose influence of the development of the early Christian faith can hardly be overstated, was a fervent follower of the Gnostic branch of Manichaeism before turning to orthodox Christianity and becoming an ardent opponent of his former faith. Early Church leaders, alarmed at the spread of Gnostic thought, vigorously sought to suppress Gnostic belief as heresy. In making this comparison, it is not intended to equate the dualistic beliefs of Manichaeism with the sadistic musings of Shan Yu; rather, it is to illustrate that Book, like Saint Augustine, has influences beyond those which most people would expect. This is in keeping with Whedon's grab-bag approach to portraying the future as an intricate mixture of East and West. Nothing (and no one) is simply what he/she/it appears to be and that uncertainty extends to Shepherd Book.

Additional evidence is presented to support the theory that the Shepherd's past was marked by violence and unsavory knowledge. In the episode "Objects in Space" (1.14), viewers get another glimpse into Book's mysterious past as River's emerging psychic abilities cause her to "overhear" random thoughts of others onboard without the solid frame of a context. As she walks through the ship, the teenager is bombarded by a flash from the gentle Shepherd in which his voice is tight with intensity as he says, "I don't give half a hump if you're innocent or not. So where does that put you?" There is no subsequent explanation for this out-of-character remark stemming from a man who is consistently portrayed as kind and giving. Perhaps it is nothing more than a random long-ago memory plucked from thousands in Book's mind or perhaps it is something much closer to the surface. The lives of past holy men can prove illustrative in this instance. For example, several popular Catholic saints had violent pasts as soldiers who actively participated in combat, including St. Ignatius of Loyola, who came to his faith following a severe injury sustained in battle (Farmer 248). A particularly apt example is found in the life of St. Thomas Becket, who led troops into battle and was for years a close confidant of King Henry II (Farmer 472 – 473). A more detailed comparison of Book and Thomas Becket is found further in this chapter, for the similarities between the two are striking and illustrate the principle that a quiet man of deep faith can originate in the chaotic clash of battle as well as on an isolated mountaintop.

Nevertheless, Book's reluctance to disclose the details of his past seems suspicious — is he the compassionate man of God he seems to be or is he merely a wolf in Shepherd's clothing, perhaps part of an elaborate plot by the Alliance government to retrieve River? This is more than idle speculation, since it becomes clear that Book's worldly knowledge extends beyond his proficiency with weaponry to include disturbing familiarity with the inner workings of the Alliance government.

In the episode "Safe" (1.05) viewers get the clearest indication of the depth of Book's shadowy past with the monolithic Alliance. Badly hurt, Book is in danger of dying and Mal uncharacteristically goes against his own self-interest by seeking medical help from an Alliance cruiser. However, help is denied by the arrogant Alliance crew until Book weakly tells the officer to check his identity card. Everything suddenly changes — Book receives state-of-the-art medical care and is returned to the ship, which is permitted to leave without so much as a cursory check. Book tries to make light of the situation, telling a very curious Mal that his solicitous treatment was the result of being a Shepherd, a point that ex-believer Mal refuses to concede.[10] Book dodges the question, saying only that he would like to tell Mal the truth, but that it won't be today. Book is willing to use whatever influence he has to save himself and those in his flock, but he will not be pushed into confessing whatever sins or secrets he believes he is carrying, preferring again to keep his troubles to himself and continuing to be one of Whedon's mysteries.

In another instance of Book having access to unexpected knowledge regarding the Alliance, it is the Shepherd who is able to advise Mal about the existence and tactics of the Operative in *Serenity*. As he explains to Mal what he can expect, Book gazes off into the distance, as if reliving some personal memories that serve as the foundation of his knowledge of these procedures. He warns Mal that he's being bird-dogged by an enemy who moves indirectly; one who will strike where Mal is weakest. As Book explains, this enemy will be fueled by intense belief. Both as a Shepherd and as whatever he may have been before, Book knows the power of belief. Further, he is well aware that belief can be used in the pursuit of both good and evil.

Deeply unsettled, Mal tries to pry some further information from the now-closed Book, remarking that he is curious and that the Shepherd will have to explain to Mal how he came by that sort of knowledge. Book's stoic gaze returns to the deepening night and he firmly declines, effectively ending the line of inquiry. In Shepherd Book, Whedon has created an interesting, nuanced man of faith who obviously has knowledge and experience beyond that of simply reading religious texts. Book's past chapters include proficiency with firearms and violence, as well as an advanced knowledge of the workings of the upper levels of Alliance military operations. However, Whedon takes the character of Book beyond being a mere cipher of "preacher man with a past." Book proves himself to be a faithful and nonjudgmental ally of the crew, regardless of their denominations or politics. In this way, Whedon instructs viewers on the nature of redemption.

A hallmark of Whedon's work is the notion that a dark, bloody past doesn't condemn a person to wear that coat for the remainder of existence. Redemption from the past is a theme Whedon constantly threads throughout his work and Shepherd Book provides an excellent example of this theme, for viewers are never precisely sure for what Book is seeking atonement.[11] He acknowledges that faith is by definition the virtual inverse of logic, telling the puzzled River that faith isn't about making sense. Rather, "it's about believing in something and letting that belief be real enough to change your life. It's about faith. You don't fix faith, River. It fixes you" ("Jaynestown" 1.07). Whedon makes it evident that Book has been redeemed from his past life of blood and intrigue and he is seeking to move forward into a different kind of life by making his home on *Serenity*.

One role the Shepherd fulfills on the ship is as the conscience and spiritual guide for the ship's residents. Book is depicted as being clearly at ease with both the crew and his own spirituality, even in the face of Mal's often-overt hostility. In "Bushwhacked" for example, the Shepherd is seen playing a variation of basketball with the crew during a rare moment of relaxation on the ship (1.03). Such inclusion indicates a level of acceptance of the Shepherd amongst them, as even Mal is seen participating in the game with no apparent problem posed by Book's presence. As has been discussed before, Whedon enjoys creating families of characters who would appear to have little in common and the "crew family" of *Firefly/Serenity* is no exception to that.

As a Shepherd, Book is regularly shown engaging in spiritual rituals, which often involve death, for as Book says, "How we treat our dead is part of what makes us different than those that did the slaughtering" ("Bushwhacked" 1.03). Based on the hints viewers see of Book's past, he very well may know both sides of this equation. In various episodes, Book is shown praying over the remains of Reaver victims, strewing dust over covered corpses and praying over the casket of a young soldier who fought with Mal and Zoe. But it is Book's actions, rather than simple ritual, that have the most direct impact on the crew, especially in his role as spiritual counselor, for among Whedon's characters, actions indeed speak louder than words and they resonate longer.

Despite his deep-rooted problems regarding faith and religion, Mal often finds himself on the receiving end of Book's counsel. Although this advice is not usually actively sought out, Mal regularly finds himself listening to and following the Shepherd's advice to look to his own higher nature, rather than taking the path of selfish ease. Such counsel goes against Mal's basic philosophy, which can be summed up as "Do unto others before they have a chance to do unto you" and Mal's steps forward into a more generous view of the 'verse are tentative at best. For example, when Book strongly suggests that the crew stop to conduct a proper funeral for the victims of a Reaver attack (supporting his position with references to the parable of the Good Samaritan), Mal reluctantly agrees. Placated, Book goes off to make his necessary preparations. Wash calls Mal on his unexpected turnabout, since Mal is not known to be one for "rituals and such" at which time Mal reveals that his acquiescence to Book's request has less to do with giving comfort to the dearly departed than with getting the time and space necessary to run a salvage operation on the stricken ship (and dealing with a Reaver-laid booby trap) without being pestered by the priest. Under Book's tutelage, Mal will move forward toward a more altruistic view of life; however, his progress (like that of most people) is made in baby steps, not giant leaps.

In *Serenity: the Official Visual Companion*, Ron Glass, who portrays Shepherd Book, comments on the relationship between Mal and Book, saying that "Book sees himself in Mal.... [Book's] intention and conviction and desire is to have Mal realize the brighter side of himself" (100). It apparently took a good deal of time and effort for Book to find that brighter side of himself, which possibly explains his patience with Mal's hard-line attitude. The Shepherd has a belief in a faith that has been able to allow him to change his outlook and his desire for Mal to experience a similar change is a recurring element in the relationship between the two characters. Whedon understands that devotion can come in many forms and should never be construed to include only the religious, although that is the path Book has chosen to walk. Whedon's Shepherd knows that the tent of faith is larger than the tabernacle, even if Mal does not yet acknowledge that fact.

Book's past certainly hints at ties to the Alliance, perhaps in some high military capacity; however, that in no way should be read as limiting his sincere desire to live a peaceful, spiritual life now. Saints (and Shepherds) are made, not born and one's past should never be interpreted as a restraint on the present. An example of the possibilities of change can be found in the life of Saint Patrick. The foreign-born patron saint of Ireland is most often remembered for the twin myths of driving the snakes from the Emerald Isle and using the three-leafed shamrock to explain the Mystery of the Trinity. However, saints are nothing more than people who continue to fumble toward God despite the odds, and St. Patrick had some dark shadows in his past, as do most humans who are worth knowing. In his "Confession," St. Patrick reveals that he had fallen into "grievous sin" in his youth. As with St. Patrick, the details of Book's past are never fully revealed, but the Shepherd's past seems to still weigh heavily on his mind.

The commonality between Book and St. Patrick involves more than a hidden past, however. Both men realize that redemption requires action within the world itself. Book may initially have been content to contemplate life behind the walls of a secluded abbey, but only when he takes the step of rejoining the vital 'verse does he impact the lives of others in a meaningful way. St. Patrick actively encouraged the Irish to embrace the Christian faith and was instrumental in organizing the Catholic Church in that country (Farmer 390). In a similar fashion, Book finds his home among the crew of *Serenity* and impacts the lives of every member of the ship, including the materialistic mercenary Jayne, with whom he forms a sincere, though unlikely, friendship.

The story of Whedon's Shepherd also contains echoes of the life of another holy man who came to his faith after a life of worldly experience, including that of combat. Once Thomas Becket became Archbishop of Canterbury, he resolutely rejected his past and shouldered his duty, embracing an austere life of religious discipline. He dared even to rebuke King Henry II, who had been a great friend of his in the past. Tensions mounted on both sides until the king called for Becket to be removed.[12] Four barons took the king literally and slaughtered Becket within the sanctuary of the cathedral. Becket's vicious murder shocked the faithful and led to public penance for the king (Farmer 472 – 473). While not identical in every detail, Book's death at the hands of underlings of the Alliance's Operative echoes Becket's murder. This is not a personal murder in the manner of Becket, for the Operative is slaying any who might offer River and the crew safe harbor.[13] However, as previously discussed, there is evidence that Book was at one time part of the Alliance's inner circle as Becket was with Henry II and like Becket, Book is killed for daring to stand in the way of the established governmental entities. In a similar fashion, as Becket's murder led to public outcry that the king be made to answer for his involvement, Book's death (as well as his dying plea to Mal to believe in *something*) is the catalyst that causes his flock on *Serenity* to actually rise up and fight back, rather than continuing to scurry in the shadows.

This action is not taken by Mal alone; indeed, it couldn't be. Book's death affects all of the crew, because all of their lives had been impacted by this singular man. In fact, it is Jayne who delivers what can be considered Book's eulogy—"Shepherd Book used to tell me: if you can't do something smart, do something right." That is the essence of redemption—trying to do something right.[14] As Whedon shows us, choosing to do the right thing regardless of the cost is rarely an easy choice to make. Further, like the path of true love, walking the path of the righteous is never smooth and the journey often involves daunting roadblocks. Key among these roadblocks is questioning whether the path is the right one in the first place. Book often doubts his own faith and his effectiveness as a spiritual leader. Far from being a fatal flaw, Book's skepticism regarding his faith is an element that adds to the character's realism, for doubt is part of faith.

Viewers see Book's doubts very early in *Firefly*. At the end of the pilot episode, Shepherd Book confesses to Inara that, after only two days aboard, he feels wildly out of place on the ship. Inara gently places a hand on the Shepherd's forehead in a gesture of benediction and blessing, reassuring him that he may be in exactly the right place.[15] That Book seeks advice and absolution from others, rather than living separate from ordinary people, reinforces the humanity of the Shepherd. Moreover, the fact that the holy man's spiritual comfort comes at the hands of Inara, who works as a high-class courtesan, emphasizes Whedon's constant theme of widespread acceptance of others, since it would be more usual for the stagecoach preacher to absolve the troubled hooker.[16]

Shepherd Book may question his own effectiveness, but this doubt does not render him ineffective. Many iconic religious figures (including Christ in the Garden of Gethsemane) have questioned their ability to perform the tasks that were set out before them, despairing that the work was too great for their puny human efforts. Queen Esther provides one such example. Although the Persian king Ahasuerus "loved Esther above all the women, and she obtained grace and favour in his sight," she doubts her ability to effectively plead for the lives of her people who face certain annihilation at the hands of a jealous court official. After all, it is death to come before the king without a royal command to appear and Esther has not been called to his presence. Her uncle Mordecai chides her for her reluctance, telling her that God may have brought her to be queen just for this purpose. Esther considers this possibility and agrees to do her best, accepting the risk with the brave statement, "I will go in to see the king; and if I perish, I perish" (Esth. 4:10–13).[17] Whedon would approve of Esther's resolve, especially in the face of an uncertain outcome. Indeed, guaranteed success to Whedon seems to be only a cheap parlor trick — if there's no risk, there can't be a reward. For example, Mal's hostility towards displays of faith is quietly understood among the crew. Nevertheless, Book is seen risking Mal's wrath in order to perform a proper burial service for the slaughtered victims of a Reaver attack, because the Shepherd believes that showing respect to the dead is the proper thing to do. While not identical to the risks Esther willingly shoulders in approaching the king to plead for her people, Book's willingness to stick his neck out to do the right thing for those who cannot help themselves has echoes in the actions of the queen.

Yet another example is found in the life of one of the greatest patriarchs of all three monotheistic religions. Moses, who has spoken to God face-to-face, doubts his ability to persuade the Egyptian pharaoh to free the Jews. His doubt causes him to attempt to bargain with God to send someone else, since he is "slow of speech, and of a slow tongue" (Exod. 4:10). Book likewise despairs over his effectiveness as a spiritual leader. However, like Moses, Book finds his answer and continues to fight the good fight, protecting his flock from the forces who wish them harm.

Doubt should not be viewed as the end of faith. One of the original disciples, who had been told of the Resurrection of Christ, refused to believe. This is logical — people who have been crucified and stabbed in the side do not survive the ordeal and people who have been declared dead and have been properly buried do not then re-appear, walking, talking, and complaining of hunger. From this skeptical disciple comes our term "doubting Thomas" (John 20:24—27). Christ understood the nature of doubt and taught that only the merest scintilla of faith was necessary to accomplish great things. He compared the required amount of faith to a mustard seed, which is an insignificantly sized seed that can become a towering tree. Christ stated to the faithful, "For if you had faith even as small as a tiny mustard seed you could say to this mountain, 'Move!' and it would go far away" (Matt. 17:20). The poet Robert Browning understood this point of view as well, stating "If you desire faith — then you've faith enough" (241). As an atheist, Whedon might disagree with the particulars of the Gospel accounts, but he would agree with Browning that when it comes to faith, regardless of that faith's center, a little can go a long way. Shepherd Book has faith, but he also has doubt about that faith — doubting whether he's doing enough or fearing that perhaps his own past is too awful to be forgiven.

Browning would say this is nonsense, as doubt just means you're thinking. In "Bishop Blougram's Apology," Browning states his position quite clearly:

> You call for faith:
> I show you doubt, to prove that faith exists.
> The more of doubt, the stronger faith, I say,
> If faith o'ercomes doubt [240].

In other words, faith and doubt are a natural pairing. Merely because Book doubts his own effectiveness doesn't mean that he is not an effective force for good and Whedon uses the Shepherd to bring about fundamental changes in the way other characters relate to the 'verse itself.

Nevertheless, Whedon's Shepherd continues to question his abilities and this persistent doubt leads Book to leave the ship, angry with himself and fearful that he is perhaps beginning to backslide into the violent ways of his past. Book doesn't want to go back to his previous life. His past isn't too bad to be forgiven, but he has to move forward and not fall back into old, destructive patterns. This is the nature of redemption — one can be forgiven for the past, but the penitent must move forward in a new direction; one must "go now, and sin no more" (John 8:11). Shepherd Book is greatly afraid that if he stays, he will devolve into what he once was and, in so doing, pull others down as well.

Most creators would permit the doubts riddling the Shepherd to cripple the character, but Whedon refuses to take the easy path. Instead, Whedon uses these well-constructed doubts as an outlet for the character to expand and grow. A Zen maxim states "Great doubt, great awakening. Little doubt — little awakening. No doubt — no awakening." Book's doubts force him to view situations from more than a single angle. Whedon uses the Operative in *Serenity* as Book's foil, for the Operative is a character who reflects the dire consequences of failing to doubt. To be sure, the Operative has faith (in his case, his faith is placed in the Alliance's overarching goal of creating "better" people) and he proceeds strictly on a "need to know" basis, refusing to entertain even a hint of a question regarding his faith by deviating from his path.[18] However, his utter failure to even once question that faith leads to bloody zealotry and total disillusionment as he discovers the end result of the Alliance's attempts to play God. The Operative's blinders are ripped away by Mal, who has been galvanized into action through his relationship with the Shepherd. Although Book does not live to see the full flowering of Mal's renewal of faith, he is the catalyst for Mal rediscovering faith and being willing, like Queen Esther, to take substantial risks for the greater good. Perhaps this is enough to enable Shepherd Book to rest easy, secure in the knowledge that he has had a positive impact on the lives of his flock.

With Shepherd Book, Whedon reinforces his position that there is a continual struggle by light to pierce the darkness. The Shepherd is clearly coded as a man with a dark past who has rejected that past in favor of leading a life marked by compassion and service to others. Just as St. Patrick reformed his life from whatever the particulars of his "grievous sin" may have been, Shepherd Book tries mightily to be a righteous man and to serve as a role model for those around him.

Whedon states repeatedly through his work that redemption is possible, but it involves action on the part of the penitent, who cannot rely on empty ritual and hollow words to achieve renewal. Whedon's Shepherd carries his violent past with him and several times Book's past experiences and knowledge are shown to be useful. In this way, Whedon emphasizes the point that people are complicated, multi-layered beings, not homogenized cogs who can be easily classified. While it is true that our past is a part of who we are; in great part we are who we *think* we are. Shepherd Book searches for meaning and faith in his life and, since he is willing to seek, he often finds.

There is an adage that sums up the Shepherd very nicely: "It matters not that we will not live to eat the fruit; still we must plant the trees." Whedon would agree with this. Although Book doesn't survive to see the sum effect he has had on others (including Malcolm, whose life is revitalized by Book's act of self-sacrifice), the Shepherd's victory is not made Pyrrhic as a result.

Measured by the impact his actions have on others, Book's life has been a success and his flock has been returned safely to the fold.

It's a struggle to leave behind the darkness of the shadows and walk in the light. Even doing that, the effect of our time in the shadows lingers, but it should be remembered that the presence of shadows can be a very useful way to mark the progress of the light. So perhaps in the end, it is the shadows crossing our lives which most define us; that best outline and throw into sharp relief the sum of our inmost character. As Whedon shows through Shepherd Book's influence on those around him, the end result of time spent in the shadows can well worth the struggle involved in finding the light.

8

Prodigal Daughter

FAITH AND HOMECOMING

A common, natural response to finding oneself in trouble is to retreat to a place of safety. Often, this response manifests as a deep desire to go home. Terminally ill patients express a wish to go home; the college student smarting from the experiences of the first semester "on his own" counts the days until he can go home (often accompanied by a sizable bag of laundry); even Hansel and Gretel want nothing more than to go home. Moreover, the well-known parable of the Prodigal Son features as one of its central themes the desire to return home after a lengthy time of atonement and anguish. Whedon's work is liberally sprinkled with characters who are seeking a place of refuge; somewhere that they can call home. Perhaps the character in Whedon's body of work who best embodies this desire to belong is Faith, who is called in Season Three of *Buffy* to be the Slayer following the death of Kendra.[1] Faith has certain similarities with the Brothers Grimms' lost children, as well as the Prodigal Son. Both will be discussed in this chapter as part of an exploration of the role penance plays in seeking redemption before one can return home, wherever that may be.

While the name "Faith" would seem to best fit a character who has firmly entrenched religious beliefs; here Whedon again plays tricks on his viewers, for the creed of this Faith is rooted totally in her own interests. This Slayer goes through her years on *Buffy* and *Angel* with "Faith" as her only name. However, when the *Buffy* role playing game was being developed, it was decided that Faith needed a surname and Whedon selected "Lehane" (Whedon "Faith's Surname"). Whedon commented that he chose the name to reflect Faith's tough South Boston roots and the name works well on that level. However, Whedon abhors single layer characters and his surname choice for Faith is no exception. "Lehane" is the anglicized version of the Irish name "O Liathain" or "O Laighin" which means "grey" (Waimate). If this is a coincidence, it is indeed a happy one, as Faith is a character who is never quite at home with being either just the hero or just the villain, although she plays both of these parts at various times. Her motives and disposition are never as pure as the driven snow nor sunless as the pits of hell — she truly is a mixture of both. As such, grey is the proper coloration for this Slayer who is so often lost without a moral compass in the dark woods of the world.

When one is lost in a shadowy, forbidding forest, it is a very good idea to know the way home. In the classic Brothers Grimm tale of *Hansel and Gretel*, Hansel plans to thwart his parents' plan to abandon the children in the forest by following a trail of breadcrumbs he has surreptitiously dropped to mark the way home.[2] However, the birds of the forest eat the breadcrumbs and the sordid tale of the enticing gingerbread house begins.[3] While her tale is not identical, Faith has certain similarities with the two children, including a remarkably grim home life. Throughout *Buffy* and *Angel*, Faith's father is never remarked upon by anyone and the woodcutter dad of the fairy tale is portrayed as weak and ineffectual to the point of being utterly unable to protect his children, leaving them to literally fend for themselves at far too early an age. He may as well be physically absent, as is Faith's father.

Moreover, the mothers in both tales are examples of extremely poor parenting.[4] In *Hansel and Gretel*, the horror of the story is compounded by the fact that it is the natural mother of the children who not once, but *twice*, convinces her husband to abandon the children to the perils of the untamed forest (Grimm 92). She is dead by the time the children return home, laden with riches from the witch's cottage (100). Faith's mother is also portrayed as being deceased by the time Faith arrives in Sunnydale and it is clear that she was, at best, a neglectful parent who preferred alcohol to caring about her daughter ("Enemies" 3.17). While Hansel and Gretel do not appear to be any the worse for wear following their adventures in the woods (it's a fairy tale, after all), Faith is clearly damaged by a harsh, unkind childhood which has left her unwilling to trust and quick to use others to meet her needs.

Faith is first seen in Sunnydale in the Season Three episode "Faith, Hope and Trick" (3.03). The title itself contains a Biblical allusion to an oft-recited verse from Chapter 14 of First Corinthians which speaks of the abiding nature of the great gifts of "faith, hope and charity."[5] In typical Whedon fashion, names serve to simultaneously conceal and reveal. Faith isn't faithful, Buffy's hope for a normal relationship with Scott Hope is thwarted by her responsibilities as the Slayer, and instead of sweet Charity, viewers get Mr. Trick, a vampire who is willing to ally himself with the "Big Bad" of Season Three, the Mayor of Sunnydale. Mayor Richard Wilkins is pivotal in putting events into motion that lead to Faith's journey into darkness. The wholly voluntary nature of Faith's turning to evil must be stressed at this point—she is never coerced or compelled; she *chooses* her path. Whedon's work always emphasizes the role choice plays in our decisions and Faith's choices, negative as they may often be, are still that—choices.

With her initial appearance in Sunnydale, Faith is already immersed in a re-telling of the classic parable of the Prodigal found in the Gospel of St. Luke. In the parable, the younger son of a prosperous family has convinced his father to give him his inheritance. He then leaves the family home for a far-off land where he squanders his gifts on "riotous living." Faith, it is learned, has fled her home with her heritage of Slaying abilities and she will waste these talents in her own version of "riotous living" in spectacular fashion in Sunnydale.

Whedon has always conceived of Buffy as the antithesis of the stereotypical "victimized blonde girl" who all too often is used only as a prop to provide the hero with a motive for revenge (Havens 20–21). Despite her increased strength, speed, and healing properties, Buffy is reluctant to fully embrace her calling. This aversion of Buffy's is a recurring theme throughout the series—she longs to have "normal" relationships that constantly seem to elude her due to her responsibilities as the Slayer. From her first appearance on the show, Faith is clearly coded as Buffy's dark side and her very costuming underscores this point. While blonde Buffy is often seen dressed in pastels or clean, true hues (such as her bridal white "Spring Fling" gown from Season One), brunette Faith is usually attired in tight clothing of black or blood-red.

Moreover, Faith is joyous about her Slaying abilities and thinks Buffy should just get with the program and quit moaning over her lot, which Faith claims most people would consider to be a gift. While not yet a sadist, Faith revels in her ability to inflict mayhem. Given the brief hints viewers have regarding her less-than-sunny childhood, Faith's delight in being physically strong and independent seems completely understandable. Even so, as William Patrick Day has pointed out, even with a traumatic childhood to provide a reason (not an excuse) for Faith's behavior, "in Buffy's world, cruelty, selfishness, self-indulgence, and indifference to others are figured not as mere psychological problems but as actual Evil" (Day 164). Coupled with her utter disdain for reliance on anyone other than herself, Faith is clearly susceptible to the influence of evil.

Faith's independent streak is excessively wide, yet she is jealous of what Buffy has—a family, friends, and security; a circle of care and concern that can only be drawn by someone who is aware of the need for community. That need and the strength provided by relationships with others is a central theme of *Buffy*. As Mary Alice Money has stated, "viewers are led to an inescapable conclusion about the hero: without the love of friends and the knowledge of the forces of evil, a Slayer is just an imperfect killing machine, almost as soulless and dead as the vampires she stakes" (Money 102). Buffy is safely wrapped in a cocoon of loving warmth and still her life involves great difficulty. Faith lacks that cocoon and, consequently, she has a much more difficult time with these same choices. For example, Buffy lives in a sheltered home with a mother who deeply loves her, even while being bewildered about her daughter's role as a Slayer. Faith is presented as an orphan who lives (again by her choice) in a sleazebag motel on the outskirts of Sunnydale. Although ostensibly proud of her self-reliance, Faith is shown to intensely desire meaningful human contact. As Eliza Dushku (who plays Faith) has observed, "No one has ever really helped Faith — helped her with her homework and watched her go to school and unconditionally loved her" (Reiss 161). Faith fiercely wants that sort of acceptance, but continued betrayals (such as the cold, manipulative actions of renegade Watcher Gwendolyn Post) cause Faith to simultaneously crave and fear such contact and the end result of this conflict is that Faith is left angry, envious and lustful.[6] For Whedon's Faith, these three deadly sins will result in a moral strikeout.

At this point, Faith sees herself as better than those she protects, viewing her Slayer abilities as granting her privileges without much in the way of corresponding responsibility. In viewing life in this way, Faith embodies certain principles espoused by Nietzsche, with a dash of Aristotle. Faith sees Slaying as something to be relished, telling Buffy that, "Slaying's what we were built for. If you're not enjoying it, you're doing something wrong" ("Bad Girls" 3.14). Aristotle argued in *Nicomachean Ethics* that the point of moral rules is to achieve happiness and that happiness is achieved by fulfilling one's nature (Aristotle 364 — 365). If Faith were to think this through, her response would likely be along the lines of *Yeah? Well, my nature's to fight the forces of evil and I'm happiest when I'm in the thick of it, knocking the hell out of the Black Hats, so take the Greek guy and get out of my way so I can do what I was made to do, okay?* However, Faith does not explore any implication of this stance beyond what gives her immediate pleasure, summing up her philosophy in "Bad Girls" as "Want. Take. Have."

To Faith, her Slayer abilities place her above such petty concerns as humility, kindness, and sympathy. Since she is stronger and faster than ordinary people, Faith reasons that she should rightfully be exempt from laws designed for those ordinary people. In this way, she reflects Nietzsche's concept of "master morality" (Schudt 28). She has higher concerns than those of the common herd and sees herself as beyond traditional morality, so her responsibility as a Slayer is to take whatever action is necessary to meet her own needs. It's a seductive worldview, but in taking this stance, Faith is ignoring the central responsibility of the Slayer, which Day has pointed out is "to do what the vampire cannot in going beyond the instinct, beyond the desire to simply live at all costs" (6). By seeing the world and those in it as existing merely to be used as her playthings, Faith continues to cut herself off from the human contact she so craves.

Faith resembles sociopaths who don't care enough to distinguish individual human beings with their own hopes, dreams, and aspirations from simple furniture that can be moved about to suit one's taste and mood. This self-centeredness has long-lasting repercussions when Faith is so blinded by her own joy in hunting and killing that she is unable to make the crucial distinction between human and vampire and stakes a human during a fight.[7] Faith deals with the aftermath of this murder[8] by hiding the body and then loudly proclaiming to Buffy that she does not care about causing the man's death, a statement she makes with a friendly, open, blood-curdling smile. To Whedon's Faith, words have power, so what is *said* has significance. She has said she doesn't care; therefore, she doesn't, no matter what dreams may come to her in the night.

As Buffy could have told Faith if she had been willing to listen, killing a human is fundamentally different from slaying the undead and Slayers aren't killers.[9] And, as Faith could have testified, saying you don't care is very different from actually not caring. However, that sort of emotional honesty is beyond Faith at this point and her rash nature and insistence on being a lone wolf has led her to this place. Without a doubt, Faith is gifted with abilities beyond those of ordinary people, but this has led to the tragic flaw of hubris. Faith's arrogance has caused her to put herself so far above others that she no longer sees others as human. As Rhonda Wilcox has pointed out, this flaw can have devastating results when a Slayer is unable to see that "the person you kill is as human as you" (Wilcox 15). Trying to conceal her responsibility in this matter only leads to Faith's further alienation from the Scooby family.

Feeling abandoned, Faith throws her lot in with the Mayor, who has been revealed to be planning something very big and undoubtedly evil for the unsuspecting town of Sunnydale. Faith knows that she is switching teams with this act, which is clearly one of betrayal. Since her delight in killing is not shown to be in the least diminished, it appears that Faith takes this course of action in furtherance of her own pleasure, rather than as an act of contrition or penance for her killing of an innocent. The Mayor is thrilled with Faith's defection and provides her with a lavish home that is full to bursting with lovely toys for a Slayer, including a wicked double-bladed knife. Although Faith is drowning in darkness, she is deluded and thinks she has finally found her way home. After all, she lives now in a secure place where both her nature and function as a Slayer are honored. Further, rather than being seen as "the other one" who is perpetually second to Buffy, the paragon of Slaying, Faith is now the petted surrogate daughter of a loving father. However, far from being home, Faith has instead stepped into the attractive candy cottage of the Grimm forest and she is moving more deeply into a fermenting maelstrom of chaos and evil. To also continue the Prodigal parallel, Faith is continuing to enjoy the high life, never realizing that the meter of the moral taxicab is continuing to run and that she is far from home.

Eager to remain in the favor of her "daddy," Faith embraces the darkness within her, as the Mayor encourages her to do. She revels even more joyously in her kills, never questioning why a particular target is chosen for her. Her willingness to obey is rewarded with open and obvious affection from the Mayor, who is quite likely the first adult male to show an interest in Faith that isn't sexual. To prove her love and worth to her substitute father, Faith shoots Angel with a poisoned arrow, making sure to miss the heart so his death will be a painful, lingering one. To Faith, this is a "two birds, one stone" moment, as Faith calculates that Buffy will be so distracted by her concern for Angel that her mind will not be firmly focused on the coming fight. Interestingly, at this point, Faith can also be read as an echo of the evil Angelus (the "bad vampire" who shares Angel's physical form), who gained tremendous satisfaction from torturing his victims, both physically and psychologically, before killing them.[10] At this juncture of her life, she is deeper into the dark woods of depravity and is unable to distinguish the true from the false.

When Faith first turns to evil, she and Buffy find themselves in a Mexican standoff, each holding a knife to the other's throat. Faith taunts Buffy, saying, "What are you gonna do, B, kill me? You *become* me. You're not ready for that yet" ("Enemies" 3.17). Circumstances have changed since that time. Fed up with trying to redeem someone who clearly is enjoying her choices and knowing that only the blood of a Slayer can save Angel, Buffy takes a proactive approach. The two evenly matched Slayers battle one another high above Sunnydale. When Buffy manages to stab Faith deeply in the gut with the Mayor's gift, Faith makes one last choice and allows herself to fall off the rooftop into the bed of a passing truck rather than be used as Angel's cure. Her injuries cause Faith to lapse into a coma. This could be the turning point for Faith, as now she might have the time for quiet contemplation of her actions, perhaps through prophetic Slayer dreams. But Faith's woods are very dark and she never carried anything to mark her way out of the forest, so her coma is just a time of deep unconsciousness. While her coma is not the start of Faith's actual "turning for home," it can be read as marking another point in the prodigal story. In the parable, the foolish younger son doesn't see a need to change his ways until his legacy has been completely spent and he finds himself penniless and friendless in a land stricken by famine — a Biblical version of the self-help language of "hitting bottom." In the parable, the starving lad takes a job as a swineherd, a task that would be both forbidden and repugnant to an observant Jew (Barclay 204). His miserable circumstances continue and he finds himself coveting the slop fed to the pigs. It takes this level of abasement before he is able to come to an awareness of himself and his need to change. By this reading, Faith's coma is the beginning of her personal "famine time." It will last for nearly a year.

Faith emerges from the coma eight months later, bewildered and searching for her surrogate father, who has been killed. The Mayor has prepared for the contingency that his machinations might not go as smoothly as planned and he has not left his Faith out of those designs. Faith is able to use a magical device to swap bodies with her blonde nemesis, leaving Buffy trapped in the body of Faith to face the consequences for Faith's earlier murderous actions while Faith enjoys the charmed life she supposes Buffy leads. Faith has an opportunity to quite literally see life through Buffy's loved and loving eyes. The resulting experience shocks Faith to her core.

While Faith at first enjoys the dark humor of this joke, glorying in the sight of Buffy being dragged off to be punished for Faith's crimes while Faith remains behind with Buffy's beloved mother, she is soon confronted with the reality of what other people expect from Buffy. She is expected to do the right thing, to set the proper example and to also accept love and respect as her due, without convoluted games or tacky scorekeeping. Faith's path to awareness can be summed up by three words, first uttered by her as a way to mock the now-absent Buffy, who Faith views as a goody-Slayer-two-shoes. The same words are said again later by Faith as a challenge to a cadre of vampires who have taken over a local church: "Because it's wrong." This attitude is the inverse of her earlier, more Nietzschean creed that was solely concerned with Faith's personal pleasure based on her supposed superiority.

Faith-as-Buffy then leaps into battle, fighting grimly and methodically, not for the sexual rush the violence gives her, or to attain any other selfish goal; rather, she is finally fighting as Buffy does — to protect the innocent, without thought of reward aside from doing what she is supposed to do. Faith is at the doorstep of understanding her true nature, but this moment of clarity does not last and she cannot yet cross the threshold, for Buffy wants her body back and she wants answers.

During the ensuing confrontation between two enraged Slayers, Faith-as-Buffy goes berserk at the sight of her former self, throwing her old body down and pummeling the merry hell out of it, all the while crying and cursing what she was, proclaiming her old self to be "Nothing! Disgusting, murderous bitch! You're nothing!" ("Who Are You?" 4.16) Greg Forster sees in Faith's violent reaction a positive step toward her moral growth. He relates Faith's repugnance of herself to Plato's account in the *Republic* of a man who forces himself to look at what simultaneously fascinates and disgusts him, stating that "Plato's point in telling this story is that it is a key feature of morally good personalities that they are ashamed and angry with themselves when they do wrong. To master one's own desires requires discipline and self-control, which is achieved ... by harnessing the emotions of anger and pride on the side of reason and against the disorderly passions" (Forster 18). Buffy-as-Faith is able to reverse the spell and put both Slayers back in their respective bodies. Shocked and repulsed by her self-knowledge, Faith flees. She can no longer deny and bury what she has learned and Faith runs to Los Angeles in another attempt to turn for home.[11]

It is well worth noting that Faith's crisis of faith is brought to a head in a church and that she flees that sanctuary to find her redemption. To Whedon, churches may be nice places with pretty windows, but they do not offer absolution for sin nor any meaningful type of redemption, for a church is merely a building and atonement must begin from within. So, like many a seeker before her, Whedon's Faith heads to the City of Angels to find answers—or to at least forget the questions. Faith's personal country is still a land wracked by moral famine and while she is reaching a point of desperation, she is not yet ready to change.

In Los Angeles, Faith seems at first to still be in "want-take-have" mode. In "Five By Five" she is seen beating a slimy hustler senseless, then robbing him of money, keys, and thick leather jacket. She dances provocatively with an anonymous guy at a club, then gleefully starts a fight when his understandably upset girlfriend protests. Most menacingly, she accepts an offer from the evil law firm of Wolfram & Hart to assassinate Angel in exchange for their legal assistance in getting all pending charges against Faith dismissed. Faith leaps into her task with zeal and borrows a page from Angelus' playbook—rather than directly attacking Angel, she stalks and harms those closest to him. Faith viciously beats Cordelia and abducts Wesley, who once served as Faith's Watcher; actions designed to get Angel "in the game." This will become important, and Whedon loves to misdirect his audience.

Wesley has always lamented his inability to save Faith from turning to darkness, but he also tells Angel that Faith is "sick," indicating that she can be made well again. In one of the darker moments of a dark series, it is Wesley who changes his stance following his prolonged torture by Faith.[12] Here again, Faith resembles the evil Angelus who once tortured Buffy's Watcher, Giles. Having Wesley as a literal captive audience, Faith rattles on at length, claiming to not think of things like fate and destiny, the road not taken and so forth; however, the mere fact she pontificates on these subjects in the first place indicates that she's thought a good deal about these concepts. Brimming with wrath, Angel arrives, ready to take revenge on this Slayer who's waltzed so long with evil that she doesn't realize it's far past time to leave the dance floor.

In another example of Whedon's layered tricking of his audience, it becomes apparent that all of Faith's activities have been designed to goad Angel, but not so that Faith can enjoy a good, boisterous battle. Rather, Faith is reminiscent of a suicidal person who can't quite bring herself to deeply slash her flesh with a razor blade and instead makes a series of "hesitation cuts" to test her resolve. Faith wants to die, to end the pain she lives in and to escape the reality she is forced to deal with in the aftermath of the body swap with Buffy. In a dark alley, with rain slicing down, Faith and Angel's battle reaches a climax as Faith weakly pounds Angel's chest, crying, "I'm bad! Angel, I'm bad! I'm bad... Please! Angel, please, just do it ... please just do it.... just kill me" ("Five By Five" 1.18). This is one of the most emotionally powerful scenes in the five years of *Angel*. One sobbing murderer crumples to the ground and is cradled by another killer who's been soaked in blood over the years, but has still managed to find purpose and redemption. In the foreground, a brutalized ex-Watcher, face unseen, drops a butcher knife to the filthy ground as he witnesses the breakdown of his torturer. Faith's "famine days" have come to an end and she is now willing to turn for home.

Making the decision to change course and "turn for home" is key to the lesson Faith teaches. Critics have pointed out that Whedon's work repeatedly illustrates the message of the possibility of redemption, regardless of the sin. "Monster" is a term that is often applied to the "others" in Whedon's shows. While these supernatural creatures are often otherworldly creations such as vampires, werewolves, or demons, it can be argued that his most terrible monsters are of the human variety — Warren, Reavers, and yes, Faith. Mary Alice Money has theorized that the monsters can become less demonized "by loving, by changing, by choosing — by becoming vulnerable to the dangers of being human" while a human becomes less human "by disregarding love, by becoming inflexible, by operating as a machine without choice, knowledge, or wisdom" (102). Faith has made choices that make her more monster than human, but as Christopher Golden points out, "true monstrosity is, in the end, defined by human behavior. *Buffy the Vampire Slayer* has shown, time and again, that monsters can find their redemption" (370). The central theme of *Buffy*, as well as the central theme of the parable of the prodigal, is one of forgiveness for past actions. However, the prodigal must sincerely desire forgiveness, as Faith now does. As is perhaps fitting for a show helmed by an avowed atheist, *Buffy* takes a skeptical view of the parable which William

Neil calls "the gospel in a nutshell" (395). In a similar fashion, Faith's story does not end with her sobbing in a dripping alley.

While Faith may have always had the seeds of redemption within her, only now is she willing to nurture those seeds into growth. Although others have offered her a helping hand before (including her Watcher, Wesley, whom she repaid with burning scorn and deep pain), Angel is the one best suited to take her hand and walk her out of the woods in which she has been lost for so long. After all, it's never a good idea to take directions from someone who has never been to the location you're trying to reach, and Angel's long history of struggling to find his own redemption makes him eminently well suited to help Faith find her path.

In fact, Angel can be read as the "father figure" in this version of the prodigal story. Faith, the wayward child, has squandered her gifts, found herself suffering and made the crucial decision to humble herself and return home, penitent and remorseful. While Angel does not drape Faith with a rich robe, new shoes, and a valuable ring, as well as order the slaughter of a fatted calf, he does offer her a place to shower and change into fresh clothes, as well as provide her with tasty doughnuts ("Sanctuary" 1.19). However, Angel is no warm, fuzzy counselor concerned that Faith may have acted out due to low self-esteem. When she complains that her feelings of remorse physically hurt and she hates that it hurts, he is unsympathetic as he dishes out a large helping of Truth: "Oh, well. It's *supposed* to hurt. All that pain, all that suffering you've caused is coming back on you. Feel it — deal with it. Then maybe you've got a shot at being free" ("Sanctuary" 1.19). To Whedon, redemption is always available, but that does not mean the penitent is not going to have to stretch to reach it. Nor does it mean that other people are always going to be cheering for the penitent to grab the gold ring.

In the Christian version of the parable, there is an older sibling who deeply resents the warm welcome given to the black sheep brother. Faith has a number of people who fit this description — Cordelia, who absents herself from the presence of Faith after first having Angel sign a stack of checks for a "paid vacation"; Wesley, who takes umbrage at what he sees as the coddling of a sadistic torturer; and Buffy, who has traveled to Los Angeles to warn Angel that Faith is conscious and on the prowl. Her shock at finding her one-time lover offering comfort to the self-proclaimed "disgusting, murderous bitch" renders her nearly speechless, a rare event indeed for the Slayer. Faith's awkward attempt at an apology falls on ears that are not deaf, but are certainly hostile.[13]

Angel attempts to bridge the gap between the two Slayers, but this task is like trying to toss a paper airplane across the Grand Canyon. When Angel tries to explain that Faith's attempts to kill him were just a "cry for help,"

Buffy responds angrily that they were no such thing; that "a cry for help is when you say 'help' in a loud voice" ("Sanctuary" 1.19). Buffy has no intention of forgiving Faith for her long list of crimes, which include (but are not limited to) murder, trying to frame Buffy for the murder, and sleeping with Buffy's boyfriend while wearing Buffy's body. Buffy is judging Faith by her actions, not by her words, which Buffy finds to be slick and hollow.[14] While Buffy may be reacting harshly to Faith's change of heart, it should be recalled that Buffy has never set herself on a pedestal as the "perfect" Slayer — certainly the Watchers Council do not think she is. Moreover, providing absolution has never been part of the Slayer job description. Buffy has tried very hard to befriend Faith, only to have her overtures rejected, so it is hardly surprising that Buffy would be skeptical that this version of Faith is sincere in her declarations to be a changed woman.

During a rooftop confrontation with Buffy reminiscent of the battle of Sunnydale, Faith finds herself with the combined forces of Buffy, the LAPD, Wolfram & Hart, and heavily armed representatives of the Watcher's Council all arrayed against her. With help from Angel, Faith manages to escape and it is then that she reaches another turning point. She realizes that she poses a danger to those who are trying to help her and she finally is willing to bear the pain and take responsibility for her actions. She goes to the police to confess her crimes and await punishment. Karl Schudt has stated that in her willingness to accept incarceration, Faith makes the leap away from her Nietzschean worldview of "Want. Take. Have" to a more Socratic position (33). According to Schudt, this stance sees beyond the individual's personal desires to include the individual's relationships with others, which can necessitate punishment for wrong actions to put the relationships into balance (33). Following the outline of the prodigal parable, key words for Faith's transformation are found in Luke 15:17. As William Barclay has noted: "'*When he came to himself*,' he said. Jesus believed that so long as man was away from God he was not truly himself; he was only truly himself when he was on the way home.[15] Beyond a doubt Jesus did not believe in total depravity" (Barclay 204). The central point is the prodigal's willingness to accept whatever burden that may fall upon him. At the end of "Sanctuary," Whedon's Faith is shown confined behind bars yet seemingly at peace and free from the demons that have dogged her steps for so long. However, jail is not Faith's final home and her journey is not yet completed, for to Whedon, accepting punishment is easy. The hard part is accepting forgiveness.

The correctional system is rarely a place for quiet contemplation and Faith's cell is that of a convict, not of a nun. Angel is shown visiting Faith in "Judgment" (2.01) and it appears from their easy give-and-take that this is a regular appointment of his. She seems to be adjusting to the society of the imprisoned and is keeping her violent tendencies in check, using her Slayer skills to defend herself against attack but not instigating any confrontations. When Angel is overcome by his vampire persona Angelus, Wesley comes to visit Faith, which seems from their high level of discomfort to be a first for them both ("Salvage" 4.13). While Faith is reluctant to get involved, the realization that Angel is in trouble — the only one who ever took her side and stayed there — helps her make the decision. She tells Wesley to "get away from the glass" and somersaults through it, an action which proves two points. First, she's a Slayer and could have left at any time. She's staying in jail because she realizes that she should accept society's punishment for her actions. Second, that she has truly changed. The woman she had been had used broken glass to torture Wesley; now she doesn't want him to get scratched by flying glass as she flings herself through the visiting-room window.[16] Faith fights the good fight, going to great extremes to vanquish Angelus while not killing Angel, including very nearly sacrificing her own life in order to restore Angel's soul. She has truly changed — instead of simply passively "doing her time" as penance for her past actions, Faith is now willing to get actively involved in the world as a force for good.

Her work in Los Angeles completed with her repayment to Angel for his unflagging belief in her, Faith is now called to Sunnydale to assist in combating the coming apocalypse of that show's Season Seven. It is time for the two Slayers to finally confront one another as the siblings of the parable. In this reading, Buffy is cast as the older sibling who resents and distrusts the younger and Faith is cast as the reformed-but-how-can-I-prove-it? younger child. Barclay underscores the resentment of the Biblical older brother by emphasizing his utter lack of sympathy for the prolonged suffering of the younger sibling. The older brother angrily questions the father about the honors being bestowed upon the returning scoundrel of a son, referring to him as "your son" rather than as "my brother" (206). There is a resentment that borders on hatred at work here and Whedon's Faith is under no illusions about what sort of home to which she is returning. But return she does, nevertheless. Buffy is not thrilled to see her, but the Slayers eventually reach the conclusion that they are actually on the same side, although they do not see eye to eye on every detail. Buffy is able to value Faith for her spontaneity which has become tempered over the years with at least a pinch of caution for those around her and Faith is able to see Buffy as a courageous leader who is able to think so far outside the box as to re-write the rules for every potential Slayer on the planet.

At this point, it may be useful to return to the text of the parable itself. The story of the Prodigal Son is not limited to the version as recounted in the Gospel of St. Luke, although that account is the most familiar. However, variations on the story are found in many belief systems, similar to the global flood myth being part of the Babylonian tale of Gilgamesh which far predates the story of Noah's Ark in Genesis. While the Christian version of the parable of the prodigal has the contrite son met by an overjoyed and loving father before he even arrives at the home he had once scorned, the Buddhists tell a different tale.

The Buddhist version of the prodigal story dates from the end of the second century AD and is part of the *Saddharmapundarika Sutra*, which is also called the *Lotus Sutra* (Valea). To summarize for readers unfamiliar with this parable: in this account, the son sneaks away, rather than demanding his inheritance. The father attains great wealth and moves to another city after the son leaves. When the starving son wanders by a rich palace, its owner has his servants call to the ragged man, who is greatly frightened, thinking he is to be punished. The father has recognized the son, but the son does not recognize his father. Wishing to help his son without frightening him further, the father has him treated as a job-seeking stranger — any "sudden restoration" would only cause more confusion and heartache. The son slowly works his way up — from scavenger to more responsible positions as he shows honesty and integrity and a willingness to work. Only after many years of slow progress is he fully accepted back into the family and acknowledged as the son (Valea). Clearly, this differs from the Christian version in which the black sheep son is joyously welcomed back into the family fold, without having to give any accounting of his activities or whereabouts. In the Buddhist version, the son must slowly earn his way back and grace is only given to the deserving, which is really no grace at all.

Whedon seems closer to the Buddhist view, although it is not an entirely comfortable fit. To Whedon, redemption such as Faith's must involve sincere repentance coupled with ongoing action, but no one is there to keep a running tally. As Angel says to Faith at the beginning of her penitent's journey: "Just because you decided to change doesn't mean the world's ready for you to. The truth is, no matter how much you suffer, no matter how many good deeds you do to try to make up for the past — you may never balance out the cosmic scale" ("Sanctuary" 1.19). To Whedon, it is the continued attempt to do right towards others that is truly important, for that not only indicates a level of moral maturity that goes beyond "Want. Take. Have" but also a desire to belong to a community, to avoid the "lone wolf" syndrome that led to Faith's isolation and despair. Faith begins her journey alone and that loneliness causes her to lash out in fear. She is saved by taking responsibility, but also by connecting with others — this is Faith's true "turning for home." She no longer thinks she is above others, but sees herself as part of a community and she is willing to adapt to circumstances as opposed to demanding that circumstances adapt to her.

Stephen Tompkins writes in his book *A Short History of Christianity* of the decision of the Jerusalem Council in AD 48 that Gentile Christians would not be required to undergo circumcision to become members of the new faith. This had become a major point of contention within early Christianity since, being Jewish in origin, the Church contained a large number of circumcised members who thought it suitable that all males be circumcised. Tomkins claims that this decision is crucial to the Christian faith because "this decision also enshrined in the inner sanctum of Christianity the idea that religion is ultimately concerned with relationship rather than the rules of ritual. By acting on the principle that different people can approach God in different ways, they made Christianity a fundamentally adaptable religion" (19). While Whedon is a nonbeliever, this sentiment would probably please him. His work centers around the desirability of relationships. Buffy constantly defies ritual, prophecy, and the status quo of what is expected and, in the case of the prodigal, what is expected is for the father to reject the penitent, scalawag son. But instead the father welcomes him home with open arms and the relationship is restored by the son's willingness to do what is necessary to regain the good graces of the father. This is also true in the Buddhist version, although the way back is harder. In both versions, however, a common theme is the *possibility* of coming home, which is a choice that only the prodigal can make.

St. Augustine teaches that God is in direct control of every aspect of worldly life and that God saves some humans and abandons others to hell. Pelagius, who was considered a heretic by the Augustinians, saw things differently. To him, "every person is responsible for their own life. Adam gives us a bad example and Christ a good example, but we are neither damned for Adam's sin, nor saved by Christ's righteousness. We choose freely and are judged by our own choices" (Tompkins 60). This is Whedon in a nutshell — personal choices and accountability. Faith has chosen to go home and is willing to accept whatever consequences await her there.

At the end of "Chosen," the final episode of *Buffy*, Faith has found her way home and is surrounded by her family — the Slayers and those who love them, for Whedon's families are rarely biological. It is a mistake to consider "home" to be only an address, for while the physical home of Sunnydale may be a smoking pit, the real home is the one you carry with you and, Thomas Wolfe notwithstanding, you can go home again. However, as illustrated by both Faith and the prodigal, sometimes it is necessary to get very far from home before you can see it. When we've gotten so far away from home that we're lost in the woods of our lives, we may require help discovering the proper direction in which to turn for home. But home can be found and once it is, the wise traveler carefully marks the location of that treasure on the map of her life so she can find her way home again after her next venture into the forest.

PART 4
ZEALOTRY: BLOOD & FIRE

Note to self — religion freaky.
— Buffy, "What's My Line? Part One" *Buffy* 2.09

9

Burning River

Witchcraft and the "Other" in *Firefly*

Whedon is quite skilled at creating complex characters who capture the interest of viewers and one of Whedon's most compelling characters is *Firefly* and *Serenity*'s River Tam. River, whose fractured mental state agitates her and those around her, is used by Whedon to explore the elasticity of the bonds of family and the lengths a family will go to in order to protect its chosen members. With River, Whedon also makes some very sharply pointed statements about the dread consequences of thinking that there is only one path to walk and that those with a different point of view are doomed to be forever outside the bounds of acceptance.

Throughout their journeys, rivers exhibit multiple characteristics — what may begin as an innocuous spring bubbling up from a cleft in a rocky glen may become deceptively calm, deep water concealing perilous currents in its depths. It may then transform into rapid whitewater crashing and tumbling over stones worn smooth by centuries of its flow, only to finally roll gently through a lazy delta to mix with the saltwater brine of the ocean. Yet all of this is the selfsame river; simply exhibiting different phases of itself at different stages of its odyssey.

In a similar fashion, the character of River Tam, like so many of Joss Whedon's creations, is a conundrum. In appearance, she is slight and frail, evoking a sense of fragility and stirring up feelings of pity and protectiveness in viewers, who are first introduced to this seemingly delicate girl-child as she is curled up naked in the fetal position, sleeping a drugged slumber in a box in which she is being transported as if cargo.

However, River is intelligent beyond the imagining of most adults, able to perceive beyond her five direct senses, and she has been trained in combat to the point she can effortlessly disable an entire tavern-full of toughs and cutthroats.

She is also at least half-mad.

The schisms of River's personality are astonishing to contemplate and they are, at least in part, the result of two years of brutal experimentation performed on the teen by the Alliance, who attempted to create in River a pliable and obedient living psychic weapon. Without a doubt, the multiple facets of River's fractured psyche make her an interesting traveling companion, but not precisely the most soothing person to have onboard *Serenity*.

Rivers are also ancient symbols of boundaries. Often a river is presented as a physical boundary, but the boundary can be a spiritual marker as well. For instance, in the Old Testament, the River Jordan is the final physical boundary that must be crossed for the Israelites to end their years of wandering in the wilderness and reclaim their ancestral home. In the New Testament, Jesus is baptized by his cousin John in the same River Jordan, thus crossing a spiritual boundary that serves to mark the official beginning of His ministry. As set forth in a previous section of this book, the character of River Tam provides a baptism of sorts for Malcolm Reynolds as he submerges into the challenges she presents and arises, re-energized and re-born, to meet those challenges. In this way, Whedon's River serves as Mal's physical boundary to separate his old, self-centered worldview from his new, more expansive view of the 'verse as well as being his "baptism" into that new way of looking at his place in the world.

Of course, Christianity is far from the only faith that sees rivers as something special. To the devout Hindu, the Ganges is a river so sacred that the mere touching of its holy water can absolve the gravest of sins, such as the killing of a Brahmin. For this reason, the Ganges is also known to Hindus as the "Saviour of the World" ("Ganga"). In fact, the very word "Hinduism" derives from the term "riverism" (Renard 77). Additionally, to followers of the Tao, water is considered the most powerful of all the elements, because it is the least resistant. In fact, the *Tao Te Ching* states that "Nothing in the world is soft and weak as water/But when attacking the hard and strong/Nothing can conquer so easily/Weak overcomes strong/Soft overcomes hard" (78). Given the strong Chinese influences in *Firefly/Serenity*, this philosophy may have provided at least partial inspiration for River Tam's name.

Throughout recorded history, mankind has sought to control rivers through techniques such as dredging and damming. This desire to tame the natural world may be driven by benevolent motives or it may be a direct result of human hubris. Either way, the desire often leads to dire consequences, such as the devastating 1889 Johnstown flood which resulted from a breached earthen dam, as well as the recent cataclysms spawned by Hurricanes Katrina and Rita which overwhelmed the levees of Louisiana.

In similar fashion, while the Alliance may sincerely have thought they had a good motive in transforming River from her natural human state into that of a highly trained weapon, once that process was begun, there could be no turning back. Quite frankly, the Alliance should have known this would not end well. They had already tried this type of behavior modification on a large scale, and the results were the loathsome wretches known as Reavers and the dead planet of Miranda.

In their desperation to find the fugitive River, the Alliance goes to extreme measures to flush her out of hiding. These efforts culminate in River's "activation" through a subliminal code buried in an insipid commercial, proving that too much TV really is bad for you. It is worth noting that the event which triggers River's forward flow into the human equivalent of whitewater occurs in the Maidenhead Bar (*Serenity*). The term "maidenhead" is slang for both virginity and the female hymen. Certainly following River's demonstration of just what she was taught at the Alliance Academy, it is safe to say that the Maidenhead has been well and truly broken. Rivers flow forward and there is simply no going back to what once was. In "Objects in Space" (1.14), the crew learns that River is a "reader," which is defined as someone with some degree of psychic ability; something that is accepted as odd and rare but not totally unheard-of in the *Firefly/Serenity* 'verse. The brawl in the Maidenhead violently reveals another facet of River's personality which must now be dealt with by a crew that views River with varying degrees of suspicion, pity, and outright fear.

Throughout the series, Whedon uses River and her fragmented psyche to fill the role of the "other" in the *Firefly* 'verse. The term "other" is used as a device to clearly distinguish one group from an(other) within a society; a sort of shorthand "us vs. them." While this device is common in science fiction (where the "other" is often portrayed as an extraterrestrial life form, which is notably *not* found within the *Firefly/Serenity* construct[1]), explorations of what it means to be the "other" are rife throughout all forms of literature and art, ranging from Grendel in *Beowulf* to the often-eerie photographs of Diane Arbus. The unifying thread throughout all uses of the "other" is the impact on the viewer — by forcing us to take an unflinching look at how the world appears to operate through the eyes of the other, we have no choice but to simultaneously turn our own gaze inward to re-examine how we view and react to the world. As an example, when River perceives a high-powered handgun in a sterile cargo bay to be an innocent tree branch in a colorful autumn meadow, the viewer is drawn into River's worldview, in which things do not "mean what you think" ("Objects in Space" 1.14). River's peculiar sense of perception coupled with her failure to realize that not everyone in the 'verse is accepting of her oddness leads her to be branded as a "witch" twice on the series; once in "Safe" (1.05) when she gives voice to a mute girl and again in "Objects in Space" (1.14) when her psychic abilities are first revealed to the entire crew.[2]

Although people who choose to live on the fringes of mainstream society may be viewed by the majority as the "other," nowhere throughout human history is there a less ambiguous example of "otherness" than the witch. Today, images of the witch in popular American culture tend to fall into three categories. The first is the witch as a comic figure, such as Witch Hazel from the Warner Brothers' Bugs Bunny cartoons. The second is the witch as a sensual, on-the-side-of-good spellcaster, such as the three sisters on *Charmed* or Glinda from *The Wizard of Oz*. The third is the witch as an evil, child-killing hag, such as the hermit lying in wait in the candy cottage depicted in *Hansel & Gretel* or the Queen in *Snow White*.[3]

Therefore, when River is condemned by the village as a "witch" in the episode "Safe" (1.05), what are the actual implications — is River being stamped as comic, sensual, or evil? The teacher, Doralee, first welcomes Simon and River as a gift from God and tries to help them see that this could be their new home, a safe place for the siblings to end their wanderings. She urges them to not be too harsh on the kidnappers who brought them there, reminding them that the Good Book says, "Judge not." From these and other dialogue references, it is reasonable to assume that this community follows some aspect of the Christian faith. However, she changes her charitable tune when it is revealed that River did not coax the mute Ruby into speaking; rather, she read the girl's mind. At this point, Doralee whispers the eight words which have condemned hundreds of thousands of men and women throughout history to painful, bloody death: "Thou shalt not suffer a witch to live" (Exod. 22:18). River as the "other" is thus viewed as a contagion within the community and her presence cannot be tolerated.

Christianity is sadly unique among the world's major religions in viewing witchcraft as a capital crime.[4] For this discussion to be useful, it is imperative at the outset to distinguish "witchcraft" from "sorcery." "Sorcery" may be viewed as the beginning of witchcraft, if one abides by Russell Robbins' definition of the act as "an attempt to control nature, to produce good or evil results, generally by the aid of evil spirits" (471). Further, acts that are commonly considered to be sorcery are both timeless and universal, being found throughout the world. These acts include both actions aimed at individuals, such as easing the pangs of childbirth or cursing a man with impotence; and actions aimed at entire communities, such as the bringing or withholding of rain. On the other hand,[5] the historic charge of witchcraft goes far beyond sorcery in its scope, as the "witch" contracts with the Devil or his minions "to work magic for the purpose of denying, repudiating, and scorning the Christian God" (Robbins 471). Moreover, this version of witchcraft is limited in range to western Europe (with a few tragic cases in colonial New England) and in time, with cases being documented from roughly 1450 to 1750.

Despite these geographic and chronologic limitations, zealots managed to ignite a bonfire of fear, superstition, illogic, and terror that swept western Europe and led to the deaths of hundreds of thousands of accused witches.[6] One key to understanding the depth of the hysteria is the fact that, far from being unruly lynch mobs, the best legal and theological minds of Europe wrestled with the difficulties posed by attempting to prove the crime of witchcraft.

The need for a standard "yardstick" to measure the actions of an accused witch to determine if the crime could be definitively proven led to the publication of a number of "handbooks" for witch hunters. Without a doubt, the most infamous of these was the *Malleus Maleficarum*, also known as *The Hammer of Witches*, which first saw the light of day in 1486. The *Malleus* was written by Heinrich Kramer, a notorious witchfinder, and Jakob Sprenger, who was the Dean of Cologne University (Robbins 337 – 338).[7] The *Malleus* took great pains to set out protocols and procedures for both ecclesiastical and civil courts. Interestingly enough, although Protestants roundly denounced the "Papist" Inquisition, the *Malleus* was readily adopted as the standard work to be used against witches following the advent of Protestantism.

In the *Malleus*, judges are instructed to be as persuasive as possible, even to the extent of retracting promises to spare a witch's life if she confessed.[8] This horrific "how to" manual also includes very specific nuts and bolts outlining the steps to be utilized in obtaining confessions from the accused, since the accused had to confess "freely" in order for the confession to be viewed as valid:

> And note that, if she confesses under torture, she should then be taken to another place and questioned anew, so that she does not confess *only* under the stress of torture.
> The next step of the Judge should be that, if after being *fittingly tortured* she refuses to confess the truth, he should have other engines of torture brought before her, and tell her that she will have to endure these if she does not confess. If then she is not induced by terror to confess, *the torture must be continued on the second or third day*, but not repeated at that present time unless there should be some fresh indication of its probable success [226 — emphasis mine].

All this on the *first day*! While River Tam was not subjected to all of these legalistic justifications of hellish torture (thank heavens for the limitations of the 44-minute television show), the outcome was to be the same — death by burning.

While River shares many characteristics with the typical accused witch in that she is female, without visible means of economic support, an outsider in the community in which she is accused, and disenfranchised within that community, not all victims of the witch hysteria fit that mold. While the legalistic fence of the *Malleus* and other such witchfinder manuals could be a high and forbidding barrier, that fence imposed limitations on the judges as well as on the accused, although very few of the accused had the means to turn this to their advantage. To illustrate this point, it is instructive to examine the case of Dame Alice Kyteler, who has the distinction of being the first woman in Irish history to be officially charged with the crime of witchcraft.

Dame Alice Kyteler was a wealthy woman living in Kilkenny, Ireland who had gained her wealth through the deaths of three husbands. Her sickly fourth husband seized on gossip and accused her in 1324 of engaging in witchcraft. When the Bishop of Ossory began a formal inquiry into the accusations, she fought back.

When Dame Alice defied the Bishop of Ossory, he excommunicated her. Dame Alice then actually imprisoned the Bishop. In retaliation, the Bishop put the entire diocese around Kilkenny under ecclesiastical interdict. As the controversy escalated, the Bishop was twice physically thrown out of the secular court, but he continued to persist in pursuing the charges against Dame Alice, who eventually fled to England to seek safety (Robbins 294).[9]

While England was not immune from the witch hysteria sweeping Europe, there were noticeable differences. Chief among these was the very nature of the charge: in England, witches were punished for *maleficia* (evil deeds), rather than heresy. The crime of witchcraft was treated as a civil, rather than an ecclesiastical, crime and therefore, witches had to be tried and punished under civil law, which forbade the tortures and death by burning found in countries on the European continent (Jong 48).

While it would appear that River Tam and Dame Alice (who disappears from history after fleeing Ireland for England) share very few characteristics beyond the obvious one of both facing death after being accused of witchcraft, the two are alike in a very important way: they are both women who step outside their assigned roles in society. Dame Alice was not "supposed" to be wealthy and independent and River is not "supposed" to be able to see ideas and memories hidden in others' heads. The seemingly sympathetic Patron of the village is willing to smooth the waters set to frothing by Doralee's accusation of River until the teenager, unable to rein in her psychic abilities, reads the man's history and reveals that he obtained his position by assassinating the previous Patron. At this point, the mask of compassion slips and he strikes her sharply across the face, accusing her of "reading minds and spinning falsehoods." He declares River to be a witch and sentences her to death ("Safe" 1.05). However, River's threat to the Patron stems not from "spinning falsehoods," but rather from her ability to discern the truth of matters the Patron needs to conceal.

In order to protect his own social position, the Patron is willing to consign an innocent teenage girl to the hellish fate of death by burning. In taking this stance, he aligns himself with the status quo, which River's mere existence as a psychic threatens to upend. It is important to note that River makes it clear as crystal throughout *Firefly/Serenity* that she does not *want* the supernormal abilities she has; indeed, her lack of ability to filter out the emotions and images she is constantly bombarded with causes her to teeter precariously on the brink of insanity. This is evidenced by her breakdown on the dead world of Miranda, as she fervently prays aloud in Chinese and English for God to turn her to stone to save her from all this *feeling* she is being forced to undergo.

In her lucid moments, River is keenly aware that her lucidity won't last long. She is also painfully conscious of the fact that she is often viewed as a burden by the crew, to whom she feels varying degrees of connection and affection. To illustrate, River once states her desire to simply "fade away" so that others onboard "could be with who they want to be with" ("Objects in Space" 1.14). It is worth mentioning that it is in this episode that the others onboard become undeniably aware of River's psychic abilities. It is therefore doubly interesting to watch the reactions of the members of the crew to River's pronouncement when they realize that she has always been fully aware of their feelings towards her. For example, Wash hangs his head in shame while Mal's face is a sestina of regret. River never asked to become the fragmented mystery that she is, but it is a burden she must shoulder.

In a similar way, another well-known victim of Europe's witch hysteria carried the burden of what many considered to be mental illness and others considered to be a sign of Divine favor. Like River, she was a formidable warrior, although she too was not even out of her teens. And, like River, Jeanne d'Arc faced death by burning. Often known by the name Joan of Arc, this teenager may be the most famous witch-who-wasn't in history.

The common misconception is that Joan was burned at the stake for the crime of witchcraft — this is not true; she was executed as a "relapsed heretic." As a side note, it is worth mentioning that people accused of witchcraft were far from the only ones subjected to legally sanctioned torture and murder during this dark time of human history. Jews, for example, could not be "witches," since the crime of witchcraft was a sort of high treason against the Christian God and therefore, only had relevance to Christians. For this reason, adherents of the Jewish faith (another of the clearest examples of the "other" throughout history) could not be persecuted for witchcraft, but were nevertheless attacked as being heretical followers of Satan. The end result was the same for both heretics and witches — sadistic torture to extract "confessions" followed by painful death. Of course, this persecution of Jews neither began nor ended with the so-called "Burning Times" of the European witchcraft hysteria. In fact, the shameful period of the twentieth-century Holocaust (itself derived from the Hebrew word for "burnt sacrifice") was led by German Christians, primarily of the Lutheran faith.

Returning to the subject of Joan of Arc, it can be said without fear of contradiction that the so-called "Maid of God" wasn't like other girls. While the outline of Joan's story is well-known, a few facts bear repeating.[10] Although she began her life as a nondescript peasant girl, she was thrust from her ordinary life when she began to hear voices that compelled her to take up arms to expel the English and secure the French throne for the Dauphin. Having convinced the Dauphin of her authenticity (through the revelation of a "sign" that has been the subject of speculation for centuries), she led French forces in a series of victories, culminating in the crowning of Charles VII in Reims Cathedral. However, victory was short-lived and soon thereafter, Joan was captured by another French faction and ultimately transferred to the English, who accused her of both witchcraft and heresy (Hobbins 2–3). While some were gleeful at the prospect of burning Joan, the charges had first to be proven to the satisfaction of the presiding judges.

The charges of witchcraft were quickly dropped, due to the difficulties of proving the "invisible crime" of witchcraft under prevailing English law. Throughout her informal hearing, Joan created quite a favorable impression, bolstered by testimony that she was both a virgin (and therefore could not be a witch, since sexual intercourse with a demonic entity was a requirement to become a witch) and of her impeccable character. Nonetheless, formal charges of heresy were prepared.

Throughout the next stage of questioning, Joan admitted to seeing and talking with various saints and angels. Although her judges attempted to trip up Joan with tricky questions, she remained undeniably clever throughout her interrogation. For example:

> [S]he was asked, "Are you in a state of grace?" which was a question without a satisfactory answer — if she said "No," it would be taken as a confession of guilt; if she said "Yes," it would be proof of her "diabolical arrogance." Joan countered with "If I am not, may God be pleased to lead me to a state of grace; and if I am, may God be pleased to keep me in it" [qtd. in Robbins 284].

Despite her adroit tap-dancing, Joan could not wholly escape the clutches of this political trial. Two principal charges remained against her — the wearing of men's clothing and her refusal to accept the Church as the sole authority over her actions. Her dilemma was this — Joan believed that she was following commands from God Himself and if the Church ordered her to take actions that were contrary to those commands, she simply could not do it, feeling compelled to follow a "higher law." As Robbins points out, "[i]n this respect, Joan of Arc was simply a premature Protestant" (285). Such a challenge to the Church's established authority could not go unanswered at this time in history. Although sentenced to death, her sentence was commuted to life imprisonment following her last minute recanting. It was to be the shortest "life sentence" in history as Joan was swiftly condemned as a relapsed heretic for the crime of wearing men's clothing when her female garb was taken from her by the guards (287). The English and their supporters were to get their pound of flesh at last.

Death by burning is horrendous and the English were not to be denied a full spectacle in the burning of this "dangerous heretic." Records indicate that the twenty-year old "Maid of God" was crowned with a miter reading "Relapsed heretic, apostate, idolater" before being placed high on the pyre so the flames and smoke would reach her slowly. When her clothing had been burned away, the hangman banked the fire so the mob could better gaze upon "all the secrets which can or should be in a woman… And when the people had satisfied themselves and watched her die, tied to the stake, the hangman built up a huge fire on the poor corpse, which was soon completely burned, and bones and flesh turned to ashes" (qtd. in Robbins 287). Heretic or early Protestant, the established authorities had made a grisly example of the peasant girl from Domrémy.

George Bernard Shaw takes the position that Joan was killed not for any actual capital crime she committed but rather for her "unwomanly and insufferable presumption" (7). Joan's spurning of the Church with her claims to know God better and more directly were a challenge the clerics could not ignore without running the very real risk that others would follow Joan's path. In River's case, the Patron is faced with the same problem — his authority is only as strong as his hold on the crowd and River's reading of how he attained that authority has just challenged that same aura of authority. She must be condemned in order to remove the threat she presents.

Joan was swept along in the rising tide of Europe's witch hysteria. This sad chapter in human history can easily be read as a reaction to the Church being in the very midst of the breakdown of medieval society and the inexorable rise of modern society. During this time at the crossroads, the Church began to face multiple challenges to its control over the people, in the form of both peasant rebellions against the nobility and the rise of so-called heretical sects threatening the authority of the Church. As economic and social conditions grew more unstable, the Church seized on the opportunity to shift blame for these conditions away from itself (and the nobility, which provided much financial support to the Church) to scapegoats found chiefly among the poor and the female. By doing so, Erica Jong argues that the Church was able to re-establish itself as the apparent guardian of the people against the dark, chaotic forces of evil at a time when people were beginning to question the Church's very relevance (39). And females, who made up the vast majority of accused witches, made easy pickings when the authorities needed a convenient target. To the undeniably feminist Whedon, the Patron provides a wonderful opportunity to preach a cautionary tale of the perils of patriarchy.

In such a rigidly patriarchal society as medieval Europe or the world in "Safe," simply to be born female is to enter the world with the scales tipped against you. Moreover, the *Malleus* made it clear that it was impossible to separate the subjects of witchcraft and gender, stating early in its text of horrors that "All witchcraft comes from carnal lust, which is in women insatiable... Wherefore for the sake of fulfilling their lusts they consort even with devils" (Kramer 47). The authors of the *Malleus* were not content to slander all of womankind in only this way; the text is riddled with misogynist myths such as: women are unfit to rule or hold professions; are liars and deceivers by nature; are feeble in both mind and body and so forth (41–47). With the inclusion of these bold statements in what would become the official text of witchfinders, these misogynist smears were given the official seal of approval of the European intelligentsia. As Jong states, with the popularity of the *Malleus* requiring multiple editions to be printed and distributed to satisfy demand, "we can only despair that the printing press has as often been a tool of oppression as of liberation" (69). This is unfortunately true, but the media has also been a tool used to promote personal freedom and independent thought.

Even during the height of the hysteria, the printing press was also used to denounce the witchfinders, for there are always a tiny few who are vocal in their opposition to delirium. During the witch trials, one of these was Friedrich von Spee, a German theologian who had accompanied a number of witches to the stake and whose investigation led him to denounce the malice and stupidity he was convinced propped up the entire process of witchcraft trials. His 1631 book, *Cautio Criminalis* (*Precautions for Prosecutors*), is a summary of the legal proceedings he had witnessed and in its pages, Spee bravely cast the clean light of reason into the dark, dank world of the witchcraft trial. In part, the book warned against the use of what Orwell would have termed "doublespeak":

9. Burning River

> There is a frequent phrase used by judges, that the accused has confessed without torture and thus is undeniably guilty. I wondered at this and made inquiry and learned that in reality they were tortured, but only in an iron vise with sharp-edged bars over the shins, in which they are pressed like a cake, bringing blood and causing intolerable pain, and this is technically called without torture, deceiving those who do not understand the phrases of the inquisitors [qtd. in Robbins 484].

Despite flickers of reason such as Spee's text, the pyres stood ready and the case of Dame Alice Kyteler, which was discussed earlier, serves as an example of how easy it was to use the charge of witchcraft as a tool to keep women in their "rightful" place in society. If a propertied and powerful woman (she had the Bishop leading the case against her imprisoned, remember) such as Dame Alice could face the pyre, what chance did a poor, powerless woman have against the charges of engaging in diabolical activities? The threat was often enough to keep women submissive and intimidated, willing to remain meekly invisible (Jong 169). To Whedon, this abuse of power is the true crime. Strength should be used to shield the weak, not to crush them.

River Tam is neither meek nor invisible. Although her safety and freedom demand that she remain cloaked from the consciousness of the Alliance, it is not possible to totally conceal a force of nature as powerful as a river. When the Operative of the Alliance manages to locate River in *Serenity*, it is through a subliminal trigger that was implanted during her time at the Academy. This trigger can be envisioned as a sort of dam in her mind which, once breached, alters River's natural flow. In a nearly balletic dance of mayhem, River smoothly attacks and incapacitates every single person in the bar who she can get her hands (or feet) on. The violence is captured on video and eventually leads the Alliance to their errant pupil. Interestingly, River's last act before becoming visible to the Alliance is to literally drop the cloak she had been wearing when she entered the bar.

Even when bound to the stake awaiting the torch in "Safe," River is not an archetypal damsel in distress. As discussed earlier, River cannot help her fractured state of mind; she has gifts and curses that she does not want, but is unable to discard. It is useful in this context to picture River's brilliant, broken mind as a fine crystal prism. Just as a sparkly prism is capable of breaking white light down into the component parts of the spectrum, River is able to perceive and project different sides to situations. Moreover, both the prism and River's mind are dazzlingly beautiful to behold in action, but both are also capable of innocently cutting the careless to the bone if mishandled. In River's case, her dangerous side is first seen in the episode "War Stories" (1.10) in which she shoots dead three henchmen without so much as looking at them, then smugly echoes Kaylee's earlier boast of "No power in the 'verse can stop me," while apparently failing to see Kaylee's fright at this sudden display of smoothly proficient violence.

In the *Firefly/Serenity* 'verse (as in ours), unstable teenage girls are not supposed to be able to kill three men with three shots. However, there is no doubt that River, like Joan, is not an ordinary girl. Like Joan, River hears voices that no one else is able to discern. As discussed previously, the Patron and the residents of the village are fully prepared to burn River alive in order to cleanse their home of the contagion she represents, although whether that contagion is read as a demonic influence or a threat to the established power structure depends on who you are in the crowd. In truth, throughout the series, River is very much a blank slate on which others project their own understanding of what a young girl *should* be, as well as providing a place to scrawl their own fears. To the Patron, River is a threat to his power and position in the community. To Doralee, River is an unnatural force, a snake introduced into her version of the Garden. To the Alliance, River is a weapon which must be neutralized. To Simon, River is simply his sister, his *family*.

Even when tied to the stake, River seems unconcerned about all the fuss. Earlier, she assured her brother that they "won't be here long. Daddy will come and take us home." Simon despairs of that, having had a series of unpleasant confrontations with their father, the ironically named Gabriel,[11] over Simon's determination to rescue his sister. However, River sees things differently from most people and she is right about this, although the "daddy" who heads up the rescue party bears no biological link to the siblings.

While River is Whedon's primary representation of the "other" in the *Firefly/Serenity* dynamic, the rest of the crew are outsiders to Alliance society as well. Rather than submitting to life under Alliance rule, Malcolm cobbles together this family (discussed in greater depth in an earlier section) with the promise of payment, adventure and, above all, freedom. The arrival of wanted fugitives Simon and River upset that applecart, causing no end of inconvenience to a man who deeply dislikes complications. But even among this group of "others," River is an outsider, so in River Tam Whedon has given us a sort of "double other."

So why does Malcolm return for River? He even admits that life would be a great deal easier without the siblings onboard the ship. Further, while Mal has been portrayed as being at least somewhat fond of River (and less so of Simon), Alyson Buckman has pointed out that, on at least two occasions, Mal refers to River as a thing, as opposed to as a person.[12] Therefore, it is worth considering why he is unwilling to sacrifice her to make his life easier, which is often a primary motivating consideration for Mal.

It is obvious that Whedon intends his audience to side with the "big damn hero" outlaws and stand in opposition to the hillfolk fanatics. Whedon makes an unmistakable statement against the perils of zealotry as Mal brushes off the Patron's insistence that the execution must proceed because River is a witch. Mal's pithy reply to this admonition is simply, "Yeah, but she's our witch. [*Cocks gun*] So cut her the hell down."[13] Mal may not believe in much at this point, but he would likely agree with Terry Pratchett that "The presence of those seeking the truth is infinitely to be preferred to the presence of those who think they've found it" (192). Certainly in this instance, the gun-toting skeptic is to be preferred far above the dead-certain zealot.

With Mal's statement, River is thereby claimed publicly as a member of his tribe, tiny and prone to squabbling as it may be. She's quirky, fractured, brilliant, and frightening in turns, but — well, she's theirs. This girl who inspires feelings of both fear (especially in Jayne) and protectiveness (especially in Simon) is *theirs*. And they, conversely, are hers. The woman who plays jacks with her on the cargo bay floor, the man whose first reaction to seeing her, tucked unconscious and naked into a box, is a noncommittal "Huh," and all the others onboard — they are *hers*. The "others" have found one another and, while all is not going to be sweetness and light for them, having each other is far better than going through the 'verse all alone. After all, a tribe of "others" is still a tribe, even on the outer fringes of society.

In returning for River, Mal is keeping faith with the teachings of Christ, who had a conspicuous affinity for outsiders of all stripes and repeatedly exhorted his followers to seek out the forsaken, the unclean, and all the "others" of society. Mal's reasoning is along the lines of *Okay, she's a mess. Not her fault, but bits of her are broken and she's at least partly crazy. Life would be easier without that brand of trouble onboard, but...* It is in the ellipsis that Mal embodies the concept of grace, which can be defined as acting with moral strength and integrity in the face of strong opposition. A good captain doesn't just abandon his crew when the corner grows tight, even when to do so would make his life simpler. No, *especially* when to do so would make his life simpler.

Christ intimately understood how difficult going against the grain could be; however, he paid no heed to the societal norms of His time. For example, the Gospel of John contains the account of the "woman at the well." Peter McWilliams points out that the woman is a Samaritan, which meant that she was considered by traditional Jews to be so unclean that merely to take water from her would render Jesus "unclean" as well. Moreover, she is drawing water from the well at noon, a task any sensible, respectable woman would perform only during the cool of morning or evening. Yet it is to this woman, this pariah and outcast that Jesus first reveals himself undeniably as the Messiah as opposed to some sort of veiled reference such as the "Son of Man" (445). Up to this point in His ministry, Christ is almost coy about His identity and it cannot be viewed as coincidental that this revelation is first made to a woman who traditional Jewish society of the time viewed suspiciously as the "other."

It was not just with unclean women that Jesus communed. In Mark 14, he tells his disciples to seek a place for what would become the Last Supper by going into the city where "a man carrying a jar of water will meet you; follow him." Drawing water was considered "woman's work." Any man performing such a chore would be viewed as effeminate and Jewish culture of that time considered effeminate men to be outcasts. As McWilliams suggests, it is as if Christ just told his disciples to "Look for a man in a dress, high heels, and a bouffant hairdo" (447). The disciples obey, the man is located, and the room is obtained. Clearly, Christ spent His ministry working to *include*, rather than *exclude*.

With such constant messages of inclusion and acceptance, there can be no doubt about which side of the "River v. Village" confrontation Christ would have chosen to align himself. Christ consigned no one to the flames of the witch pyre, although what has been done in His name must make Him shake His head in despair at the stubbornness and myopia of mankind.

Mal often protests that he has no use for (or belief in) God. He creates his own family in his crew and, in his creed, you have to look after your crew. In this way, Mal views himself as his brother's keeper, provided his "brother" is a member of his crew. This point of view is logical to both believers (God expects us to look after one another) and non-believers (since there is no God to look after us; we had better take care of one another). Whedon's Mal may not be a traditional hero, but that doesn't mean he's willing to take the easy way out when it means leaving a mentally fragile teenage girl and her loyal-to-a-fault brother behind.

Meanwhile, the believers in the village stack cordwood, preparing to cleanse themselves of the "other" in their midst through fire. Ultimately, their efforts will be futile, for you simply cannot burn a river. Rivers have their own flow and purpose and, while it is possible to divert that flow and delay that purpose, such a strong natural force cannot be eternally confined.

To Whedon, confinement of the human spirit is wrong. Fearing what we do not understand is wrong. And roasting someone alive for seeing more (or differently) than you do is certainly wrong. So Mal goes back. People of faith don't do things because they are *easy* but because they are *right*, and while it is easy to know what should be done; it is often quite difficult to have the moral courage to do it.

While Whedon and the writers of the Gospels would disagree on nearly everything, there is one point on which they would agree; namely, that in the final analysis, there is no "other." There is only us. We make our own witches, just as the Alliance made both River and the Reavers. Every time we continue to be frightened of the unknown, the unusual, or the alternative by branding it "wrong" (if not "of the Devil"), we are aligning ourselves with the superstitious mob. When we continue to be unwilling to open our hearts and minds to include all into our idea of "us" rather than isolating some off as "them," we continue to add wood to the pyre. And when we continue to divide the world into "ourselves" and the "other," we continue to be willing to burn River.

10

No Girls Allowed

CALEB AND THE EVILS OF MISOGYNY

No less an authority on *Buffy* than Joss Whedon has remarked that Season Seven was intended to serve as a return to the series' beginnings; hence the use of the newly rebuilt Sunnydale High School as a locus for much of the action. However, for many viewers, one element of Season Seven seems to ring a false note — the introduction of the character of Caleb in the final five episodes. In the seven years *Buffy* aired, Joss Whedon had achieved his desire to create a new feminist icon with Buffy Summers, the petite blonde who could hold her own with the forces of evil and still look good doing it. *Buffy* reimagined so many of the standard tropes of network television that to many viewers, Caleb appeared to be a step backward rather than a step forward to complete the circle begun with Season One. After all, as an evil ex-preacher with a pathological hatred for women, Caleb was not only undemonic but seemed at first blush to be a delivery from the Stock Villains Warehouse. Let's see — Caleb was not a master vampire (Season 1), or a demonic ex-lover bent on destroying the world (Season 2), or a human who craved "ascension" to a pure demon form (Season 3). Neither was he a monstrous amalgam of demon, man, and machine (Season 4), or a clotheshorse of a hellgod (Season 5) or a best friend gone mad with grief and supernatural power (Season 6). No, Caleb was human. Evil, but still only human — and *Buffy* had never before had a "just plain human" serve as the "Big Bad," although Warren in Season Six comes close. However, for *Buffy*, a show that continually focuses on issues of female empowerment, the use of the profoundly misogynistic Caleb as antagonist is actually a sublime end note, since the character embodies so much of what Whedon feels must be fought against in this world.[1]

Of course, Caleb isn't even the true "Big Bad" of Season Seven. That role is filled by the First Evil (the "First"), who had been introduced in the Season Three episode "Amends" (3.10). The First predates demons, vampires, and even the first evil act perpetrated on the Earth — the First is beyond the very *concept* of evil. Like every evil, the First has a weakness — it is incorporeal and therefore, needs physical beings to carry out its designs. The First's need for others to perform necessary tasks is the dark mirror of the prayer of St. Teresa of Avila who reminded the faithful that:

> Christ has no body now but yours
> No hands, no feet on earth but yours
> Yours are the eyes through which He looks compassion on this world
> Christ has no body now on earth but yours.

The First can only achieve evil through the actions of others, much like the concept of misogyny can only harm and degrade men and women when the abstract concept becomes concrete action.

The First finds a willing servant in Caleb, a woman-hating ex-priest who takes obvious joy in vicious sadism long before he meets the First. This is evidenced by Caleb's fond reminiscence of his murder of a choirgirl in Knoxville who "even screamed on key"; a murder that Caleb mentions took place before he ever meets the First. Like all hobbyists, Caleb enjoys looking back over his past accomplishments and the First is willing to reward its faithful servant by playing a perverse version of "dress up" that permits him to repeatedly relive his sadistic slaughter of girls and young women. In this way, the character of Caleb is clearly coded as an antagonist whose twisted views of the female will be pitted against the very female savior figure of Buffy.

The wardrobe of this wolf in priest's clothing is important. Of course, the character of the fanatic decked in the trappings of religious faith is not Whedon's unique contribution to popular culture. In Marlowe's version of the Faust legend, the damned doctor tells Mephistophilis to appear before him as "an old Franciscan friar; / That holy shape becomes a devil best." As Marlowe knows, the awful is made more terrible by appearing as the familiar, an idea that is expounded on further in this chapter. Another example of the collision between religion and evil is Robert Mitchum's portrayal of Harry Powell, a psychotic preacher who believes God has told him to murder women in the frightening 1955 film *The Night of the Hunter*.[2] Moreover, Caleb's preferred outfit of Roman collar and black jeans has been seen before in Garth Ennis's creation of Jesse Custer from his *Preacher* comic series.[3]

Whedon gives viewers a depraved trickster in Caleb. Whedon has done this before, of course. Just as Mayor Wilkins presents a socially acceptable face that conceals his plan to ascend to full demon status in Season Three,

Caleb is initially presented as a saving grace for Shannon, a Potential who is fleeing for her life from the Bringers, who are minions of the First. When she flings herself into Caleb's truck, he appears confused and concerned, asking her if she's all right ("Dirty Girls" 7.18). Viewers are relieved that Shannon seems to have escaped the bloodthirsty Bringers, but Whedon is never satisfied to let an archetype remain the status quo.[4] Rather than finding sanctuary with the young preacher, Shannon discovers that she faces a larger danger when Caleb asks her, "Did you ever think that maybe they were chasin' you because you're a whore?" He proceeds to terrify the young Potential, branding her with a red-hot cross and pinning her to the seat with a wickedly sharp hunting knife. Then, in a shot framed to make this human-shaped monster resemble an ardent lover whispering endearments to his sweetheart, he murmurs a message for Shannon to deliver to Buffy before roughly removing the knife and flinging her from the speeding truck. While Caleb may wear the outfit of a soulful man of the cloth, Whedon clearly codes him as a predator in the service of evil, rather than as a protector on the side of good. In this way, the coming battle is set as being not just between good and evil, but is also between misogyny and acceptance.

Over the seven year run of *Buffy*, viewers became accustomed to amazing monster effects, ranging from grotesque vampire visages to the lovable floppy-eared Clem. However, Caleb lacks any obvious physical tag such as fangs or claws to mark him as the evil "other." This very ordinariness of Caleb, the fact that he looks "like us," is the very thing that makes him scarier than anything Whedon has given his audience before. Previously, viewers could rationalize the evil in *Buffy* in symbolic, metaphoric terms: vampires could be read as the desire to dominate and overwhelm those weaker than ourselves; werewolves could be read as the struggle to contain the beastly impulses within us; and so on. The character of Caleb removes that safe distance between "us" and "other," for he is not a metaphor or a symbol of some type. He is real, just as he is, and the lesson Whedon uses Caleb to teach is that evil doesn't need fierce fangs or clicking claws to be horrifying. While most viewers would agree that vampires, demons, and the like do not stalk the streets of our towns, one unfortunately need only pick up the newspaper to discover that there are Calebs hunting their prey in our communities — and that's about as scary as hell gets.

The decision to make this sociopath have any sort of link to religion is not likely to soothe those who have trouble grasping *Buffy* on religious grounds, and the fact that "Dirty Girls," the episode in which Caleb first appears, originally aired during the Christian Holy Week of 2003 was viewed as bordering on blasphemous by some opponents.[5] Indeed, the timing and content of "Dirty Girls" was read by the Parents Television Council ("PTC") as an example of Evil, Impious Hollywood deliberately throwing gasoline on

Easter eggs. The introduction of Caleb was denounced by the PTC as a "bigoted slap in the face to Christians everywhere." Then again, the PTC didn't seem to expect much from a show that they characterized as being "known for displaying scenes of graphic violence and inappropriate sex to its young teen audience" ("*Buffy the Vampire Slayer* Mocks"). The PTC and like-minded groups miss the point Whedon is making with his ex-preacher about evil not necessarily looking evil. In fact, their outrage would probably cause Caleb to grimly chuckle, probably as he cleans his knife of the "polluted blood" of yet another victim who believed that *he's a preacher; he must be safe.*

Whedon may identify himself as an atheist, but it is a mistake to mark Caleb as some sort of ham-fisted swipe at the organized Church. Drew Goddard, the writer of "Dirty Girls," addresses this issue on the commentary track for the episode, stating that the idea behind Caleb is that he is emphatically *not* a member of any church; indeed, that no faith would have him. The roots of Caleb's pathological hatred of women are never addressed; perhaps if viewers had any explanation for why he is so frightened of the potential power of women that he feels the need to slaughter them, there would be a temptation, however slim, to rationalize his sadism and bloodlust.[6] However, the fact that Whedon presents Caleb as a man of one-time faith cannot be lightly brushed aside, either. After all, if Whedon had wanted an evil plumber, viewers would have gotten an evil plumber. So what is the viewer to make of this preacher; this willing lapdog of evil who speaks softly while, if not carrying a big stick, gleefully snapping necks and eviscerating women who have made the fatal mistake of trusting his gentle drawl?

As has been demonstrated again and again, names are valuable keys to understanding characters in Whedon's work. With that in mind, it becomes fascinating to learn that the name "Caleb" is considered to have two meanings, both of Hebrew origin. The name can be translated as either "faithful" or "dog" (Kolatch 49). It is doubtful that the "dog" meaning is intended as a slur, but should instead be read as a statement regarding that animal's steadfast faithfulness, since the Biblical Caleb, who has "wholly followed the Lord" is proclaimed by God to be the only person in his generation who will live to see the promised land of Canaan (Num. 14:20–24). Throughout the five episodes in which he appears it is very clear that, while *Buffy*'s Caleb is not faithful to the ideals of the Roman collar he wears, the moniker Whedon has given him still fits him and his actions quite well, for Caleb is faithful unto death to the First.

The First Evil intends to tip the scales of good and evil over to the side of darkness and thereby gain the ability to become corporeal in this dimension. As Whedon establishes, the First cannot physically manifest until this is accomplished, but it is able to appear in the form of any human who is (or has been) dead and is quite talented at planting ghastly suggestions and goading humans into taking action that the First itself is unable to do. For example, by appearing as Warren, the First is able to trick the hapless Andrew into murdering Jonathan. The First may not be able to take physical action itself, but it is quite able to get others, such as Caleb, to perform its bidding. And it has a special task in mind for this particular faithful servant.

In order to sufficiently tip the scales and also remove a potential threat to its power, Whedon has the First plot to end the line of Slayers. Since Slayers can only be female, this means a great number of girls and their protectors (the Watchers) must be eliminated. To be given such a purpose must feel to Caleb like being let loose in a particularly lethal candy store. The Watchers are dispatched from a distance by explosives placed within the Watchers Council, but the girls — well, that's up-close, personal work — just the sort a misogynistic sadist would relish. And for a feminist such as Whedon, there can be no more fitting confrontation than to have his beloved Buffy face the forces of misogyny that have sought for millennia to bring women to heel.

Whedon has Caleb throw himself into his mission and viewers see the results of his zeal throughout Season Seven, long before they actually meet him. It is interesting to realize that when Whedon has the First appear to its misogynistic minion as the twice-dead Buffy, Caleb has no reaction other than dismissing the apparition as being "just another dirty girl." When the First tells Caleb to look more deeply, viewers see reverent recognition dawning on him that this is to be his reward for all his hard work — he will meet the Slayer, an opponent worthy of a true misogynist's hatred and fear. Caleb is elated at the prospect and stretches out his hand with the only tenderness he ever displays to stroke the cheek of his prize; the finest woman he will ever attempt to slaughter. However, the First is still noncorporeal so Caleb can only gaze upon the vision of his trophy kill — what he fears and seeks to conquer is something he is even denied the ability to touch. This fits Whedon's feminist philosophy in a beautifully symbolic way, since real-life misogynists also cannot connect with women and view the female as merely a construct to be dominated and subjugated.

Through his words, it becomes evident that Caleb's pathological hatred of females is rooted in a fear of the sexual power of women over men. Caleb views women as temptresses who seek to corrupt men by enticing them away from the True Path. Unable to see women as anything beyond their genitalia, he habitually refers to females as "dirty," "polluted," "whores," and (most vile) "splits."[7] With the First, Caleb has literally formed an unholy alliance. He is under no glamour or spell, but knows exactly what he is doing and serves quite willingly as the incorporeal First's hands in this world. He knows that his actions are calculated to pry open doors for evil such as mankind has never known before and he goes about his business with joy. All concrete actions, whether good or evil, are rooted in abstract ideas and thoughts. So although Caleb's actions are ruled by the intangible concept of hatred of the female, the intangible First gives its faithful servant a veritable buffet of tangible young women to slaughter and dominate. Whedon gives the character of Caleb an awful purpose to fulfill and Caleb is overjoyed at the certainty of knowing his purpose in the grand plan. Caleb's violence and sadism renders him the very inverse of the faith symbolized by his Roman collar.

Further, Caleb has an obsession to *know*, and while knowledge may be power, it is also true that power is often a corrupting force. In "Dirty Girls" (7.18), Caleb states that he has spent far too much time "looking for the Lord in the wrong damn places," to which the First asks Caleb in amusement if he considers the First to be God. Offended, Caleb replies that he certainly does not, since he is beyond such concepts. Caleb has betrayed his name and is no longer faithful to the light, if indeed he ever was. He has rejected faith, which by definition contains elements of that which cannot be objectively proven. Like Marlowe's Faust, Caleb wants only certainty and knowledge. To Caleb, lack of knowledge coupled with the general weakness of the human condition is the tragic fate from which the First is rescuing him. In fact, after his first encounter with Buffy, he relates a story to the First (Jesus is not the only one who teaches in parables) that Buffy "was filled with darkness, and despair, and why? Because she did not *know*." In Caleb, Whedon shows viewers the devastating effects of deep-seated certitude and zealotry in belief systems.

The homicidal Caleb is always seen wearing a priest's collar, which for him is a form of lure designed to coax the innocent to draw nearer. Whedon's Caleb has exercised free will in choosing to serve evil in return for knowledge that will elevate him beyond mere humanity. In contrast, Buffy wears whatever the current style may be,[8] but defends the innocent to the point of being named "Class Protector" during her senior year of high school. Using a Christian cross as a literal weapon against the forces of Darkness, Buffy is repeatedly shown as having been *chosen* to be the Slayer, a role that is presented as her unchangeable destiny. While it is extremely doubtful that Whedon is a closet Calvinist, this deliberate set-up of Caleb's use of free will versus Buffy's predestination should not be dismissed with a shrug. It must be remembered that one of *Buffy*'s recurring themes is that people are defined far more by choices than by destiny and it is Buffy's refusal to accept her destiny as hers and hers alone that ultimately leads to the defeat of the First. Simply put, Whedon seems to be saying that destiny and choice are more interrelated than they may appear at first glance.

Whedon has Caleb choose to seek knowledge at all costs. His thirst for knowledge is echoed in the beliefs and practices of certain sects of ancient

Gnostic Christian thought as well as modern-day fundamentalism. Both will be discussed in turn; however, an interesting nugget to consider before turning attention to Gnostic beliefs in detail is that among the Gnostic pantheon of deities is a goddess named Edem who is the principle who causes evil on Earth, although she herself is not necessarily evil (Carlyon 337). It makes you wonder exactly what Whedon was reading around 2003 as the First begins to appear wearing Buffy's feminine form. While Gnostic beliefs are neither the beginning nor the end of the long chain of theological distrust of the female, there are additional links between some Gnostic writings and the Caleb/First arc that should not be ignored.

For centuries, nearly all knowledge regarding these early sects of Christianity was viciously suppressed by the orthodox keepers of the Christian faith, who viewed the Gnostic scriptures as anathema, since they contradicted and even reversed so many basic concepts of traditional Christian belief. When those who held the orthodox point of view prevailed, the Gnostic texts disappeared and later scholars could only rely on the words of the early Christians to determine the doctrines followed by the vanquished Gnostics. Since the early Christians opposed these doctrines and only one side was able to speak, an accurate picture seemed impossible to obtain.[9] But in 1945, a large cache of primary Gnostic texts, now known as the Nag Hammadi library, was uncovered in Egypt and the Gnostics had a long-overdue chance to voice their thoughts.[10]

"Gnosticism" is a term that is often used as if it encompasses a single, unifying school of theology, which is patently untrue. However, despite multiple differences among these splintered sects, two commonalities emerge throughout Gnostic writings. According to Anne McGuire, the two essential features of Gnostic belief are an emphasis on the saving power of knowledge (which is "gnōsis" in Greek, from which the movement derives its name) and a worldview that sharply distinguishes the superior realm of the divine from the inferior realm of the mundane (258). The Gnostics roundly rejected the idea that the world was created by a benevolent Deity; rather, they believed that the world was the result of a sort of cosmic disaster by the actions of a god who is "at best a botcher or ignoramus, or at worst a spirit of malevolence" (Bloom 51). According to pupils of this school of thought, God is the king of deceivers and only by transcending the ties of the material world could humans hope to return to heaven. This transcendence could only take place by learning "the truth about ourselves, the world around us, how we came to be here, and how we can escape" (Ehrman 45–46). Caleb embraces portions of this worldview, particularly the idea that God does not wish His creations to attain enlightenment and acts only to confuse and obscure the true knowledge which is required for humans to ascend beyond this miserable existence. Caleb, of course, believes that the answers to his questions have been found in serving the First, rather than a paltry god. Moreover, Caleb believes that this knowledge is the key to attaining the higher existence promised to him by the First. As an atheist, Whedon may consider the whole discussion an empty intellectual exercise but as a human, he may wish people would put more of their energies into making this world a better place, rather than worrying so much about the next.

The orthodox were greatly angered by the notions put forth by the Gnostics, who presented a serious threat to their authority during the first four centuries of the Common Era. At that time, Christianity was struggling to define itself and crossovers between Gnostics and non–Gnostic theologies were not unknown. For example, the major Gnostic thinker Valentinus sought election as Pope in 397 and St. Augustine spent the first part of his life as a Gnostic (Barnstone xviii). While the doctrines of what would become Christianity were somewhat malleable at this point in history, the early Church was unwilling to embrace what it saw as the heresies of the Gnostics, which included the teachings of Manichaeism. In this theology, Eve gives life to Adam and the serpent is actually a liberating force that urges the couple to eat from the Tree of Gnosis in order to begin the journey toward self-knowledge and salvation (xviii). It has even been suggested that the New Testament canon of Christianity was established as a result of the provocation of the early Gnostic Marcion of Sinope (xviii). In the canonical version of Genesis, Eve is given a threefold punishment for eating of the forbidden fruit. As a result of her disobedience to God's express commands, women "shall bear children in intense pain and suffering; yet even so, you shall welcome your husband's affections, and he shall be your master" (Gen. 3:16). This idea of the "Divine curse" of male superiority repeatedly being used to justify forced female submission will be discussed further; however, it is proper to mention that Caleb also interprets his murderous behavior as having Divine sanction — uppity women (and to his mind, this encompasses *all* women) must be returned to their proper place. Whedon is using his creation of Caleb to establish the necessary parties for an inevitable showdown between a despiser of women and a powerful woman. For just as Caleb thinks he is working under the auspices of a dark Divine presence, Buffy is repeatedly shown to be an avatar of the forces of Good. The battle between these two foes would not be nearly as compelling to watch if both sides were not equally matched.

Just as Buffy is consistently portrayed as a complex woman, capable of showing multiple facets of her personality, the portrayal of women in the Gnostic texts is likewise complicated. While some scholars read the primary texts as containing what Anne McGuire refers to as a "preponderance of positive female imagery," other scholars note the opposite, arguing that the many negative references to women "betray the devaluation and subordination of women" (259). As is often the case, the truth is more likely found in the middle than on either extreme end of the spectrum of argument. However, the fundamentalist demand to determine a single, "correct" reading of any text so swimming with diverse points of view (be it Gnostic, Biblical, or *Buffy*) is doomed to failure and frustration.

The Gnostic story of Sophia ("wisdom" in Greek) is illustrative of the gender tension found throughout Gnostic texts. While many versions of the Sophia story exist, the basic facts are these: Sophia was a member of the Divine, but she reached beyond her established boundaries by desiring someone other than her correct consort. The result of this union is the God of the Old Testament and for her transgression, Sophia is sharply rebuked. McGuire eloquently spells out the lesson taught by Sophia's punishment, stating that "the calamitous consequences of independent female activity and the benefits of restoring the rebellious female to her proper place [serves to reinforce] ideologies of gender relations by idealizing redemption and marriage alike as coming about through the hierarchical union of a superior, perfect, and dominant male and an inferior, imperfect, and subordinate female" (262). Whedon's Caleb may not be familiar with the story of Sophia, but he would wholeheartedly agree with the outcome of the tale, since he despises females as being the epitome of all that he considers to be bad. Indeed, it is doubtful that Caleb views females as people at all, stating as he does to Shannon that women are born without souls. Since he believes that women cannot be redeemed, but only removed, his wholesale slaughter of the Slayer line is to him a holy crusade, with Buffy as the Jerusalem that can only be saved by being destroyed.

Misogyny is marked by a deep revulsion for the sexual power of women, which is usually viewed by those holding this view as an improper power women exercise over men. The Gnostics were certainly not of one mind on this concept; in fact, detractors such as Clement of Alexandria cited wild, licentious behavior such as "free love" among Gnostic believers as proof of their heresy (McGuire 265). However, there was also a strong strain of asceticism running throughout many Gnostic sects, who favored renouncing this world to pursue the purer values and priorities of knowledge. Ehrman states that "since bodily pleasure above all else is what ties us to this world, making us long for more and more of what we can acquire in this material existence, it is precisely bodily pleasure that must be rejected" (71). Caleb can be defined as an ascetic of this type. He not only rejects bodily pleasure, he views sexual urges as the fault of women, who, as he explains to Shannon, are "born ... with that gaping maw that wants to open up, suck out a man's marrow" ("Dirty Girls" 7.18). Whedon clearly uses this character to emphasize the inherent evil of devaluing human beings on the basis of gender.

Caleb views any display of sensuality as subhuman behavior. When the First expresses envy at the Scoobies' ability to touch and connect through physical intimacy, Caleb is befuddled, reasoning that human contact in the form of sex is nothing more than the nauseating behavior of animals and surely the First is beyond such desires. As Caleb says with reverent wonder to the First, the rutting Scoobies are "just sinners, but you — you are *sin*." Yes, the First concedes, but it still longs to be able to "wrap my hands around some innocent neck and feel it crack." Caleb well understands that desire, concluding the discussion with a quietly impassioned, "Amen." Caleb has found the knowledge he has long sought — the knowledge of the fullness of sin and, as Damrosch states in his exploration of Satan in *Paradise Lost*, this knowledge of sin "has been gained in the only way possible, by sinning" (101). Like Faust, there can be no turning back for Caleb, who has found his dark light in the glow of the First.

Although the possibility of redemption for horrific past acts is a theme that Whedon repeatedly weaves throughout his work, forgiveness must be sought. It is not a salvific shirt flapping on a clothesline available to any who pass by. Caleb doesn't think he needs redeeming, so redemption remains out of his grasp. However, Whedon places Caleb firmly on the side of evil, so Caleb would spurn redemption in any event, for he has found his purpose in serving the First.

It seems that Caleb fits into many of the clothes hanging in the roomy Gnostic closet. He feels deceived by God; he has found his perceived salvation through knowledge and experience; and he has a revulsion toward earthly things such as sensuality, viewing it as unnecessary deadweight. His hatred of women, however, is hardly a concept that is unique to certain sects of Gnosticism. Indeed, although he may not consciously realize it, the Roman collar he wears is emblematic of an institution that has long sought to define the female faithful as less worthy than the male — the organized Christian church. That Caleb was at one time a member of some denomination cannot be denied, since when questioned by the First as to his choice of wardrobe, he replies that a man "can't turn his back on what he came from."[11] While Whedon's Caleb comes from a Christian background, it is abundantly clear that he has long since left that in the dust in favor of the darker, less complicated worldview espoused by the First.

Caleb gives every indication of being a man who has more than a passing familiarity with Christian scripture. He often employs Biblical imagery in his speech, musing about the wine list at the Last Supper and referring to Faith as playing Cain to Buffy's Abel. He claims to be beyond the very concept of God, and certainly has no fear of Satan, whom he refers to as a "little man." In a perversion of the Lord's Prayer, he tells the First that the "kingdom, the power, and the glory are yours, now and forever." Moreover, he explains to the First that Buffy will come to the vineyard with the Potentials, because curiosity is woman's first sin and he has offered "her an apple. What can she do but take it?" thereby casting himself as the serpent in the Garden of Eden story.[12]

As an atheist, Whedon is unlikely to spend much time attempting to rectify the paradoxes raised by the scriptures of any particular faith. However, his choice to have Biblical imagery issue repeatedly from the mouth of a man who has so thoroughly rejected the very principles espoused by Christian beliefs underscores the fact that Christian theology is riddled with paradoxes and is subject to multiple interpretations. Philosophers from Donne to Kierkegaard have wrestled with the deeper meanings of the Christian faith; however, the exploration of these thorny problems interests Caleb not a whit. While Whedon often explores the deeper questions of what it means to be human, including the role of faith in answering those questions, his creation of Caleb deliberately doesn't bother. Caleb wants quick, easy answers and he doesn't want nuance and subtlety. Simply put, Caleb has found *an* answer, so he stops seeking, which prevents him from finding anything beyond the point at which he currently stands. Whedon has Caleb find his answer in the straightforward worldview presented by the First — a mindset can be summed up as an echo of *Lost in Space*'s robot: "Crush. Kill. Destroy." This desire to reduce the complex down to the basic is a hallmark of fundamentalism and, while few fundamentalists are fanatical, murderous zealots, it cannot be denied that of such theologies suicide bombers and Timothy McVeighs are made. Whedon's creation of Caleb can be read as clearly distrusting the "easy answer." Instead, Whedon seems to be advocating the position that life is complicated and attempts to boil the complex down to the fundamental can yield a dark, poisonous sludge, rather like the ichor that is seen streaming from Caleb during his final battle with Buffy.

It is Caleb as the fundamentalist believer in knowledge who partially blinds Xander to punish him for being the "one who sees everything," an event which will be explored in more detail later. In keeping with the Biblical references that flock around the character of Caleb, this battle takes place in the "Shadow Valley Vineyard," which Tammy Kinsey has pointed out is a clear a reference to the Valley of the Shadow of Death from the Twenty-third Psalm. This is a particularly apt reference, since the forces of good truly are walking like lambs into a very dark and forbidding place. Many additional examples of Biblical imagery being associated with Caleb abound throughout the five episodes in which he appears, but there is one telling reference. When the Scoobies capture a Bringer, they cast a spell designed to compel the Bringer to divulge the plans of the First. When forced to "talk" through Andrew, the

Bringer refers to Caleb as "teacher," a title that was also used by Christ's disciples to refer to Him ("Touched" 7.20). In this way, Whedon makes yet another statement about Caleb's role as a false prophet; one who wears the outward clothes but has not the inner light of a spiritual leader.

While Caleb's murderous sprees would not be tolerated in any parish today, the organized Church unfortunately has often treated its female faithful as less worthy than its male members, so in some ways, Caleb is the latest bloody link in a very long, woman-hating chain. The authorities of the early Church worked tirelessly to bury what they viewed as Gnostic heresy, but distrust of the female had been deeply woven into the warp and woof of everyday life long before the emergence of the Christian faith. Whedon's desire to offer an antidote to this deep-rooted misogyny was one of his touchstones in creating the icon of Buffy in the first place.

The historical bias against women can be illustrated with examples from many places and eras. The ancient Greek philosophers, for example, believed that women were mentally weak and subject to the whims of their baser emotions and therefore, had to be protected from themselves through a system of male guardianship (Thompson). In fact, women in ancient Greece were unable to make purchases beyond inexpensive everyday objects and were forbidden from owning property or entering into any form of contract (Thompson). The famed Roman Empire was not much better in its treatment of women. As Thompson states, a woman usually remained under the control of one man or another throughout her life, regardless of her status as slave or free. While in theory this male (the *pater familias*) had absolute legal control over every aspect of life within the family, Thompson points out that this control was most often limited to economic matters, although the choice of a spouse for daughters was considered such an economic matter that it could not safely be left to the flighty mind of a female. While the founders of the early Church were not necessarily woman-haters, they were the result of their various societies, all of which viewed women as being of a lower status than men, a view with which Caleb as Buffy's antagonist vigorously agrees.

Christianity is, of course, rooted in the Jewish tradition. While a woman in ancient Israel could keep her own property at marriage and the husband was obligated to provide economic support to his wife, the man had much more freedom within the matrimonial relationship than did the woman. Since the continuation of a husband's lineage through sons was essential to Jewish culture, the birth of sons was considered to be the greatest achievement to which a woman could aspire and a man could easily divorce a barren wife. Since slavery was also common within this society, a loophole developed to permit a wife to consider any children conceived between her husband and the wife's "handmaiden" to be the wife's children (Thompson). Having established the acceptability of such "handmaid's children" in the Biblical account of the childless Sarah, who gives her Egyptian slave Hagar to her husband Abraham in Gen. 16:1–4, things take a truly bizarre turn in Chapter 30 of Genesis. Jacob had married two sisters (polygyny was acceptable in order to increase the chances of extending the male line and as long as Jacob didn't marry his *own* sister, this disturbingly straight family tree was socially acceptable); Leah was fertile, Rachel was not. Fearing the loss of her husband's affections, Rachel gives Jacob her servant-girl Bilhah, who conceives two sons, thus elevating Rachel's status above that of her sister Leah. The second of Bilhah's children is named "Naphtali" by Rachel, which means "Wrestling" since "I am in a fierce contest with my sister and I am winning!" In retaliation, her sister Leah gives *her* slave-girl Zilpah to her husband and names the resulting child "Gad" meaning "My luck has turned!" (Gen. 30:9–13) By having Leah and Rachel compete for the attentions of their husband in this manner, a powerful lesson is being taught — women must willingly play into the system of patriarchy in order for it to continue.

This use of slave-girl surrogates continues until all twelve sons who will form the twelve tribes of Israel (which is Jacob's new name, given to him after he prevails in a wrestling match with an angel in Gen. 32) are present and accounted for. Jacob is presumably content with this competition (and, one assumes, with the slave girls warming his bed); the slave girls' thoughts on the matter are not recorded. After all, accounts are written by the winners, and Bilhah and Zilpah do not fall within that category. Caleb, who rejects the religious title of "Father" since he himself is (thankfully) childless, would be no doubt repulsed at the repeated sexual encounters of this story. However, he would approve of the underlying idea that the identity of the mother of the children is secondary, since to him and all men in this tradition, all important history and lineage comes through the male.

As truly weird as the account of Leah and Rachel seems to be by most twenty-first century standards,[13] it is crucial to remember that a woman's worth was measured primarily by the number of sons she was able to produce. Only by fulfilling this function could a woman achieve a measure of security in her relationship with her husband; childless women were viewed as basically useless and divorce was easy for a man to obtain in such circumstances. While this seems patently one-sided and unfair, it must be remembered that this arrangement was viewed as the natural order of things, dating back to Eve's punishment in the Garden of Eden. Unfortunately, the position of women did not improve with the emergence of Christianity, despite Christ's often-recorded radical take on equality between the genders. Whedon's Buffy, with her egalitarian army and proven record of self-sacrifice, certainly comes far closer to fitting the Christ model than do most of the early

Church fathers. Buffy continually strives to use her powers to protect the weak and the innocent, a goal Whedon clearly feels is more worthy than accruing power for its own sake.

In "Dirty Girls," Caleb states that "Paul had some good stuff to say ... but overall, I find it a tad complicated" and since Paul's influence on the development and spread of the early Church cannot be denied, he seems to be a good starting point for this discussion. It is important to remember that Paul was a *convert* to the Christian faith — not only was he not an original disciple, he is first introduced as an eager opponent of the new faith. In fact, it is at Paul's feet that the murderers of Stephen, the first Christian martyr, lay their cloaks as they prepare to execute Stephen by stoning him to death (Acts 7:57–58). Wishing a more active role than that of cloak-check girl, Paul talks the High Priest into essentially deputizing him so Paul can flush out other Christians and drag them back to Jerusalem in chains, but has his famous conversion experience on the way to fulfill his mission. Filled with a heavenly zeal, this one-time persecutor of the faith becomes one of its most ardent supporters.

Whedon's Caleb is the inverse of Paul in this respect for, while both Caleb and Paul jump to other bandwagons, Paul moves from persecuting to proselytizing while Caleb merely uses the physical trappings of Christianity (the collar and the cross) to trap the innocent for slaughter, such as the choir-girl he mentions killing in Knoxville. Whedon makes the case that clothes certainly do not make the man — just because Caleb looks like a kindly man of God doesn't mean he is one and, in the case of Caleb, appearances can be deadly deceiving.

As is fitting for someone who whipsawed from one side of the faith to the other, the writings attributed to Paul are filled with contradictions. Ehrman points out that the material cannot really be used to definitively "establish what Paul himself said or thought, but it does show us what later Christians wanted Paul to think" (94). A classic example of this tension is found in First Corinthians, which scholars acknowledge is (at least mostly) the work of Paul. Verses 34–35 of Chapter 14 are often used to support the position that women are not to hold positions of authority within the Church, since Paul states that women are to be silent in church and not to take part in any church discussions or express any opinions, since their role is to be subordinate to men. This is a position the villainous Caleb would take even further, since he desires that women keep deathly silent, preferably by his hand.

However, Paul's position on the subject is complicated by his statement merely three chapters earlier in Chapter 11:13–16, in which he states that women are to cover their heads when praying in public and prophesying in church. Now, one cannot prophesize and keep silent simultaneously. Bart Ehrman's studies have indicated that the troubling verses in Chapter 14 appear to be later additions made by persons who "wanted the apostle to be on the side of those who believed women should not participate in the worship services as active members of the congregation" (94). First Corinthians does not contain the only "perils of Pauline" for those attempting to discern a sole, unified meaning in these writings. It is a mistake to attempt to distill a single meaning from any source so rich with layers, but it is worth noting the existence of (as well as the exasperation that can be caused by) the multiple layers. Many of Whedon's characters (including Buffy) have echoes here, as they cannot be neatly tucked into precise pigeonholes.

For example, while some of his writings insist that women take a subservient role, Paul also writes repeatedly of women occupying positions of authority within the early Church. Ehrman points out three women mentioned prominently in Paul's letter to the Romans; a deacon named Phoebe; Prisca, who supported a home church; and Junia, whom Paul refers to as "foremost among the apostles" (159). Yet in 1 Timothy, he explicitly forbids women to teach or even speak in church and indicates that only through childbirth can women be cleansed of the sin of being tricked by Satan in the Garden (1 Tim. 2:12–15). This prohibition is a reiteration of the early Church's prevailing ideas that only through submission to the male can the "Divine curse" placed on women in Genesis be negated and that "good" women should never strive for any position other than that of mother. Ehrman strives to untangle this contradictory skein by presenting evidence with which most Biblical scholars agree: that the Pastoral Epistles, which include 1 Timothy, were written in the *name* of Paul, but not actually *by* Paul (159). As a misogynist who is coded as Buffy's antagonist, Whedon's Caleb would simply cut through the whole tangled rat's-nest of contradictions and reject any interpretation that posits that women are worthy of any respect, including honoring women for their role as childbearers. As amply illustrated, this is a point of view with which Whedon emphatically disagrees.

Some very interesting accounts of powerful female leaders of the Church can be found by studying the books that did not make the canonical cut as the New Testament was being assembled. Thecla, for instance, is a grossly overlooked early Christian with a story that pushes the envelope of fantastic. Thecla was a female convert of Paul's and, for centuries, she had a following that nearly rivaled that of Mary herself (Ehrman 145). Despite being a longtime follower of the Christian path, she somehow never got around to being baptized. She is captured and flung into the arena to face a gruesome death from the claws and teeth of many beasts. However, a lioness lies down at her feet and proceeds to kill any creature that dares approach the holy woman, until the brave lioness herself is killed grappling with another lion. Sensing her death is near, Thecla spies a large barrel of water and hurls herself into it in an act of self-baptism. Unfortunately, the barrel is teeming with man-eating seals.[14] God saves Thecla by striking the barrel with a lightning bolt, which miraculously kills only the seals. Released by the amazed governor, Thecla dresses herself in men's garments and seeks Paul.[15] Upon finding him and relating her tale, Paul, delighted with the faith of his convert, does not order her to keep silent, but instead instructs her to go forth and teach the word of God (Barnstone 452–453). One assumes that Thecla is wise enough to steer clear of Sea World in her ministry.

Thecla may receive her marching orders from Paul, but Buffy has rejected the authority of the Watchers Council and blazes her own path instead. Nevertheless, the peculiar tale of Thecla teaches us several lessons we can apply to Whedon's characters and themes, especially when contrasted with canonical scriptures. First, we learn from this feast of contradiction that scripture (canonical or not) can be used to support just about any position, whether that position is equality or slavery, the blessings of saving grace or the heavy boot of punishing law. Second, we learn that early Christianity has some wildly implausible tales that may have caught the fancy of early believers who were accustomed to the hijinks of the prevailing Roman and Gnostic gods. Third, we learn that stories which prominently feature powerful women were deemed unsuitable for inclusion in the "official" text of Christianity, the New Testament, where the exploits of men are celebrated and those of women are buried deep within the texts.[16] And fourth, we learn a valuable lesson about the continuing marginalization of women which can be seen as running in an unbroken line from Thecla the Seal Slayer to Buffy the Vampire Slayer, both of whom are often brushed aside by those in authority, Thecla by the early Church and Buffy by most adults in Sunnydale.

Many problems emerge when people refuse to acknowledge the inconsistencies which are inherent in any work, such as the New Testament, assembled decades (and even centuries) after the events it is relating. Memories fade and yes, agendas emerge. Yet some adherents insist on seeking only one reading, wearing blinders to the existence of anything that contradicts that reading. This results in rendering faith as something as uselessly immobile as a fly encased in prehistoric amber, rather than permitting faith to grow wings and take flight. In addition, such a reading ignores the very intention of the Bible's New Testament, which was never meant to be simply dry, disinterested recitations of historical events; rather, it is "meant to show that the life, death, and resurrection of Jesus brought salvation — that is, they had a theological agenda" (Ehrman 42). To insist that there is one and only one meaning is to engage in theological myopia which strips faith of any meaning beyond that of a curiously rendered antique from an earlier era. This is a position Whedon would steadfastly oppose. His penchant for layered language and shifting allegiances among his characters support his existentialist beliefs that meaning is where you find it and is therefore unique to the individual seeker.

The struggle between a narrow, exclusive reading of religion and a broader, more exclusive definition of faith continues. Unfortunately, both sides often become strident and shrill in stating their positions, rather than displaying Christ's qualities of compassion and tolerance. This idea of the "continuing struggle" is a theme that Whedon often explores. For example, at the end of Season Five, Buffy is clearly depicted as a valiant Christ-figure, hurling herself into the abyss to save the world through her act of sacrifice. However, that is not the end of Buffy's story, as she is literally resurrected in Season Six and must struggle to re-define her place in the material world. This is a fight that continues until the very last episode (and beyond), pitting Buffy against demons, both literal and metaphoric.

Part of Buffy's struggle is against a society that views her—a young, attractive woman—as someone to be taken lightly. This is another result of the wholesale institutionalization of misogyny. Entire societies expend tremendous amounts of energy to define the "proper place" for women and then make sure they stay there. In the previous chapter, the tool of criminal charges of witchcraft to suppress women's independence was discussed. Often, societies have utilized either clothing or body modifications to achieve this goal. Three examples will illustrate the universality of this desire for societal subjugation and physical control of women.

First, for a thousand years, it was common for Chinese girls to have their feet broken by tight bindings applied in early childhood, often as early as three years of age. This excruciatingly painful (and dangerous) practice was designed to achieve the ultimate in feminine beauty as defined by that society—freakishly high-arched feet measuring four inches or less in overall length that hobbled natural movement ("Chinese Girl"). Readers may remember that Whedon created a Chinese Slayer who is killed by Spike during the Boxer Rebellion. While footbinding was still practiced during this time, it would seem that this Slayer had not been subjected to it, given her agility and combat skills as she battles Spike. While she loses the battle, the war continues, for another Slayer is called to replace the fallen.

Second, consider the nineteenth century corset, which was designed to create a tiny, delicate waist by reducing a woman's natural waist by up to eight inches. In order to accomplish this ideal of feminine beauty, up to twenty-one pounds of pressure was continually placed on a woman's internal organs, which were both displaced and deprived of natural blood flow. Miscarriage was common among corseted "ladies of leisure" (Pierson and Cloe). Viewers of *Buffy* may remember Whedon's Civil War era Slayer, Lucy Hanover. Like the unnamed Chinese Slayer, Lucy also appears to have bucked the system. Being uncorseted had to have been more effective for fighting the forces of darkness than being beautiful by the prevailing standards of her society. It seems that Buffy's stubborn insistence on doing things her way might be a more common trait among Whedon's Slayers than first thought, despite Buffy's obvious interest in fashion.

Third, the wretched practice of female genital mutilation is practiced today on girls as young as four in countries such as Egypt and Somalia. In this nightmarish procedure, a girl's external genitalia are sliced away in an overt attempt to control the girl's sexuality by obliterating any form of pleasure she might naturally obtain from sexual intercourse. Although roundly derided by medical authorities as unnecessary and inhumane, the World Health Organization estimates that over 100 million women have undergone this obscenity ("Female"). Quite often, the bloody procedure is done in primitive and unsanitary conditions, greatly increasing the risk of life-threatening infections and complications. This desire to physically control the sexuality of women through destroying the very body parts that permit a woman to experience pleasure is a practice which Caleb would no doubt approve, since Whedon has tagged him to be fearful of women's sexuality.

Despite their far-flung cultural origins, what all of these practices have in common is the overwhelming desire to control and dominate women. It would be a mistake to think that our own culture is immune from this. Despite our desire to consider ourselves "more civilized" than those who would break their daughters' feet or slash their private parts, our youth-obsessed culture actively promotes unhealthy ideals of feminine beauty, leading to the willingness of women to starve themselves, inject toxins into their faces to temporarily achieve a smooth, more youthful countenance, or have their bodies resculpted under general anesthesia with substances such as saline and silicone. Whedon demonstrates his understanding of the urgent drive for youth that permeates popular culture (after all, the Chosen One in every generation is one *girl*, not one *woman*), but he also makes statements about the hazards of pursuing youth at all costs. For example, the *Angel* episode "Eternity" (1.17) features a television actress whose desperate yearning to remain youthful leads to her willingness to be transformed into a death-dealing vampire in return for stopping the aging process. The actress's desires are shown to be shallow and foolish.

To paraphrase A. Whitney Brown, at some point, the only way to keep someone down in the gutter is to get down there yourself and hold her there (143). Despite the slime and mess found in gutters, many seem quite willing to do just that. For example, Pat Robertson writes that "[t]he feminist agenda is not about equal rights for women. It is about a socialist, anti-family political movement that encourages women to leave their husbands, kill their children, practice witchcraft, destroy capitalism, and become lesbians" (Pelletier). That explosive rhetoric could have been culled directly from the witchfinder manuals of the 1500s. Both Whedon's Caleb and Robertson seem to believe that the gutter is the natural habitat for women and they are both willing to get into the muck themselves to guarantee women don't rise from it. In Caleb, Whedon reminds viewers how dangerous and evil this worldview can be.

This brings up an important point about misogyny—the high price that it also requires of men. Whenever a society so rigidly defines gender roles for one sex, it is by default defining the acceptable roles for the other. Whedon commented on this very point in May 2006 when he was honored at an Equality Now event, saying that

> [E]quality is not a concept. It's not something we should be striving for—it's a necessity. Equality is like gravity—we need it to stand on this earth as men and women. And the misogyny that is in every culture is not a true part of the human condition. It is life out of balance and that imbalance is sucking something out of the soul of every man and woman who is confronted with it ["On the Road"].

Therefore, while this pernicious, poisonous desire to subjugate half the human race harms women in a myriad of ways, men are likewise affected. E. M. Forster commented on this in his novel *A Room with a View* when the character of George says, "This desire to govern a woman—it lies very deep, and men and women must fight it together before they shall enter the garden" (195). Whedon agrees with Forster that this is a battle that must be fought by *both* genders. No one gets to be a conscientious objector in this war, for we are all wounded by the adamant refusal to allow people of both genders to achieve their full potential as people simply because they do not fit a particular cookie-cutter shape of acceptable behavior, ambition, or gender. As Buffy demonstrates, if the game is rigged so that you can't win, the proper response is to change the game. Nevertheless, many people continue to prefer bystander status, arguing that misogyny really has no effect on their lives. To these people, Whedon argues that if you're not seeing the harm, you're deliberately not looking, for only by wearing blinders is it possible to see so little.

The image of wearing blinders is especially apt in this context, since eyes and vision feature so prominently in the Caleb arc. Whedon shows Caleb willingly entering into the First's embrace with his eyes quite literally wide open. Like Marlowe's Faust, Caleb has achieved his desire to know (in his case, to gain knowledge of sin) and even though he is only seeing part of the overall picture, he is content with that simplistic answer. The Bringers, who he refers to as "his boys," have no need for eyes, since they are merely interchangeable cannon fodder, working tirelessly to tip the scales which will permit the First to enter this world in full physical form. And then Whedon has Xander, who has so often been the heart of the Scooby Gang, lose an eye to Caleb, echoing the high price paid by many mythic heroes.

That the character of Caleb is a sadistic woman-hater has been clearly established. He joyfully eviscerates women with a phallic knife, slashing open their abdomens, the location of the womb. He goads Buffy about how Shannon's "polluted blood" has soiled his truck to the point of rendering the vehicle unusable. He degrades women by referring to them as "splits," a clear reference to genitalia that amazingly was able to sneak by Standards & Practices. This devaluing of women to nothing more than the level of sex organs has some interesting echoes in contemporary American society, in which men are often insulted by being identified through female references such as "sissy," "bastard," "son of a bitch," or even "pussy." This dates back centuries: Queen Elizabeth I is said to have chided one of her chancellors for showing disrespect to her by saying, "Had I been born crested rather than cloven, you would not speak to me thus." Like Elizabeth, Whedon's Buffy stands in opposition to wholesale dislike of women. She is repeatedly shown as being at ease with her femininity and (also like Elizabeth), she harbors no secret, hidden desire to be "crested."

Caleb is ultimately defeated by Buffy, although he gives her a strong run for her money. Since Whedon's work is wonderfully circular, Caleb's own slurs come back to defeat him, along with a very sharp, femininely curved Scythe. Refusing to die after being deeply slashed with the Scythe, he taunts Buffy that she can't kill him, since she doesn't have the... Rather than letting him finish the insult, Buffy hacks at his crotch with the Scythe, castrating him with the quip, "Who does, nowadays?" before ripping the blade upward to literally turn him into a "split," a death Whedon has said he found fitting.[17]

Most of us don't have mystical Scythes to fight misogyny. Of course, most of us don't have to face sadistically minded ex-preachers to save the world, either. All of which begs the question — according to Whedon, how do ordinary people — men *and* women — fight this scourge? After examining the degree to which hatred of the female has been entrenched into the foundations of our society, it would appear that we can't; that the game is rigged to ensure the continuation of the status quo. However, that is not the end of the equation, for through Buffy, Whedon has shown us a path that allows us to know that we don't have to fight alone. After all, as the Guardian tries to tell Buffy, the Scythe is a powerful weapon, but it is not her only one.

The First, in one of its final lies, taunts the demoralized Buffy that the Slayer prophecy holds the ultimate Truth for her as it recites the words viewers have memorized over seven years: "Into each generation, a Slayer is born.

She alone... There's that word again. What you are. How you'll die. Alone" ("Chosen" 7.22). The First expects Buffy to accept the "you must be alone" rule because, well, no one has ever thought of challenging that. The First sneers at Buffy's apparent weakness when she leaves Caleb alive in order to save her friends. It is this expectation that "what is, must be" which permits the status quo to remain firmly entrenched. It is the reason why Leah and Rachel gave slave-girls to their husband when they were unable to bear children; why countless generations of Chinese women broke their daughters' feet; why modern Egyptian women mutilate their daughters to deprive them of joy in sexual intercourse; and why you can easily find pro-anorexia websites supporting an American woman's right to self-starvation.

Whedon has Buffy refuse to buy the lies the First is peddling, so there's a poetic beauty in the fact that the First is wearing Buffy's form as it plants the seed of its very destruction. There is a Zen concept that within every problem nestles its solution and these solutions very often lie within us, as opposed to being found beyond us. Buffy has never played by the rules, whether those rules were set by the Watchers or by ancient prophecy. Her ability to forge ahead, smashing expectations of what is proper and acceptable behavior for the Slayer has been remarked upon again and again, but Spike's comment early in Season Two sums it up succinctly: "A Slayer with family and friends. That sure as hell wasn't in the brochure!" ("School Hard" 2.03) Remembering that her strength has always rested in her relationships with others, she reaches the startling conclusion mentioned earlier: if you can't win the game because the game is rigged, change the game. If the problem is that you are alone in the fight, don't be alone any more. So with Willow's help, Buffy gives away what she has always been led to believe makes her unique among her generation. Every Potential becomes a full-fledged Slayer and the battle is won. The battle, yes; but not the war, which like good and evil, is forever ongoing.

Like evil itself, the First is an unkillable foe who has been temporarily vanquished, but it will return again to attempt to regain our dimension once it has formulated a new plan and located another willing vessel such as Caleb. Only by standing together, shoulder to shoulder, can we hope to push back the forces of darkness, which include the foulness of misogyny. In this battle, men must join with women or neither can be full persons. Whedon has said, "When I created Buffy, I wanted to create a female icon but I also wanted to be very careful to surround her with men who not only had no problem with the idea of a female leader but were in fact engaged and even attracted to the idea" ("On the Road"). We may not face the battle armed with a mystical Scythe, but as Whedon has shown us, we don't really need it, provided we have each other.

Conclusion

BUFFY GOES (BACK) TO SCHOOL

If you earn your living as an academic and you also spend a large chunk of your time examining and writing about popular culture, sooner or later you're going to begin to feel as if you're a lone voice crying in the wilderness. While your colleagues may nod sagely if you tell them you're working on a new biography of Charles Dickens or a treatise on the influence of Marxist theory on the Victorian novel, the same reaction does not occur when you excitedly reveal that you're working on a book which delves into the portrayals of belief and the consequences of choice in the work of Joss Whedon. Trust me on this, I know. Therefore, it is absolutely imperative that you take the time to mix with those who also cry in the wilderness. This not only gives you the opportunity to present your work to a critical, thoughtful audience; it also provides an opportunity to access the work that others are doing and realize that other people really do think deeply about this material. In fact, coming back from a Whedon-centric conference such as *Slayage 2*, I began to feel that, far from being a lone voice in the wilderness, the woods were downright crowded!

However, as I was putting together this book, I came to the startling realization that I didn't want to write about Buffy. Now this was a puzzlement to me — Buffy is, after all, the queen of Whedon's work and there is so very much to discuss about her. After all, Buffy saves the world on a near-weekly basis, even dying twice, yet still emerges in this world to fight for those who cannot. After studying my reluctance, I came to the conclusion that so much brilliant work has already been done on Buffy that I would prefer to concentrate on some of the lesser-discussed characters, such as Melaka Fray and Doyle.

But you can't simply ignore Buffy, especially in a book that focuses on Whedon's lessons and the mythos of Western Christianity.[1] Up to this point, all the material in this text has consisted of thoughts, observations, and (hopefully) supportable theories. Partway through drafting the manuscript, I became passionately interested in how Buffy (both the character and the show) would translate in a real-world setting. Could I take the theories and present them to students—both established fans of the show and non-fans who had an interest in the positions I was taking? This is the true challenge of the academic study of popular culture in a nutshell: can fans be persuaded to look more deeply into the text and can non-fans be coaxed to care about the text at all? Well, there comes a time when theories just have to be tested, so I decided to assemble a proposal for a short course and suggest that it be offered as a continuing education class.

I knew I wanted to keep the focus on *Buffy* and that the show would provide an overabundance of material, so my first challenge was to decide what to cover in such a limited time frame. How could I introduce so many characters and relationships to a new viewer and still have the show seem cohesive and relevant without showing every episode? I also knew I wanted to focus on the broad concepts of heroic morality as being based in some idea of faith—whether that was faith in a Divine creator, or faith in humanity, or faith in the idea that this life can be something finer and better than what it currently is, or faith in something completely different didn't really matter. Key to the course would be the notion that one's particular idea of faith could transmute and change. Finally, I narrowed my initial desire to teach what I was beginning to understand was a sort of a "*Buffy* Grand Unified Theory of Everything" down to something that was marginally manageable for a four-week course.

I received invaluable assistance as I was putting the course proposal together from both Diane Wilson, who created a wonderful outline for a much-lengthier course called "The Unitarian Slayer" and from Dr. Rhonda Wilcox, who led a workshop on the gut-wrenching Season Five episode "The Body" that I was fortunate enough to attend at the Popular & American Culture Associations in the South Conference in 2006. Both were kind enough to respond favorably to my requests to incorporate parts of their materials into the class, which was enthusiastically backed by the Powers That Be at my college.

I knew there were some closeted *Buffy* fans in the area, but I especially wanted students who were intrigued by the ideas I was proposing to study, but who were not familiar with the show itself. Of course, I was also concerned about how these two groups might interact. It was either going to be a glorious ride or an absolute train wreck and I wasn't at all sure which was more likely. Buffy may have gone to college back in Season Four, but would college come to Buffy?

I needn't have worried. Throughout the four weeks the course met, discussion was lively between the established fans and the curious not-yet-fans. Responses were animated and discourse didn't stop at the classroom door. I discovered that two of my "non-fans" were setting up a "Buffy club" to watch all the episodes in order and another student had decided to switch his research paper topic in his English composition class to something more "Buffy-centric," even going so far as to order four of the essay collections when he got frustrated at not being able to find them locally. (I took in samples every week, but explained that I wasn't running a lending library!) By looking more deeply and critically at the show in order to analyze what was in the frame, non-fans became fans and fans became scholars. Probably the best thing any instructor can hear is, "I never looked at it that way before" and I heard that multiple times. Far from sucking the joy out of the viewing experience, students seemed to truly enjoy seeking out meaning and looking behind the sofa cushions of the narrative to see what loose change was rolling around back there.

So — will college come to *Buffy*? I don't know yet — while other versions of a "Whedon class" have been offered elsewhere, the overall sample is still too small to serve as definitive empirical evidence. But I know there is interest in the texts that goes far beyond, "Spike is *so hot!*"

The journey Whedon will take you on is a very, very interesting one and is one well worth taking, especially if you are willing to occasionally stray from the path. Staying on the path is the way of formulaic plots and lemming-like imitation; qualities Whedon seems to neither demonstrate nor admire. Therefore, it is my hope that what is found within his work will continue to resonate in many diverse areas — economics, aesthetics, philosophy, gender studies, and (of course) film and television studies. It's a big tent, with plenty of room for mavericks of all stripes.[2] While I hope thoughtful academics will continue to closely examine Whedon's work, I also hope his influence is seen outside traditional academia.

Back in the Introduction of this text, I identified the "ABCs" of Whedon's work as being *acceptance, belief,* and *choice*. As I reach the close of this text, I would like to mention a specific example of how Whedon fans embody these ABCs to work toward making this world a better place for all who inhabit it.

In May of 2007, Whedon posted on Whedonesque.com, an Internet site devoted to his work, about his despair over the death by stoning of a young Iraqi girl named Dua Khalil Aswad. Dua (whose name ironically means "prayer" in Arabic) was barbarically executed in a so-called "honor killing" in which a family's besmirched "honor" is restored by spilling the blood of the disgraced family member. What made this particular killing so especially repugnant to Whedon was the fact that it was all captured on cell phone cameras for later sharing with those who missed the supposed fun. Part of his post read:

> I have never had any faith in humanity. But I will give us props on this: if we can evolve, invent and theorize our way into the technologically magical, culturally diverse and artistically magnificent race we are and still get people to buy the idiotic idea that half of us are inferior, we're pretty amazing. Let our next sleight of hand be to make that myth disappear [Whedon "Let's Watch a Girl"].

Now, I personally think Whedon has a great deal of faith in humanity, so I'm willing to chalk that portion of the past up to a momentary and understandable feeling of hopelessness when faced with the enormity of the misogyny that permeates human cultures. It's difficult to decide to take a stand on any issue this large. However, we all can *choose* to do so. We can all *accept* that our families are larger than mere biological ties and we can all *believe* in our ability to make the world a better place through our actions and efforts. Whedon fans chose to take a stand.

Whedon has credited his mother, the late Lee Stearns, as being a huge influence on his life and work (Havens 6). Stearns was also a strong influence on many people outside her immediate family. One of her former students, Jessica Neuwirth, co-founded Equality Now in 1992, a group which exists to address issues that were not included as part of the agenda of other human rights organizations, such as human trafficking, honor killings, and female genital mutilation ("Frequently Asked Questions"). Whedon was known to support the work of the charity so, when a group of *Firefly/Serenity* fans (known as "Browncoats") in Portland, Oregon were considering how to get *Serenity* back on the big screen at the end of 2005, the idea of a charity screening was born (Dundas). Thanks to the Internet, the idea spread like wildfire, albeit a well-organized one.

In 2006, charity screenings of *Serenity* were held in dozens of cities spread across three continents and in excess of $65,000 was raised for Equality Now ("2006 Screenings"). Pleased with their efforts and perhaps spurred on by awareness of Dua's horrific murder, global Browncoats upped the ante for the 2007 screenings. As of this writing, the worldwide tally for the 2007 screenings stands in excess of $114,000 ("Amount Raised"). In addition to these fund-raising efforts, Whedon got in on the act, auctioning himself off as a dinner guest at San Diego's 2007 Comic-Con, with all proceeds earmarked for Equality Now. The final tally for the auction (which included five dinner guest spots as well as some nigh-impossible-to-attain collectibles) exceeded $60,000 (Cabri).

None of this negates the fact that Dua Khalil Aswad was viciously murdered by the very people who should have been her protectors and that her murder was recorded by the rabid mob who joined to participate in her execution. However, through the efforts of the *Firefly/Serenity* fanbase, many, many more people have been made aware of the existence both of honor killings and of organizations that fight to halt them.

Perhaps the light shining out from these efforts is only a flickering candle in the midst of a very dark night. It's easy to despair that the winds of cruelty have blown out the fragile spark put forth by humanity's nobler impulses, but I have to think that we are stronger than the darkness. Whedon's characters, from Book to Angel to Buffy herself, sometimes question whether redemption is possible for them. It is, for we're all worth saving. However, that is only true if we are willing to take action and not allow the seductive darkness to overwhelm us. In the end, as Whedon reminds us again and again, it's not what we carry in our blood that makes us worthwhile. It's what we choose to do.

Chapter Notes

Author's Note

1. Lawyers have to have notes. It's a thing. This one is to let you know that, at the time, I was also familiar with the fertile octogenarian, the officious intermeddler, and a host of other characters that you, tender reader, are most glad to avoid.

2. And yes, we both passed the bar examination.

Introduction

1. Joss Whedon is the grandson of John Whedon, who wrote for *The Donna Reed Show* and *The Andy Griffith Show* and the son of Tom Whedon, who wrote for shows such as *Alice* and *Benson* (Havens 3).

2. For example, the Virgin Mary was never to be portrayed barefoot. (Heins 170).

3. No doubt it would be flippant of me to point out any similarities between the Church's behavior in this desire for total control of the faithful and the behavior of the Alliance in the *Firefly/Serenity* 'verse. I'm sure there's nothing to it.

4. Both works hang in New York's Metropolitan Museum of Art and are considered among the height of artistic achievements of the Enlightenment. *The Toilet of Venus* (painted by François Boucher in 1751) has been denounced for depicting bestiality and nudity for its inclusion of naked cherubs and a nude Venus cradling a dove to her breast. *The Death of Socrates* (painted by Jean-Louis David in 1787) has come under attack for depicting assisted suicide and homosexuality due to the placement of a man's hand on Socrates' thigh (McWilliams 751).

5. As McWilliams notes, these somewhat bizarre etchings could more accurately be titled *Naked Man, Naked Woman, and Four Naked Children Writhing in the Water and on a Wet Rock* and *Selected Body Parts of an Attractive Young Woman Being Examined by Four Men Prior to Being Eaten by Dogs* (McWilliams 588).

6. An example of "cultural gatekeepers" in America can be found in the Hays Code, which was used for decades to regulate the content of motion pictures in the United States. Among the restrictions codified in the Hays Code were prohibitions against using ministers "as comic characters or villains" and showing any religious faith in a light that invited ridicule. Whedon has shattered both of these restrictions.

7. Among the touching moments contained in *Dogma* is the observation made by a celestial Muse to Bethany that people nowadays "don't celebrate your faith. You mourn it" and among the hilarious twists is the decision of the Catholic Church to retire the crucifix as "too depressing" and replace it with the more upbeat "Buddy Christ."

8. *See* http://en.wikipedia.org/wiki/Garth_Ennis. I know of no other mass produced comic series that is so totally and completely *not* for children! However, as an adult, I view Garth Ennis' work in this series as both brilliant and thought-provoking.

9. Regarding the above-referenced charges, many sources are available. One of the most helpful and thoughtful I found can be accessed at http://rogerebert.suntimes.com.

Chapter 1

1. As well as discovering that Sunnydale apparently has a large, foreboding castle that no one has ever noticed before. Talk about uncontrolled growth!

2. In the dream, Tara also tells Buffy that, "You think you know ... what's to come ... what you are. You haven't even begun." This cryptic warning applies not only to Buffy, but also to Dawn, as the series continues to progress and lives continue to unfold in some very unexpected ways.

3. But no one gets turned into a cricket, so that's something.

4. The Disney version is based on the Charles Perrault tale *The Princess of the Sleeping Wood*. It should be noted that in the Perrault version, "Dawn" is the name of the daughter of the unnamed princess, not the name of the princess herself. *See Tales from Perrault* as translated by Ann Lawrence.

5. It is interesting to note that Glory and Dawn mirror in each other in some important ways. Glory is on the wrong side of a locked door; Dawn is the Key. Also, both are non-human entities and, while only Dawn is in the physical form of a teenager, Glory often acts like a spoiled adolescent, demanding that the very fabric of the universe bend to suit her whims.

6. This is not a foolproof solution. Those who are "outside reality" (such as the clairvoyant or the insane) see Dawn in her natural state — that of a glowing globe of energy. This is shown in Season Five episodes such as "Real Me" (5.02) or "Listening to Fear" (5.09). Also in "Listening to Fear," Joyce, the putative mother of Dawn, can see that Dawn is not truly her daughter when Joyce is adversely affected by a brain tumor.

7. With Dawn, the typical teen lament of "Well, I never asked to be born!" takes on a whole new poignancy. And I'm not even getting into the Ben as host/Glory as parasite discussion that plays a part in Season Five. In fact, Season Five takes Whedon's skills at misdirecting his audience to a higher level as, for at least part of the season, Dawn can be read as quite possibly being the concealed "Big Bad" of the season.

8. While many faiths have traditions that consider the mentally ill to be in some way "touched by God," it is doubtful that Glory's "brain drains" are what the faithful had in mind. *See* http://news.bbc.co.uk/1/hi/health/321622.stm for a discussion of the Islamic view on this topic and http://www.saintjohnofgod.org/sjog_story/story.php for a Catholic view.

9. Whedon's Dawn therefore can be seen as a continuation of a noble science fiction tradition of non-human sentient beings. One example of this tradition are the "replicants" from Ridley Scott's classic film *Blade Runner*, which is based on Philip K. Dick's novel *Do Androids Dream of Electric Sheep?* By being outside the usual human experience to the point of being "born" in such an unusual way, Dawn also fits neatly into the template provided by classical mythology and seen in figures such as Athena and Aphrodite. In Christianity, this concept is seen in the virgin birth of Christ.

10. Buffy's relationship with Dawn often seems to be more mother-child than that of sisters, especially following the tragic death of Joyce, the matriarch of the Summers clan, a heartbreaking event which takes place towards the end of Season Five. In fact, in Season Seven, Principal Wood initially mistakes Buffy for Dawn's mother. When you consider that the monks used some of Buffy's blood to give Dawn her physical form, this seems apt, for in a way, Buffy *is* Dawn's mother.

11. As Spike puts it, "'Cause it's always got to be blood.... Blood is life ... Course it's her blood" ("The Gift" 5.22).

12. Significantly, Buffy's attitude will change. In "Grave," (6.22), Buffy will tell Dawn that "I don't want to protect you from the world. I want to show it to you."

13. In a similar fashion, the Gospels of both Matthew and Luke recount the story of Jesus retreating to the harshness of the Judean desert where he was tempted by the Devil for the span of forty days and nights. Apparently, it is a common theme for great spiritual leaders to isolate themselves and be tempted by the promise of an easier path before beginning their ministries. *See* Matt. 4:1–11 and Luke 4:1–13.

14. The record is silent on whether or not the "street called Straight" was also narrow.

15. While "Saul" is a name with Jewish origins — Saul was the name of the first king of Israel — "Paul" is a Romanized name meaning "small." *See* "The Apostle Formerly

Known as Saul" on www.thirdmill.org. This new name could be a indication of Paul's feeling that he is merely a vessel for the spirit of the Lord and as such, a "small thing." Or maybe not. The writings attributed to Paul have always been heavily influential on the development of the Christian Church, including being a primary driving force behind the Reformation of the sixteenth century (Renard 127). Paul's conversion experience is a major point in the development of the early Church, and accounts can also be found in Acts 22:6–21 and 26:12–18, as well as in Gal. 1:12–16.

16. In fact, the Eightfold Path can be summed up as consisting of rightness of understanding, purpose, speech, conduct, vocation, effort, alertness, and concentration. *See* Burtt 4.

17. Certainly Buffy is shown to be distraught at being forcibly returned to this world by the actions of her friends in the beginning of Season Six. Far from rescuing her from a hell dimension, viewers learn that Buffy was at peace, enjoying an afterlife that she likens to Heaven. One central theme of Season Six involves Buffy's reconciling herself to life back here on earth, where "everything is ... hard, and bright, and violent" ("After Life" 6.03). Dawn is not the only one in Season Six who has to make some hard choices. Ultimately, Buffy chooses to live, rather than merely exist, and it is significant that she claws her way out of her grave alone in the dark at the beginning of Season Six, but re-enters the world in sunlight accompanied by Dawn in the final episode of the season.

18. Sure, she uses it on Xander in "End of Days" (7.21) rather than on the hordes of hell, but it's understandable. Xander was obeying Buffy's directive to drive himself and Dawn out of the coming battle so Buffy wouldn't be distracted worrying about their safety. Dawn's having none of this by the last few episodes of Season Seven and tasers Xander.

19. As Principal Snyder puts it in "Band Candy" (3.06), "Summers, you drive like a spaz!" The relationship between Buffy and cars doesn't really improve. After Dawn tasers Xander, she switches to the driver's seat and heads back to Sunnydale.

20. Which will earn him an eye-gouging from the psychotic ex-priest, Caleb, before the end of the season. This is a significant event which is discussed in greater detail in the final section of this book.

21. Indeed, with the advent of the "Season Eight" comics scripted by Whedon that began publication in March of 2007, the story of Dawn and the rest of the Scooby Gang continues to be told. Already it is clear that Whedon has (ahem) *big* plans for Dawn.

Chapter 2

1. It should not be considered accidental that Dawn is working on an art assignment dealing with "negative space" when Buffy arrives to break the news of their mother's sudden death in the heartbreaking episode "The Body" (5.16), as discussed by Kaveney (79).

2. Of course, humans exist who override this "moral compass," such as Caleb in Season Seven or psychopathic killers such as Ted Bundy in life outside Whedon's created worlds.

3. These same biblical passages are used by members of the Watch Tower Bible and Tract Society to justify the refusal of blood transfusions. Members of this faith are more popularly known as Jehovah's Witnesses. *See* http://www.jw-media.org/medical/medical_care.htm.

4. Angel was turned into a vampire by Darla, while Spike was turned by Drusilla, who had been turned by Angel. For a time, the quartet of vampires live together as a family, albeit one that has broken every taboo, including that of incest as Spike and Angel both have passionate love affairs with the women who "mothered" them into Unlife.

5. The fact that Liam is Irish while William is English is a subject that is worthy of deep examination in terms of Anglo-Irish relations, but is, unfortunately, beyond the scope of this chapter.

6. Buffy seizes on an outdated fashion sense to identify the vampires in a crowd, proof that it's just hard for the Undead to move beyond their own time period. As she tells one vampire, "Okay, first of all — what's with the outfit? Live in the now, okay? You look like Debarge!" ("Welcome to the Hellmouth" *Buffy* 1.01)

7. A vampire may be "sired" by either a male vampire or a female vampire; the term is gender-neutral. In this way, the term "sire" takes on more of a parent or "master" connotation. Although the latter term is not gender-neutral, it does indicate a power hierarchy.

8. In keeping with Whedon's thoughtful naming of his characters, it is worthwhile to

note that "Drusilla" is the name of the favorite sister of the crazed Roman emperor Caligula. It is also the name of Caligula's daughter by his fourth wife. The little girl was said by the Roman historian Suetonius to be prone to attack her playmates and attempt to claw out their eyes. There is also a brief mention of a "Drusilla" in the book of Acts, in which she comes with her husband to hear the preaching of St. Paul.

9. By having this scene take place in a church confessional, Whedon underscores his belief that religion offers very little practical assistance in most matters. By having Angelus pose as a concerned priest, viewers see the ultimate in negativity—a priest who has foresworn good to embrace evil. Whedon will return to this concept in Season Seven of *Buffy* with his creation of Caleb, who is discussed in the final section of this book.

10. While the bread and the wine of communion is generally regarded to be a metaphorical consumption of the body and blood of Christ, ingested in a gesture of remembrance of His suffering and death, transubstantiation (the belief that the bread and wine become the *actual* body and blood of Christ) is dogma within the Roman Catholic faith. *See* Panati 174.

11. The power of Christian symbols to act as "vampire repellent" gives rise to a comedic moment in the *Buffy* episode "Passion" (2.17) when Willow muses on her Jewish father's likely reaction to her protective measures. When Buffy asks if Willow's actions will really bother him, she replies, "Ira Rosenberg's only daughter nailing crucifixes to her bedroom wall? I have to go to Xander's house just to watch *A Charlie Brown Christmas* every year."

12. When a horde of vampires take over a church in "Who Are You?" (*Buffy* 4.16) one exclaims, "It's hard to believe. I've been avoiding this place for so many years, and it's nothing!" In another twist on the traditional vampire mythos, Whedon's vampires also can move about during the day, although full, direct sunlight can severely injure them.

13. Although this is an ancient belief, dating back at least to the time of the Greeks (*see* Bunson 64), Whedon has stated that he was unaware of this origin myth for vampires. *See* Golden 90.

14. Anya is a good example of this. In "Selfless" (*Buffy* 7.05), Anya has reverted back to her previous status of vengeance demon. She seeks to have her mentor, D'hoffryn, undo the horrible effects of a curse she caused and discovers that the price is the "life and the soul" of a vengeance demon. Anya thinks D'hoffryn means to kill her, but the price is higher than that and her friend, Halfrek, is sacrificed instead.

15. Settled, yes; assimilated, no. To this day, the Rom maintain allegiance far more to internal clan designations than to countries.

16. Whistler is not the only "good demon" Whedon creates. Demons, it turns out, are much like humans—you can't paint them all with the same brush. Doyle, another good demon who serves as Angel's guide for a time, is the focus of a later chapter of this book.

17. This is "white magic" (a spell used to produce a positive effect) utilized by Willow which has very dark results. It's all in the timing and, in this case, the road to Hell truly was paved with good intentions. Willow continues to use magic throughout *Buffy* and continues to have some very uneven results.

18. Whedon has commented that Dickens is among his favorite writers and indeed, much of Dickens' serialized style can be seen in Whedon's long, intricately plotted story arcs. *See* Havens 41 as well as the Introduction of this book.

19. As Angelus, he would occasionally leave sketches of his victims behind to taunt and terrify the survivors. This is memorably shown in the episode "Passion" (*Buffy* 2.17) in which Angelus carefully sets the scene in Giles' apartment with rose petals, champagne and the soaring strains of Puccini, all designed to lead Giles upstairs to the bedroom, where Jenny Calendar's still-cooling corpse is arranged in bed. As an extra souvenir, Angelus has left behind a sketch of her dead body with its blankly staring eyes.

20. He is quite delighted to discover that the chip does not prevent him from harming demons. As long as he gets to hit something, Spike is usually satisfied.

21. This is not the first time the fickle Drusilla has left Spike. In addition to being Angelus' lover, there was also a chaos demon in South America.

22. A turn of events that Angel feels is patently unfair. As he puts it, "Fair? You ask for fair? You asked for a soul; I didn't. It almost killed me. I spent a hundred years trying to come to terms with infinite remorse. You spent three weeks moaning in a basement and then you were fine! What's fair about that?" ("Just Rewards" *Angel* 5.02)

23. The title of the episode—"Beneath

You"—is itself a reference to the way both Cecily and Buffy have referred to William/Spike. Both have rejected him by claiming that he is "beneath" them and therefore unworthy of their affections.

24. Angel's assistant Winifred ("Fred") Burkle would say that it doesn't matter; that prophecies are mere guidelines. As she put it so eloquently in "Offspring" (*Angel* 3.07), "Can I say something about destiny? Screw destiny!... Destiny is just another word for inevitable and nothing's inevitable as long as you stand up, look it in the eye and say, 'You're evitable!'" It's safe to assume that Fred is not a big believer in the Calvinist view of predestination.

25. Whedon stated in the commentary track to "Chosen" (*Buffy* 7.22) that it is Spike's soul that both elevates and kills him. It's a sacrifice Spike makes willingly, just as Buffy made hers in Season Five. Then again, Buffy "saved the world. A lot." It says so right on her tombstone.

Chapter 3

1. Other examples of twinning utilized by Whedon include the *Buffy* episode "The Replacement" (5.03) in which Xander is split into two separate individuals. One retains his more self-doubting, immature characteristics while the other exhibits his more confident, adult characteristics. Much of the episode centers on Xander's subsequent internal grappling to determine which is the "real" Xander. Interestingly enough, Nicholas Brendon, the actor who played Xander, is an identical twin. His brother (who goes by the stage name Kelly Donovan) was cast as the "other" Xander. Also, in *Serenity*, the crime bosses Fanty and Mingo are played by identical twins Yan and Rafael Feldman.

2. Whedon has a deep and abiding adoration for Kitty Pryde. This desire for the representation of "girls who can fight [and] stand up for themselves" was a driving force behind the creation of the character of Buffy Summers. *See* the "Foreword" to the collected issues of *Fray* for additional details.

3. In a lovely metanarrative nod, one of the Slayers in training is seen in issue #3 of the new *Buffy* comic reading a copy of *Fray*.

4. While *Maus* focuses on the Holocaust and its aftermath on Spiegelman's family, it is not the only instance of comics being used to document and convey contemporary (and often horrific) events that seem to defy understanding. Interested readers may benefit from reading Joe Kubert's *Fax from Sarajevo*, which recounts one family's experiences during the siege of that city or Spiegelman's *In the Shadow of No Towers*, which is a heartrending account of 9/11. Of course, this method of handling serious issues in a visual medium predates the contemporary comic book. For example, consider Hogarth's engravings of *The Harlot's Progress* and *The Rake's Progress* made in the 1730s.

5. It may be that this immediacy of information found in the visual explains the existence of the MPAA, while books (at least those without pictures) are free from such ratings.

6. Maybe it was destiny for me to write this particular chapter. As I was conducting my research, I discovered that, apart from "Dale Arden" of *Flash Gordon* fame (who I already knew about), Dale Conner Ulrey had been the second artist to work on the long-running strip *Mary Worth* and that Dale Messick was the creator of the comic strip *Brenda Starr*. *See* Horn's *Women in Comics*, v. 3. It appears that comics and "girl-Dales" go together nicely. I am honored to continue the trend.

7. While all of Shakespeare is considered part of the canon of Western literature, not all of Shakespeare's plays are routinely taught in school. Notably missing from the standard curriculum is *Titus Andronicus*, which contains the magnificently morbid stage directions "Enter Lavinia, her hands cut off, and her tongue cut out, and ravished" and later "Enter a Messenger with two heads and a hand." Quentin Tarantino should take note. Of course, it should not escape mention that Shakespeare's plays fit well within the definition of popular culture of his time and violence and sex sold quite well in Elizabethan England.

8. The Internet, with its staggering amount of freely available information, is likewise viewed with suspicion by these self-appointed cultural watchdogs.

9. Some stories list Castor and Clytemnestra's parents as Leda and Zeus, while attributing the parentage of Pollux and Helen to Leda and her earthly husband, Tyndareus, although Helen's unearthly beauty would seem more likely to result from a liaison with a god. It will get much more tangled and quite bloody before it's all over. If invited to a family reunion of this clan, find something else to do that day.

10. A case in point is Iphigenia, Agamemnon's daughter with Clytemnestra. Iphigenia was sacrificed to Artemis by her father both as a penance and in order to obtain a favorable wind to Troy. *See* Wolverton 86.

11. I am indebted to both the Campbell and Moyers text *The Power of Myth* and a Website operated by the Maricopa Community Colleges which details the steps of Campbell's hero's journey (which can be accessed at www.mcli.dist.maricopa.edu) for portions of this section.

12. "Erin" is also a traditional name for the country of Ireland. By using this name, Whedon is continuing to showcase the influence Irish themes and names have in his work. As just two examples of this, consider that Angel was born and raised in Galway and that Angel's original connection to the Powers That Be was a half-Irish/half-demon named Doyle.

13. Whistler in *Buffy*, for example. Whedon distrusts simple math such as "demon = bad." His moral equations are more complex and often require a calculator, preferably one with sine functions.

14. While this would seem to be at odds with the finale of *Buffy* in which all Potential Slayers are gifted with the full talents of "the" Slayer, Whedon glosses over that point. *Fray* is set in a post-apocalyptic world where the order and structure of Watchers and Slayers has been replaced by sharp divisions between the haves and have-nots and that's enough explanation for him.

15. It's not unusual for the so-called "normal" character to act violently when war is brought to the doorstep. After all, in *High Noon*, Grace Kelly plays a Quaker who shoots a man in the back to protect Gary Cooper.

16. Although it's actually far more gory than that.

17. Vampires didn't kill Loo — they have to be invited inside a dwelling. I told you Fray filed that information away, but she needed to fight her war before acting on her hard-won knowledge.

Chapter 4

1. Jes Battis' *Blood Relations: Chosen Families in "Buffy the Vampire Slayer" and "Angel"* provides a wonderful starting point for any student of Whedon's family structures.

2. Mal's conflict between seeking peace and presenting himself as a stone-cold criminal is examined in much greater depth in the next section of this book.

3. A large part of Mal's character development is centered on his gradual change from this attitude toward one that is far more accepting of people on their *own* terms.

4. *Star Trek*'s captains tend to fall into this archetype. In fact, there is an insightful (and hilarious) essay comparing the *Enterprise* crew to the crew of *Serenity* by Roxanne Longstreet Conrad contained in the Jane Espenson-edited collection *Finding Serenity*.

5. It's a close race, but the title of "most innocent" probably goes to Kaylee by a nose.

6. This was especially true for female pilots, who were commonly called "aviatrixes" in the early days of powered flight. Beryl Markham and Amelia Earhart were certainly figures of admiration, but they also shattered the mold of conventional female behavior into unrecognizable shards.

7. Remember "War Stories" (1.10) and the moment of "Zoe's Choice"?

8. Religious faith is not an option for River, who is seen "correcting" Shepherd Book's Bible to rid it of logical fallacies in "Jaynestown" (1.07).

9. Why Mal returns for the Tam siblings is discussed at greater length in the final section of this book.

10. Indeed, great trouble results when River and Simon attempt to leave the ship in an effort to protect the rest of the family from the pursuit of the Alliance in the film *Serenity*.

11. This system is not perfect. The sadistic crime lord Niska does not wear a hat, nor does the Operative.

12. He is also shown delightedly brushing Helen's hair. Helen is the prostitute he picks out at the Heart of Gold. He also remains with the same girl throughout the crew's time at the brothel.

13. While never specifically mentioned in a show, this is Gina Torres' idea and it is a lovely explanation for why viewers always see this necklace on Zoe after the war. *See Firefly: The Official Companion* 1:40.

14. Sadly, viewers only see Zoe wearing "slink" as she carries a funeral taper to her husband's gravesite.

15. I can only assume that in the *Firefly* 'verse, any sort of hyphenated ethnic identifier has long gone the way of the dodo. If there is no "America" (a reasonable assumption since the past tense is used to refer to "Earth-That-Was"), there could not be "African-

Americans," "Chinese-Americans," "Irish-Americans," or any other such ilk.

16. The Simon/River dynamic is one of the very few positive "blood family" relationships in Whedon's work. Biological family is often shown to be a negative influence on its members. For example, Tara is told from childhood that she is destined to become a demon on her twentieth birthday and is protected from her biological family by the Scoobies, who are themselves primarily single children from distant, dysfunctional family structures. Willow's parents don't pay attention to the fact that their daughter has dyed her hair and begun the study of witchcraft, Xander's parents bicker so harshly that he sleeps outside every Christmas Eve, and Cordelia's parents neglect to pay their taxes, thereby putting the family's security at risk.

17. Then again, it could be out of jealousy. Kaylee's never given Jayne the sort of attention she longs to give Simon.

18. Book's shadowy past and his heroic efforts to live a peaceful life are detailed in a chapter in the next section of this book and will therefore not be discussed fully here.

19. The Mal/Book relationship is also discussed more fully in subsequent chapters.

20. In fact, as Mal shows off the ship to Zoe and explains his plans to use the vessel to remain free of the influence of the Alliance, part of his plans involve hiring a cook ("Out of Gas" 1.08).

21. A television show listed among the writing credits of John Whedon, the grandfather of Joss Whedon (Havens 3).

Chapter 5

1. Actually, Angel is guided by two "good demons." The first is Whistler, who seeks Angel out when the soul-filled vampire is still wandering aimlessly through his Unlife, wracked by guilt and remorse. In an effort to make Angel a force for good, Whistler takes Angel to Los Angeles to observe Buffy, who has just been called to be the Slayer. The experience causes Angel to rouse himself from his overwhelming despair and get involved in the human world ("Becoming, Part One" *Buffy* 2.21). In the second part of this episode, Whistler is the one who convinces Buffy to take the necessary action to halt the evil Angelus. In addition to both being "good demons," both Whistler and Doyle seem to share the same fashion sense, including an affinity for loud bowling shirts and questionable hats. The clothes hound hellgod Glorificus would probably have them both flayed for their lack of style.

2. Think of the floppy-eared Clem who seems cuddly, but includes kittens in his diet.

3. Attempts to equate The Powers That Be with God are met with this rather coy response from Whedon: "We keep it vague for a reason. If people want to believe it's God, we're not going to say it's not any more than we're going to say it is" (qtd. in Golden 4).

4. In another example of Whedon's fun with gender-based names, Doyle also has a lovely blonde wife (later his ex-wife) named "Harriet" who he consistently refers to as "Harry." She is the only one to call Doyle by his given name of Francis, who Doyle seems to regard as someone he once was, but is no longer. This is explored in greater depth further in the chapter.

5. The parallels between the Scourge and groups devoted to so-called "ethnic cleansing" are both obvious and intentional. In particular, the portrayal of the jackbooted, militaristic Scourge has strong echoes with Nazis. This comparison grows stronger when the viewer sees the half-blood Lister demons in "Hero" (1.09) hiding in secret compartments in the basement and running desperately to escape the country, much as European Jews did during the time of the Third Reich.

6. Although beyond the scope of this chapter, it is worth noting that the half-Irish Doyle is guilty here of violating the ancient Celtic law of hospitality, which obliged all to extend food, drink, entertainment, and a bed to any who appeared on their doorstep, regardless of the guest's social status, destination, or even identity. In fact, the failure to extend suitable hospitality was considered an embarrassment and was punishable by a "blush fine." *See* http://www.ancientworlds.net/aw/Article/617978.

7. Although both Joshua and the child Samuel appear to come through these encounters unscathed. *See* Josh. 1:1–9 and 4:1–7 as well as 1 Sam. 3:1–14.

8. Fever dreams, if you ask me, but dreams in any event. Also worthy of note is the fact that Matthew recounts that the wife of Pontius Pilate has a dream about Jesus that is so vivid that she attempts to dissuade her husband from having anything to do with his trial (Matt. 27:19). Her efforts are, of course, futile.

9. Interestingly, in this way, Doyle can also be considered to be filling a traditional woman's role in a patriarchal society. Of course, as a half-demon, Doyle is a constant outsider. Humans fear the demon; demons distrust the human. Doyle's best fit comes with the other "misfit toys" like Angel, who has a foot in two worlds, but feels comfortable in neither. If only he'd met Lorne...

10. The effects of the visions are bad enough for the half-demon Doyle; they will nearly kill the human Cordelia when the visions are passed on to her. Cordelia will ultimately make the choice to become part demon herself in order to withstand the pain, rationalizing that the usefulness of the information contained in the visions is worth the cost. "Cordelia" is also the name of King Lear's youngest daughter, the one who is disinherited for speaking the bald truth, instead of syrupy, sugar-coated flatteries. Whedon again shows his strong grounding in the classics by giving this name to Angel's often-tactless friend and occasional office manager.

11. It's a lovely legend of the power of non-violence, but in fact never occurred. No order for Danish Jews to ever wear the loathsome symbol was ever issued by the Nazi command. *See* http://www.snopes.com/history/govern/denmark.htm. However, the Danes did make an organized effort to transport their Jewish citizens to the safety of Sweden, so the spirit of the legend is true, even if the specific details have been romanticized.

12. Of course, Angel has a similar motivation, although in Angel's case, he spent a century actively causing the terror and mayhem to the sort of innocents he now seeks to protect. Again, his are sins of *commission*, as opposed to Doyle's sins of *omission*.

13. The effort fails. Doyle, it seems, is not even a good gate-crasher. In a way, this is another echo with the problems of the "good vampire" Angel, who cannot enter a home without the express invitation of the owner.

14. Doyle has an overabundance of Irish charm. As viewers learn, it's not an unadulterated gift, as charm can often be a type of curse.

15. He also gives Cordelia the kiss of a lifetime, as the power to receive the visions are transferred to her by The Powers That Be. Perhaps this is a sign that Doyle has been released from his service; that his atonement is complete.

Chapter 6

1. I have wondered if over the years, Mal has ever even fleetingly thought that he would have preferred to be standing just slightly off to the side at this moment. Readers of the *Serenity: The Official Visual Companion* learn a bit about the immediate aftermath of the war. Suffice it to say that the few remaining Browncoats were not sent home with forty acres and a mule.

2. There is a quote in Boris Pasternak's *Doctor Zhivago* that fits the post-war Mal very well: "Everything had changed suddenly—the tone, the moral climate; you didn't know what to think, whom to listen to. As if all your life you had been led by the hand like a small child and suddenly you were on your own, you had to learn to walk by yourself" (127).

3. In the film *Serenity*, Mal replies to the Operative's remark that River is "an albatross" by saying, "Way I remember it, albatross was a ship's good luck, til some idiot killed it," effortlessly referencing Coleridge's "The Rime of the Ancient Mariner," a feat which greatly surprises the sophisticated Inara.

4. It is interesting to note that "peacemaker" was also the nickname for the Colt .45 pistol, the so-called "Gun That Tamed the West." Variations on the Colt .45 are common in the *Firefly* 'verse for, while advanced weaponry such as portable lasers exist, they are presented as expensive and unreliable. Traditional firearms, on the other hand, are plentiful and bullets are cheap.

5. The eye rolling previously mentioned would probably escalate if Prov. 22:6 were mentioned. "Train up a child in the way he should go; and when he is old, he will not depart from it." If he were in an uncommonly good mood, Mal might reply, as he did in another situation, "[W]hy don't we just ignore each other, 'til we go away?" ("The Train Job" 1.02)

6. In many ways, River, resting at the bottom of her box, is cast in this role for Mal. Just as in the Greek myth of Pandora, she may be concealed beneath a host of troubles for him, but she also presents him with hope in a better day to come—and one that he will view as worth fighting for.

7. In fairness to Mal, it should be pointed out that all of these admittedly violent acts can be easily justified. Dobson had already shot Kaylee and was currently holding a gun to River's head; Crow had expressed his mur-

derous intentions toward Mal and his crew for Mal's refusal to complete the job Niska had hired him to do; and Jayne had attempted to sell River and Simon out to the Alliance, which Mal took as a personal affront. This instance will be discussed in greater detail later in this chapter.

8. Although outside the scope of this chapter, the brother-sister relationship between Mal and Kaylee is worthy of thoughtful consideration, as she is the only character routinely seen offering affection to and receiving affection from Mal, ranging from her kissing him on the cheek and exclaiming, "I love my Captain" in the pilot episode to Mal kissing her on top of her head in "Our Mrs. Reynolds" (1.06). Many other examples abound, which make this verbal slap of Mal's so stinging.

9. Events detailed in the three-issue comic "Those Left Behind" which bridges the time period between *Firefly* and *Serenity*. While viewers know from "Heart of Gold" (1.13) that Inara has decided to leave the ship, Book's departure is less expected and is discussed in greater detail later in this chapter.

10. There is also a certain irony is the fact that the crew's robbery and the Reaver attack occur during Sunday church services. While the citizens who followed Mal's orders to seek refuge in the vault survive, those attending church are mercilessly butchered. This can be read as another statement by Whedon as to the lack of protection provided by organized religion in the face of violence.

11. I begin to sympathize with Mal's issues regarding organized religion at this point and heartily approve of his solution to the problem posed by the mob and the woodpile. Occam's Razor is often a useful problem-solving tool.

12. Mal refers to the earlier nautical practice of keelhauling traitors, lamenting his lack of a keel. This brutal practice involved trussing the traitor with ropes so that he was unable to swim, then tossing him overboard, where he was hauled either under the ship's keel or "swum" from stem to stern. Either way, the man was generally dead by the time the punishment was complete. *See* http://www.fff.org/freedom/0495a.asp.

13. The actions of her brother Simon are motivated entirely by his desire to rescue River and keep his broken sister safe, no matter the personal cost.

14. Unfortunately, despite all the practice Mal gets with hand-to-hand combat, he never really obtains much in the way of finesse, remaining an effective, yet graceless, bar brawler. The Operative in *Serenity* is his opposite in this regard, fighting with focused skill and smooth grace.

15. From a costuming point, it is interesting to note the contrast between Mal, who is dressed in light tones during the swordfight, and Wing, who is arrayed in dark, somber hues. Mal may be the "bad outsider," but his clothing codes him as the "good guy" in this duel.

16. Also known to viewers as "Yo-Saf-Bridge" for her overabundance of names, which changed depending of which scam she was running at any given time. Her real name, like woman, remains a mystery. Oddly enough, it is from Mal's interactions with Saffron that viewers learn the majority of what is known about his past; specifically, that he hails from a planet called "Shadow," which seems appropriate for a character who is so often depicted as being layered with midtones and darkness contrasting with his lighter, more noble, characteristics.

17. Saffron is far from the wet-behind-the-ears piece of fluff she presents herself to be. When Mal finally catches up with the treacherous vixen, she pays him a backhanded compliment, saying, "You know, you did pretty well. Most men ... they're on me inside of ten minutes. Not tryin' to teach me to be strong and the like" ("Our Mrs. Reynolds" 1.06). Little wonder that Mal often ponders the value of being a good guy.

18. Of course, it can be argued that Mal never has left Serenity Valley and that the battle is the defining moment in his life. What better reason to christen the ship after the decisive battle of a failed war than to ensure that he never has to move beyond that moment? In one of the most beautiful moments of an episode filled to bursting with them, viewers see Mal absently patting one of the overhanging pipes of the ship as if caressing a faithful Labrador as he orders his crew to abandon the ship.

19. The captain of the other ship is a true pirate, complete with a brilliant red sash that stands out in sharp contrast to the greys and browns of the cargo bay where Mal is ambushed. Mal refuses to succumb, despite being shot by the opposing captain. Without a doubt, this is a bloody episode, beginning with Mal entering the frame by crashing to the floor of the cargo bay and the camera almost lovingly following his dripping blood

as it falls through the open grating of the floor. As the episode progresses, viewers see Mal's blood smearing nearly every surface on *Serenity*, symbolizing the depth of sacrifice he is willing to make for this ship.

20. It was love at first sight for Mal. In a flashback scene in "Out of Gas" (1.08), viewers see Mal ignore a barker's patter regarding a larger, quite possibly better, ship as he falls hopelessly in love with the broken grace of the Firefly-class ship that will become *Serenity*.

21. This is during what must be described as the funniest torture scene ever committed to film and yes, I know how sadistic that sounds. It also serves as a testament to the skills of Alan Tudyk and Nathan Fillion that the scene also reads as both inspiring and heartbreaking.

22. Dickens' Ebenezer Scrooge, to serve as one example. A good discussion of the intricacies of the meaning of "agape" can be found at http://mb-soft.com.

23. The "Seven Deadly Sins" have undergone alteration since they were originally proposed in the sixth century C.E. Late in the seventeenth century, the list was codified as listed in the text (Panati 179–180).

24. This comment is in Mandarin in the comic; see http://kernelm.livejournal.com for the English translation of the original Chinese.

25. Nathan Fillion, who played Malcolm Reynolds, has said this regarding the Mal/Book dynamic: "But whenever Book says something to Malcolm Reynolds, Malcolm Reynolds listens.... Book is very knowledgeable about a lot of things. Mal holds a lot of his feelings within him. He doesn't say a lot of who he is or how he is or why he is, nor does Book. That is something that Malcolm sees and doesn't press him about. So if Malcolm had a guide, it was Book" (*Firefly Visual Companion* 2:22). The Mal/Book dynamic is discussed further in the next chapter.

26. It's a beautiful scene, with Mal's darkened face covered in cross-hatched shadows projected by the gridwork, reminiscent of prison bars, as he looks up from his personal well of despair.

27. Malcolm Reynolds shares much with William Wallace in that both men have a central creed that insists that people have an inherent right to decide for themselves how to live and conduct their lives, free from governmental interference into those personal affairs.

28. The thirty million settlers lived on "Miranda," which is named for the daughter of the magician who renounced magic in Shakespeare's *The Tempest*. The planet is located on the outer edge of the "Burnham Quadrant," a reference to Birnam Wood that spelled death and defeat for the mad king Macbeth. Whedon loves his Shakespeare and it shows. The entire "Miranda" plotline takes on a truly frightening resonance when you consider events such as the MK-ULTRA experiments conducted by the Central Intelligence Agency in the 1950s and 1960s. Truth is stranger than fiction, even when it's science fiction.

29. Whedon's Shakespeare influences are in full flower as Mal delivers what can best be described as the "*Serenity* St. Crispin's Day speech" to inspire his crew to back his decision to venture forth and fight rather than cower before overwhelming odds. Prince Hal, meet Mal.

30. Wash's display of plastic dinosaurs is still intact on the console. Memorials take many forms.

Chapter 7

1. Of course, Malcolm Reynolds, the angry skeptic, also possesses these qualities. Whedon never claims that the moral high ground can only be occupied by the traditional, recognizable "good guys."

2. Although that should be taken with a caveat, since viewers learn of this theology through the recitations of the amoral minx Saffron.

3. It is interesting that we meet Book, a believer in the risen God, on a world named for the Queen of the Underworld.

4. In the episode "Heart of Gold" (1.13), Book is explicit about this, commenting that for quite a while he has been "following the footsteps of a carpenter," which is a clear reference to Jesus Christ. Christ referred to himself as a "good shepherd" who would lay down his life for his sheep. *See* John 10:11–16.

5. This is a discovery that the rough-hewn Jayne finds intriguing, albeit in the manner of a sixth-grade boy furtively looking at certain *National Geographic* reports; a sort of oh-God-how-can-people-live-like-that sort of way.

6. While not the Garden of Eden, it seems logical to assume from the quantity and variety of foods brought onboard by the Shepherd that the abbey gardens are lush and

verdant places. At the table, reference is made to both tomatoes (a forbidden fruit during the Middle Ages) and rosemary, which has been associated with remembrance since at least Shakespeare's time and is mentioned in both *Hamlet* and *The Winter's Tale*. Much more regarding food and the communal table of the ship can be found in the previous section of this book.

7. Book also acts in his spiritual role, praying over the injured Kaylee after Simon completes surgery on her. Later, when the crew is discussing just what to do with Dobson, Book stoutly remarks, "I'll not sit by while there's killing here," prompting Jayne to reply, "Shepherd's got a mean streak" ("Serenity" 1.01).

8. Again, it is Jayne who comments on the incongruity of a holy man knowing firearms so intimately. Jayne doesn't buy Book's excuse that the abbey's residents shot rabbits for stew, but doesn't press the issue.

9. "Shan Yu" is also the name of the villain in the 1998 animated Disney film *Mulan*, which was a retelling of a Chinese legend.

10. As he puts it, "[m]en of God make everyone feel guilty and judged." Mal's issues regarding religion are very near the surface here.

11. This continuing mystery sets him apart from other Whedon creations such as the vampires Spike and Angel, who are shown murdering innocents with the unbridled enthusiasm of a Reaver. While both vampires eventually seek redemption for these actions, viewers know exactly how awful their past was; with Book, it's left up to the viewer to fill in the very large blank spaces.

12. While there is no evidence that King Henry II actually cried, "Will no one rid me of this meddlesome priest?" it is an undeniably powerful line, especially when uttered by Peter O'Toole in the film *Becket*.

13. It is beyond ironic that the planet on which Book is murdered is named "Haven." Certainly there is no safety for him there, nor for his adopted flock who are all massacred as part of the Operative's scorched earth policy.

14. It's even better if it's also something smart, but Shepherd Book knows that sometimes you just have to take what you can get.

15. Despite her profession as a Companion, Book and Inara quickly reach a level of respect and peace with one another, beginning with his refusal to lecture her about "the wickedness of her ways" ("Serenity" 1.01).

16. The topsy-turvy dynamic between Shepherd and Companion is seen again in "The Train Job" (1.02) when Book confesses to Inara that he feels worthless aboard the ship. Inara suggests that he pray for the crew's safe return, to which Book comments that he thinks the captain probably wouldn't really like that, since he is well aware of Mal's hostility. With an enigmatic smile, Inara suggests that the Shepherd take a page from her book and just keep it a secret that he prays for Mal, as she does.

17. The wicked plot is exposed and the Jews are saved. The raucous holiday of Purim commemorates these events.

18. Another Whedon creation who represents this "failure to doubt" is the foul misogynist Caleb from *Buffy*'s final season. Caleb is discussed in the final section of this book.

Chapter 8

1. Kendra was called to act as Slayer following Buffy's death at the hands of the Master in Season One. There is speculation that Buffy's death ended her "Slayer line" even though she was quickly resuscitated. Since Buffy is on the KIA list of Slayers, this could explain why no additional Slayers are shown as being "activated" following Buffy's second death in Season Five.

2. The story also echoes the classic Greek myth of Ariadne, who assists Theseus in his quest to slay the Minotaur by providing him with a ball of thread for him to unwind as he traverses the labyrinth so he can find his way out again.

3. Hansel and Gretel are also referenced in the *Buffy* episode "Gingerbread" (3.11) in which a hideous demon tricks the residents of Sunnydale into nearly consigning Buffy, Willow, and Amy to a fiery death. The demon does this by taking on the form of two cherubic children whose apparent deaths in a brutal type of ritual sacrifice have whipped the townspeople into a mindless frenzy of revenge.

4. When I began researching *Hansel and Gretel* for this chapter, I was shocked to discover this — I had convinced myself that the story featured a typical "evil stepmother." Two separate versions of the Grimm tale refer to the maternal figure as the mother of the children, which I contend makes the story that much more horrible.

5. "Charity" is replaced by "love" in some versions. The concept remains the same.

6. Shortly after meeting the Scooby Gang

for the first time, Faith nonchalantly comments that slaying always makes her "hungry and horny" ("Faith, Hope and Trick" 3.03).

7. Faith kills Allan Finch, an aide to Mayor Wilkins. Whedon's attention to detail is evident with even this relatively minor character, whose name is reminiscent of the ultimate good father figure of "Atticus Finch" from Harper Lee's classic novel *To Kill a Mockingbird*.

8. Okay, maybe it's not a "murder" so much as it's "manslaughter." Then again, Faith definitely meant to kill *somebody*. While Finch was just in the wrong place at the wrong time, legally speaking, Faith's premeditated homicide equals "murder." Since the river of denial runs deep in Sunnydale, most jurors probably wouldn't believe that Faith meant to kill an Undead vampire. I would advocate pursuing a vigorous insanity defense at trial.

9. Buffy had also accidentally killed a human before, in the episode "Ted" (2.11). While Ted turned out to not actually be a human, Buffy didn't know that when she used her Slayer strength to cause his death. She had to face the consequences of her actions, and so will Faith, for whom the road will be far rockier.

10. More about Angel/Angelus can be found in the first section of this book.

11. Phil Colvin points out that Faith's redemption cannot be found in Sunnydale which is "a place of absolutes" (21). Taken as a whole, the series *Angel* deals much more with the "Lehane grey" of moral dilemmas than the far stricter binary reading of good/evil which *Buffy* often employs.

12. For instance, Faith identifies the "five basic torture groups" as "blunt, sharp, cold, hot and loud." When Wesley refuses to choose a group, she smashes a picture frame and holds up a jagged shard of the broken glass and announces that they'll move on to sharp.

13. Eliza Dushku has commented of the fascination many viewers have for Faith: "With Faith, one of the things that made her so appealing to people is that she's got all the bad girl attributes. She's next to Buffy, this blonde, blue-eyed, good girl from a good family. And then there's Faith: dark. A 'bad' girl. But then you find that she goes so much deeper than that and that Faith is not just evil. You find that she can change. People were surprised that they could still love Faith and feel compassion and empathy for her after she'd done such awful things. But what we hate most in other people is often what we hate the most about ourselves" (Reiss 164).

14. A great deal of Buffy's rage can be explained by her comment to Faith during another rooftop fight in "Sanctuary" when she states: "I've lost battles before but nobody else has ever made me a victim."

15. Emily Dickinson may have thought the two concepts were linked tightly together when she wrote that "home is the definition of God."

16. Although beyond the scope of this chapter, it is worth noting that, as Faith has walked toward the light, Wesley has been steadily marching into darkness. In the next episode, "Release" (4.14), Wesley is shown to be quite willing to use pain to extract information from a drug-addled human. Faith is repulsed by his actions but Wesley is unwilling to take counsel from the woman who tied him up to inflict unspeakable pain upon him, cutting her off by saying, "This is the part where you tell me you've turned a new leaf, found God, inner peace? We both know that isn't true. You haven't changed. You can't." Even if he is goading her rather than really meaning his words, he does not hesitate to hurl her sins back into her face.

Chapter 9

1. It should be noted that, while there are no extraterrestrial forms of life within *Firefly/Serenity*, the rage-filled Reavers come close to filling that role. It cannot be considered coincidence that the insane mental states of both River and the Reavers are created by Alliance meddling, nor should the similarity in names be dismissed with a casual shrug. As the *Tao* states, "True words resemble their opposites" (78).

2. While much of the discussion in this chapter will center on the events in "Safe," other instances from *Firefly* and *Serenity* will be referred to as well.

3. The Disney version of *Snow White* is frightening enough, but the original source material is truly horrific. For instance, in one version, the evil witch-queen eats what she believes to be Snow White's heart. Later, the seven dwarfs get their revenge by having the queen dance at Snow White's wedding in red hot iron shoes until she falls down dead.

4. Even within the pages of the Bible, not all "witches" are viewed harshly. *See* 1 Sam 28

for the account of King Saul's visit to the so-called Witch of Endor to consult with the spirit of the dead Samuel.

5. Interestingly enough, "the other hand" refers to the left hand (*sinister* in Latin), and a left-handed person has often be considered to be prone to occult activities such as witchcraft and consorting with unclean spirits.

6. The total number of the victims of the "Burning Times" is, of course, subject to speculation. While many were executed publicly through burning, strangulation, or hanging, countless others died in the custody of their inquisitors as a result of the dungeon-like conditions of their prisons or through tortures so foul they cause a compassionate person to shudder when contemplated.

7. Robbins points out that Sprenger was not given a requiem Mass by his university colleagues upon his death in 1495, which may have been due to his death away from Cologne, but may also have been rooted in accusations of academic dishonesty in including a misleading letter in later editions of the *Malleus*. This letter purported to be an official letter of support from the university faculty for the work of the *Malleus* when in fact, only four faculty members signed the letter, which actually contained only very conditional support for parts of the book (340).

8. "[T]he promise to spare her life should be kept for a time, but that after a certain period she should be burned. [Alternatively,] the Judge may safely promise the accused her life, but in such a way that he should afterwards disclaim the duty of passing sentence on her, deputing another Judge in his place" (226).

9. Ireland had very few witch trials— Robbins writes of fewer than ten documented cases from that of Dame Alice to the last case in 1711. However, as late as 1895, the accusation that a woman (Bridget Cleary) was actually a "changeling" was used as a defense to her murder. Bridget's husband was convicted of the crime and sent to prison. He was released in 1910, at which time he emigrated to Canada.

10. There are many informative texts on Joan of Arc. One that readers may find especially helpful is the English translation of *The Trial of Joan of Arc* by Daniel Hobbins.

11. The Hebrew meaning of "Gabriel" is "my strength is God" (Room 198). Gabriel Tam, who abandons his children to retain his social position, utterly fails to live up to his moniker.

12. The first is just after he "unthaws" River—as Simon is cradling her, trying to soothe her down from her obvious hysteria and fright, Mal's question is, "What's this?" (as opposed to "Who's this?") The second occurs when the "Big Damn Heroes" arrive to rescue the Tams in "Safe" as Mal remarks to the mob, "Y'all got something that belongs to us and we'd like it back."

13. Although Mal's hostility towards God and religion has been detailed earlier in this book, I can't help but wonder if he is a fully confirmed member of the Church of the Gun at this point. I'm pretty sure Jayne is an elder in that particular sect.

Chapter 10

1. In one of the bonus commentary tracks on the Season Seven DVD set of *Buffy*, writer Jane Espenson agrees with this position, stating, "This is a show about a woman with power. The perfect ending for this series is this man whose entire reason to exist has to do with denying women power."

2. Later, Mitchem would also play the abominable rapist Max Cady in the 1962 film *Cape Fear*. In the 1991 remake, the religious fanaticism of the Cady character (played by Robert DeNiro) is emphasized through the dialogue and, indeed, the vast array of religious tattoos adorning Cady's body.

3. Just a quick reminder—*Preacher* featured an Irish vampire named Cassidy who was a buddy (and then a betrayer) of Jesse, the reluctant antihero of the series. In addition, several issues of *Preacher* featured a gang of vampire wannabes. *Preacher* was published from 1995 to 2000, and was therefore often running simultaneously with *Buffy*. As Joss Whedon is a self-proclaimed "comics geek," it is only proper to note the similarities in the two works.

4. Although "Dirty Girls," the episode which introduces Caleb to the audience, is credited as being written by Drew Goddard, his commentary states that this "teaser" scene was actually written by Whedon. According to Goddard, Season Seven is a season-long exploration of the ways in which men attempt to take power away from women; a "Big Bad" that squares neatly with the theory that the concept of misogyny is central to Season Seven's "Big Bad."

5. Whether the timing was deliberate or not is subject to speculation; however, the

standard television season is 22 episodes in length and is subject to some degree of flexibility in scheduling. My personal opinion is that the network executives either didn't realize when Holy Week fell in 2003 (Easter is a moveable feast, after all) or they believed that feather-ruffling was inevitable, since the broadcasts of two earlier episodes of *Buffy* had been postponed. The broadcasts of both "Earshot" (3.18) and "Graduation Day, Pt. 2" (3.22) were delayed due to sensitivities over content following the Columbine High School massacre.

6. While Whedon has addressed issues of misogyny before (Tara's family legend of all the women in the family turning into demons (*Buffy* "Family" 5.06) and the *Angel* episode "She" (1.13) for instance), nowhere is the idea of misogyny being the embodiment of evil developed as fully as it is with Caleb.

7. This last is a term that will come back to haunt him.

8. Indeed, in "Earshot" (3.18), Buffy picks up on Giles' thought that "If a fashion magazine told her to, she'd wear cats strapped to her feet."

9. *Firefly*'s Malcolm Reynolds (played by Nathan Fillion, who also portrayed Caleb) would remind us that this is not surprising, since the prerogative of writing history belongs to the winners of any conflict.

10. It appears that Xander was right when he stated in "Dead Man's Party" (3.02) that, "You can't just bury stuff, Buffy. It'll come right back up to get you."

11. Not to mention "black is slimming. Everyone knows that." Vanity, thy name is Caleb.

12. Caleb is right about Buffy's reaction to the "apple," which is the message given to the wounded Shannon that Caleb has something of the Slayer's. Buffy takes the bait and walks her troops smack into disaster. In this instance, Buffy has echoes of Caleb's own desire to seek knowledge — Buffy hates fighting blind. Interestingly enough, the Bringers (who are minions of the First) are portrayed as being without eyes. Minions don't need to know the big picture.

13. Jerry Springer's guests really don't have anything that surprising to share with anyone who has actually *read* the Bible. And I'm not even getting into the Leah-and-the-mandrake-roots story.

14. Don't ask. There's another story in the Apocrypha that involves Peter bringing a smoked tuna fish back to life. Seriously.

15. Women wearing men's clothing is another traditional taboo. In fact, this was one of the chief offenses that caused Joan of Arc to be sentenced to die as a "relapsed heretic," as discussed in the previous chapter. It is interesting to consider that Thecla may now be valued by Paul since she is appearing before him dressed as a male rather than as a "less worthy" female.

16. Interestingly, the very words "testament" and "testify" are derived from the word "testicles." Peter McWilliams goes into this in more detail, stressing the importance of honesty when castration was a punishment for deception (327). Since females lack the requisite part on which honesty was sworn, a woman's testimony was nearly valueless.

17. I'll admit it; it's a death I find deeply emotionally satisfying. I worry about me sometimes. Then again, on the commentary track to "Chosen" (7.22), Whedon says this regarding Caleb's exit from this life: "And I thought that splitting him in half from the crotch up was ... maybe a little on the nose as a radical feminist statement goes, but for his character, I really thought he'd earned it."

Conclusion

1. I won't even attempt to create a definitive list of outstanding Buffy-related essays and articles. But the curious reader could do worse than examine the material and links found on the *Slayage* Website, which can be accessed at http://slayageonline.com/.

2. Hmm. Striped mavericks. Well, that's a mangled metaphor.

Primary Sources — *Buffy the Vampire Slayer*

(JW=Joss Whedon)

Season One

Title (and Writer)	Director	Original Air Date
"Welcome to the Hellmouth" (JW)	Charles Martin Smith	3 Mar 1997
"The Harvest" (JW)	John T. Kretchmer	10 Mar 1997
"Witch" (Dana Reston)	Stephen Cragg	17 Mar 1997
"Teacher's Pet" (David Greenwalt)	Bruce Seth Green	24 Mar 1997
"Never Kill a Boy on the First Date" (Rob Des Hotel & Dean Batali)	David Semel	31 Mar 1997
"The Pack" (Matt Kiene & Joe Reinkemeyer)	Bruce Seth Green	7 Apr 1997
"Angel" (David Greenwalt)	Scott Brazil	14 Apr 1997
"I, Robot ... You, Jane" (Ashley Gable & Thomas A. Swyden)	Stephen Posey	28 Apr 1997
"The Puppet Show" (Dean Batali & Rob Des Hotel)	Ellen S. Pressman	5 May 1997
"Nightmares" (David Greenwalt & JW)	Bruce Seth Green	12 May 1997
"Out of Mind, Out of Sight" (Ashley Gable Thomas A. Swyden & JW)	Reza Badiyi	19 May 1997
"Prophecy Girl" (JW)	Joss Whedon	2 June 1997

Season Two

Title (and Writer)	*Director*	*Original Air Date*
"When She Was Bad" (JW)	Joss Whedon	15 Sep 1997
"Some Assembly Required" (Ty King)	Bruce Seth Green	22 Sep 1997
"School Hard" (David Greenwalt & JW)	John T. Kretchmer	29 Sep 1997
"Inca Mummy Girl" (Matt Kiene & John Reinkemeyer)	Ellen S. Pressman	6 Oct 1997
"Reptile Boy" (David Greenwalt)	David Greenwalt	13 Oct 1997
"Halloween" (Carl Ellsworth)	Bruce Seth Green	27 Oct 1997
"Lie to Me" (JW)	Joss Whedon	3 Nov 1997
"The Dark Age" (Dean Batali & Rob Des Hotel)	Bruce Seth Green	10 Nov 1997
"What's My Line?—Pt. 1" (Howard Gordon & Marti Noxon)	David Solomon	17 Nov 1997
"What's My Line?—Pt. 2" (Marti Noxon)	David Semel	24 Nov 1997
"Ted" (David Greenwalt & JW)	Bruce Seth Green	8 Dec 1997
"Bad Eggs" (Marti Noxon)	David Greenwalt	12 Jan 1998
"Surprise" (Marti Noxon)	Michael Lange	19 Jan 1998
"Innocence" (JW)	Joss Whedon	20 Jan 1998
"Phases" (Rob Des Hotel & Dean Batali)	Bruce Seth Green	27 Jan 1998
"Bewitched, Bothered & Bewildered" (Marti Noxon)	James A. Contner	10 Feb 1998
"Passion" (Ty King)	Michael E. Gershman	24 Feb 1998
"Killed by Death" (Rob Des Hotel & Dean Batali)	Deran Sarafian	3 Mar 1998
"I Only Have Eyes for You" (Marti Noxon)	James Whitmore, Jr.	28 Apr 1998
"Go Fish" (David Fury & Elin Hampton)	David Semel	5 May 1998
"Becoming—Pt. 1" (JW)	Joss Whedon	12 May 1998
"Becoming—Pt. 2" (JW)	Joss Whedon	19 May 1998

Season Three

Title (and Writer)	*Director*	*Original Air Date*
"Anne" (JW)	Joss Whedon	29 Sep 1998
"Dead Man's Party" (Marti Noxon)	James Whitmore, Jr.	6 Oct 1998
"Faith, Hope & Trick" (David Greenwalt)	James A. Contner	13 Oct 1998
"Beauty & the Beasts" (Marti Noxon)	James Whitmore, Jr.	20 Oct 1998
"Homecoming" (David Greenwalt)	David Greenwalt	3 Nov 1998

(Season Three, continued)

Title (and Writer)	Director	Original Air Date
"Band Candy" (Jane Espenson)	Michael Lange	10 Nov 1998
"Revelations" (Douglas Petrie)	James A. Contner	17 Nov 1998
"Lovers Walk" (Dan Vebber)	David Semel	24 Nov 1998
"The Wish" (Marti Noxon)	David Greenwalt	8 Dec 1998
"Amends" (JW)	Joss Whedon	15 Dec 1998
"Gingerbread" (Jane Espenson & Thania St. John)	James Whitmore, Jr.	12 Jan 1999
"Helpless" (David Fury)	James A. Contner	19 Jan 1999
"The Zeppo" (Dan Vebber)	James Whitmore, Jr.	26 Jan 1999
"Bad Girls" (Douglas Petrie)	Michael Lange	9 Feb 1999
"Consequences" (Marti Noxon)	Michael Gershman	16 Feb 1999
"Doppelgangland" (JW)	Joss Whedon	23 Feb 1999
"Enemies" (Douglas Petrie)	David Grossman	16 Mar 1999
"Earshot" (Jane Espenson)	Regis B. Kimble	21 Sep 1999
"Choices" (David Fury)	James A. Contner	4 May 1999
"The Prom" (Marti Noxon)	David Solomon	11 May 1999
"Graduation Day – Pt. 1" (JW)	Joss Whedon	18 May 1999
"Graduation Day – Pt. 2" (JW)	Joss Whedon	13 July 1999

Season Four

Title (and Writer)	Director	Original Air Date
"The Freshman" (JW)	Joss Whedon	5 Oct 1999
"Living Conditions" (Marti Noxon)	David Grossman	12 Oct 1999
"The Harsh " Light of Day (Jane Espenson)	James A. Contner	19 Oct 1999
"Fear Itself" (David Fury)	Tucker Gates	26 Oct 1999
"Beer Bad" (Tracey Forbes)	David Solomon	2 Nov 1999
"Wild at Heart" (Marti Noxon)	David Grossman	9 Nov 1999
"The Initiative" (Douglas Petrie)	James A. Contner	16 Nov 1999
"Pangs" (Jane Espenson)	Michael Lange	23 Nov 1999
"Something Blue" (Tracey Forbes)	Nick Marck	30 Nov 1999
"Hush" (JW)	Joss Whedon	14 Dec 1999
"Doomed" (Marti Noxon & David Fury & Jane Espenson)	James A. Contner	18 Jan 2000
"A New Man" (Jane Espenson)	Michael Gershman	25 Jan 2000
"The I in Team" (David Fury)	James A. Contner	8 Feb 2000

(Season Four, continued)

Title (and Writer)	Director	Original Air Date
"Goodbye Iowa" (Marti Noxon)	David Solomon	15 Feb 2000
"This Year's Girl" (Douglas Petrie)	Michael Gershman	22 Feb 2000
"Who Are You?" (JW)	Joss Whedon	29 Feb 2000
"Superstar" (Jane Espenson)	David Grossman	4 Apr 2000
"Where the Wild Things Are" (Tracey Forbes)	David Solomon	25 Apr 2000
"New Moon Rising" (Marti Noxon)	James A. Contner	2 May 2000
"The Yoko Factor" (Doug Petrie)	David Grossman	9 May 2000
"Primeval" (David Fury)	James A. Contner	16 May 2000
"Restless" (JW)	Joss Whedon	23 May 2000

Season Five

Title (and Writer)	Director	Original Air Date
"Buffy Vs. Dracula" (Marti Noxon)	David Solomon	26 Sep 2000
"Real Me" (David Fury)	David Grossman	3 Oct 2000
"The Replacement" (Jane Espenson)	James A. Contner	10 Oct 2000
"Out of My Mind" (Rebecca Rand Kirshner)	David Grossman	17 Oct 2000
"No Place Like Home" (Douglas Petrie)	David Solomon	24 Oct 2000
"Family" (JW)	Joss Whedon	7 Nov 2000
"Fool for Love" (Douglas Petrie)	Nick Marck	14 Nov 2000
"Shadow" (David Fury)	Daniel Attias	21 Nov 2000
"Listening to Fear" (Rebecca Rand Kirshner)	David Solomon	28 Nov 2000
"Into the Woods" (Marti Noxon)	Marti Noxon	19 Dec 2000
"Triangle" (Jane Espenson)	Christopher Hibler	9 Jan 2001
"Checkpoint" (Douglas Petrie & Jane Espenson)	Nick Marck	23 Jan 2001
"Blood Ties" (Steven S. DeKnight)	Michael Gershman	6 Feb 2001
"Crush" (David Fury)	Daniel Attias	13 Feb 2001
"I Was Made to Love You" (Jane Espenson)	James A. Contner	20 Feb 2001
"The Body" (JW)	Joss Whedon	27 Feb 2001
"Forever" (Marti Noxon)	Marti Noxon	17 Apr 2001
"Intervention" (Jane Espenson)	Michael Greshman	24 Apr 2001
"Tough Love" (Rebecca Rand Kirschner)	David Grossman	1 May 2001
"Spiral" (Steven S. DeKnight)	James A. Contner	8 May 2001
"The Weight of the World" (Douglas Petrie)	David Solomon	15 May 2001
"The Gift" (JW)	Joss Whedon	22 May 2001

Season Six

Title (and Writer)	Director	Original Air Date
"Bargaining — Pt. 1" (Marti Noxon)	David Grossman	2 Oct 2001
"Bargaining — Pt. 2" (David Fury)	David Grossman	2 Oct 2001
"After Life" (Jane Espenson)	David Solomon	9 Oct 2001
"Flooded" (Douglas Petrie & Jane Espenson)	Douglas Petrie	16 Oct 2001
"Life Serial" (David Fury & Jane Espenson)	Nick Marck	23 Oct 2001
"All the Way" (Steven S. DeKnight)	David Solomon	30 Oct 2001
"Once More, with Feeling" (JW)	Joss Whedon	6 Nov 2001
"Tabula Rasa" (Rebecca Rand Kirshner)	David Grossman	13 Nov 2001
"Smashed" (Drew Z. Greenberg)	Turi Meyer	20 Nov 2001
"Wrecked" (Marti Noxon)	David Solomon	27 Nov 2001
"Gone" (David Fury)	David Fury	8 Jan 2002
"Doublemeat Palace" (Jane Espenson)	Nick Marck	29 Jan 2002
"Dead Things" (Steven S. DeKnight)	James A. Contner	5 Feb 2002
"Older and Far Away" (Drew Z. Greenberg)	Michael Gershman	12 Feb 2002
"As You Were" (Douglas Petrie)	Douglas Petrie	26 Feb 2002
"Hell's Bells" (Rebecca Rand Kirshner)	David Solomon	5 Mar 2002
"Normal Again" (Diego Gutierrez)	Rick Rosenthal	12 Mar 2002
"Entropy" (Drew Z. Greenberg)	James A. Contner	30 Apr 2002
"Seeing Red" (Steven S. DeKnight)	Michael Gershman	5 May 2002
"Villians" (Marti Noxon)	David Solomon	14 May 2002
"Two to Go" (Douglas Petrie)	Bill Norton	21 May 2002
"Grave" (David Fury)	James A. Contner	21 May 2002

Season Seven

Title (and Writer)	Director	Original Air Date
"Lessons" (JW)	David Solomon	24 Sep 2002
"Beneath You" (Douglas Petrie)	Nick Marck	1 Oct 2002
"Same Time, Same Place" (Jane Espenson)	James A. Contner	8 Oct 2002
"Help" (Rebecca R and Kirshner)	Rick Rosenthal	15 Oct 2002
"Selfless" (Drew Goddard)	David Solomon	22 Oct 2002
"Him" (Drew Z. Greenberg)	Michael Gershman	5 Nov 2002
"Conversations with Dead People" (Jane Espenson & Drew Goddard)	Nick Marck	12 Nov 2002
"Sleeper" (David Fury & Jane Espenson)	Alan J. Levi	19 Nov 2002
"Never Leave Me" (Drew Goddard)	David Solomon	26 Nov 2002

(Season Seven, continued)

Title and Writer	Director	Original Air Date
"Bring On the Night" (Marti Noxon & Douglas Petrie)	David Grossman	17 Dec 2002
"Showtime" (David Fury)	Michael Grossman	7 Jan 2003
"Potential" (Rebecca R and Kirshner)	James A. Contner	21 Jan 2003
"The Killer in Me" (Drew Z. Greenberg)	David Solomon	4 Feb 2003
"First Date" (Jane Espenson)	David Grossman	11 Feb 2003
"Get It Done" (Douglas Petrie)	Douglas Petrie	18 Feb 2003
"Storyteller" (Jane Espenson)	Marita Grabiak	25 Feb 2003
"Lies My Parents Told Me" (David Fury & Drew Goddard)	David Fury	25 Mar 2003
"Dirty Girls" (Drew Goddard)	Michael Gershman	15 Apr 2003
"Empty Places" (Drew Z. Greenberg)	James A. Contner	29 Apr 2003
"Touched" (Rebecca R and Kirshner)	David Solomon	6 May 2003
"End of Days" (Douglas Petrie & Jane Espenson)	Marita Grabiak	13 May 2003
"Chosen" (JW)	Joss Whedon	20 May 2003

"Season Eight"

Buffy the Vampire Slayer Issues #1–#4 "The Long Way Home." Written by Joss Whedon. Milwaukie, OR: Dark Horse, 2007. Issues continue to be published monthly.

Primary Sources — *Angel*

(JW=Joss Whedon)

Season One

Title (and Writer)	Director	Original Air Date
"City Of" (David Greenwalt & JW)	Joss Whedon	5 Oct 1999
"Lonely Heart" (David Fury)	James A. Contner	12 Oct 1999
"In the Dark" (Douglas Petrie)	Bruce Seth Green	19 Oct 1999
"I Fall to Pieces" (JW & David Greenwalt)	Vern Gillum	26 Oct 1999
"Rm w/ a Vu" (David Greenwalt & Jane Espenson)	Scott McGinnis	2 Nov 1999
"Sense and Sensitivity" (Tim Minear)	James A. Contner	9 Nov 1999
"The Bachelor Party" (Tracey Stern)	David Straiton	16 Nov 1999
"I Will Remember You" (David Greenwalt & Jeannine Renshaw)	David Grossman	23 Nov 1999
"Hero" (Howard Gordon & Tim Minear)	Tucker Gates	30 Nov 1999
"Parting Gifts" (David Fury & Jeannine Renshaw)	James A. Contner	14 Dec 1999
"Somnambulist" (Tim Minear)	Winrich Kolbe	18 Jan 2000
"Expecting" (Howard Gordon)	David Semel	25 Jan 2000
"She" (David Greenwalt & Marti Noxon)	David Greenwalt	8 Feb 2000

(Season One, continued*)*

Title (and Writer)	Director	Original Air Date
"I've Got You Under My Skin" (David Greenwalt & Jeannine Renshaw)	R. D. Price	15 Feb 2000
"The Prodigal" (Tim Minear)	Bruce Seth Green	22 Feb 2000
"The Ring" (Howard Gordon)	Nick Marck	29 Feb 2000
"Eternity" (Tracey Stern)	Regis B. Kimble	4 Apr 2000
"Five By Five" (Jim Kouf)	James A. Contner	25 Apr 2000
"Sanctuary" (Tim Minear & JW)	Michael Lange	2 May 2000
"War Zone" (Garry Campbell)	David Straiton	9 May 2000
"Blind Date" (Jeannine Renshaw)	Thomas J. Wright	16 May 2000
"To Shanshu in L.A." (David Greenwalt)	David Greenwalt	23 May 2000

Season Two

Title (and Writer)	Director	Original Air Date
"Judgment" (JW & David Greenwalt)	Michael Lange	26 Sep 2000
"Are You Now or Have You Ever Been?" (Tim Minear)	David Semel	3 Oct 2000
"First Impressions" (Shawn Ryan)	James A. Contner	10 Oct 2000
"Untouched" (Mere Smith)	Joss Whedon	17 Oct 2000
"Dear Boy" (David Greenwalt)	David Greenwalt	24 Oct 2000
"Guise Will Be Guise" (Jane Espenson)	Krishna Rao	7 Nov 2000
"Darla" (Tim Minear)	Tim Minear	14 Nov 2000
"The Shroud of Rahmon" (Jim Kouf)	David Grossman	21 Nov 2000
"The Trial" (Douglas Petrie, Tim Minear & David Greenwalt)	Bruce Seth Green	28 Nov 2000
"Reunion" (Tim Minear & Shawn Ryan)	James A. Contner	19 Dec 2000
"Redefinition" (Mere Smith)	Michael Grossman	16 Jan 2001
"Blood Money" (Shawn Ryan & Mere Smith)	R. D. Price	23 Jan 2001
"Happy Anniversary" (JW & David Greenwalt)	Bill Norton	6 Feb 2001
"The Thin Dead Line" (Jim Kouf & Shawn Ryan)	Scott McGinnis	13 Feb 2001
"Reprise" (Tim Minear)	James Whitmore, Jr.	20 Feb 2001
"Epiphany" (Tim Minear)	Thomas J. Wright	27 Feb 2001
"Disharmony" (David Fury)	Fred Keller	17 Apr 2001
"Dead End" (David Greenwalt)	James A. Contner	24 Apr 2001

(Season Two, continued)

Title (and Writer)	Director	Original Air Date
"Belonging" (Shawn Ryan)	Turi Meyer	1 May 2001
"Over the Rainbow" (Mere Smith)	Fred Keller	8 May 2001
"Through the Looking Glass" (Tim Minear)	Tim Minear	15 May 2001
"There's No Place Like Plrtz Glrb" (David Greenwalt)	David Greenwalt	22 May 2001

Season Three

Title (and Writer)	Director	Original Air Date
"Heartthrob" (David Greenwalt)	David Greenwalt	24 Sep 2001
"That Vision-Thing" (Jeffrey Bell)	Bill Norton	1 Oct 2001
"That Old Gang of Mine" (Tim Minear)	Fred Keller	8 Oct 2001
"Carpe Noctem" (Scott Murphy)	James A. Contner	15 Oct 2001
"Fredless" (Mere Smith)	Marita Grabiak	22 Oct 2001
"Billy" (Tim Minear & Jeffrey Bell)	David Grossman	29 Oct 2001
"Offspring" (David Greenwalt)	Turi Meyer	5 Nov 2001
"Quickening" (Jeffrey Bell)	Skip Schoolnik	12 Nov 2001
"Lullaby" (Tim Minear)	Tim Minear	19 Nov 2001
"Dad" (David H. Goodman)	Fred Keller	10 Dec 2001
"Birthday" (Mere Smith)	Michael Grossman	14 Jan 2002
"Provider" (Scott Murphy)	Bill Norton	21 Jan 2002
"Waiting in the Wings" (JW)	Joss Whedon	4 Feb 2002
"Couplet" (Tim Minear & Jeffrey Bell)	Tim Minear	18 Feb 2002
"Loyalty" (Mere Smith)	James A. Contner	25 Feb 2002
"Sleep Tight" (David Greenwalt)	Terrence O'Hara	4 Mar 2002
"Forgiving" (Jeffrey Bell)	Turi Meyer	15 Apr 2002
"Double or Nothing" (David H. Goodman)	David Grossman	22 Apr 2002
"The Price" (David Fury)	Marita Grabiak	29 Apr 2002
A New World" (Jeffrey Bell)	Tim Minear	6 May 2002
"Benediction" (Tim Minear)	Tim Minear	13 May 2002
"Tomorrow" (David Greenwalt)	David Greenwalt	50 May 2002

Season Four

Title (and Writer)	Director	Original Air Date
"Deep Down" (Steven S. DeKnight)	Terrence O'Hara	6 Oct 2002
"Ground State" (Mere Smith)	Michael Grossman	13 Oct 2002

(Season Four, continued)

Title (and Writer)	Director	Original Air Date
"The House Always Wins" (David Fury)	Marita Grabiak	20 Oct 2002
"Slouching Toward Bethlehem" (Jeffrey Bell)	Skip Schoolnik	27 Oct 2002
"Supersymmetry" (Elizabeth Craft & Sarah Fain)	Bill Norton	3 Nov 2002
"Spin the Bottle" (JW)	Joss Whedon	10 Nov 2002
"Apocalypse, Nowish" (Steven S. DeKnight)	Vern Gillum	17 Nov 2002
"Habeas Corpses" (Jeffrey Bell)	Skip Schoolnik	15 Jan 2003
"Long Day's Journey" (Mere Smith)	Terrence O'Hara	22 Jan 2003
"Awakening" (David Fury & Steven S. DeKnight)	James A. Contner	29 Jan 2003
"Soulless" (Sarah Fain & Elizabeth Craft)	Sean Astin	5 Feb 2003
"Calvary" (Jeffrey Bell & Steven S. DeKnight & Mere Smith)	Bill Norton	12 Feb 2003
"Salvage" (David Fury)	Jefferson Kibbee	19 Feb 2003
"Release" (Steven S. DeKnight & Elizabeth Craft & Sarah Fain)	James A. Contner	12 Mar 2003
"Orpheus" (Mere Smith)	Terrence O'Hara	19 Mar 2003
"Players" (Jeffrey Bell & Sarah Fain & Elizabeth Craft)	Michael Grossman	26 Mar 2003
"Inside Out" (Steven S. DeKnight)	Steven S. DeKnight	2 Apr 2003
"Shiny Happy People" (Elizabeth Craft & Sarah Fain)	Marita Grabiak	9 Apr 2003
"The Magic Bullet" (Jeffrey Bell)	Jeffrey Bell	16 Apr 2003
"Sacrifice" (Ben Edlund)	David Straiton	23 Apr 2003
"Peace Out" (David Fury)	Jefferson Kibbee	30 Apr 2003
"Home" (Tim Minear)	Tim Minear	7 May 2003

Season Five

Title (and Writer)	Director	Original Air Date
"Conviction" (JW)	Joss Whedon	1 Oct 2003
"Just Rewards" (David Fury & Ben Edlund)	James A. Contner	8 Oct 2003
"Unleashed" (Sarah Fain & Elizabeth Craft)	Marita Grabiak	15 Oct 2003
"Hell Bound" (Steven S. DeKnight)	Steven S. DeKnight	22 Oct 2003
"Life of the Party" (Ben Edlund)	Bill Norton	29 Oct 2003
"The Cautionary Tale of Numero Cinco" (Jeffery Bell)	Jeffery Bell	5 Nov 2003
"Lineage" (Drew Goddard)	Jefferson Kibbee	12 Nov 2003
"Destiny" (David Fury & Steven S. DeKnight)	Skip Schoolnik	19 Nov 2003

(Season Five, continued)

Title (and Writer)	Director	Original Air Date
"Harm's Way" (Elizabeth Craft & Sarah Fain)	Vern Gillum	14 Jan 2004
"Soul Purpose" (Brent Fletcher)	David Boreanaz	21 Jan 2004
"Damage" (Steven S. DeKnight & Drew Goddard)	Jefferson Kibbee	28 Jan 2004
"You're Welcome" (David Fury)	David Fury	4 Feb 2004
"Why We Fight" (Drew Goddard & Steven S. DeKnight)	Terrence O'Hara	11 Feb 2004
"Smile Time" (JW & Ben Edlund)	Ben Edlund	18 Feb 2004
"A Hole in the World" (JW)	Joss Whedon	24 Feb 2004
"Shells" (Steven S. DeKnight)	Steven S. DeKnight	3 Mar 2004
"Underneath" (Sarah Fain & Elizabeth Craft)	Skip Schoolnik	14 Apr 2004
"Origin" (Drew Goddard)	Terrence O'Hara	21 Apr 2004
"Time Bomb" (Ben Edlund)	Vern Gillum	28 Apr 2004
"The Girl in Question" (Steven S. DeKnight & Drew Goddard)	David Greenwalt	5 May 2004
"Power Play" (David Fury)	James A. Contner	12 May 2004
"Not Fade Away" (Jeffery Bell & JW)	Jeffery Bell	19 May 2004

Primary Sources — *Firefly*

(JW=Joss Whedon)

Episodes are listed in the order they were intended to be viewed. As you can see from the "Original Air Date" column, *Firefly* aired out of date and three episodes never aired commercially. Fortunately, the episodes are all available on DVD.

Season One

Title (and Writer)	Director	Original Air Date
"Serenity" (2 Pts.) (JW)	Joss Whedon	20 Dec 2002
"The Train Job" (JW & Tim Minear)	Joss Whedon	20 Sep 2002
"Bushwhacked" (Tim Minear)	Tim Minear	27 Sep 2002
"Shindig" (Jane Espenson)	Vern Gillum	1 Nov 2002
"Safe" (Drew Z. Greenburg)	Michael Grossman	8 Nov 2002
"Our Mrs. Reynolds" (JW)	Vondie Curtis Hall	4 Oct 2002
"Jaynestown" (Ben Edlund)	Marita Grabiak	18 Oct 2002
"Out of Gas" (Tim Minear)	David Solomon	25 Oct 2002
"Ariel" (Jose Molina)	Allan Kroeker	15 Nov 2002
"War Stories" (Cheryl Cain)	James Contner	6 Dec 2002
"Trash" (Ben Edlund & Jose Molina)	Vern Gillum	Never Aired
"The Message" (JW & Tim Minear)	Tim Minear	Never Aired
"Heart of Gold" (Brett Matthews)	Thomas J. Wright	Never Aired
"Objects in Space" (JW)	Joss Whedon	13 Dec 2002

Primary Sources — Other

Those Left Behind (2005)

This is the three-issue comic (or "graphic novel") which serves as the bridge between events depicted in the television series *Firefly* and the feature film *Serenity*. It is available both as three single issues (2005) or collected into a single volume (2006).

Whedon, Joss and Brett Matthews. *Serenity: Those Left Behind.* Art by Will Conrad. Milwaukie, OR: Dark Horse, 2006.

Serenity (2005)

Serenity. Written and Directed by Joss Whedon. Universal Studios, 2005.

Bibliography

"We're Starting a book club?"
— Mal to Niska ("War Stories" *Firefly* 1.10)

Abbott, Stacey. "Walking the Fine Line between Angel and Angelus." *Slayage: the Online International Journal of Buffy Studies* 9 (2003):27 pars. 20 May 2007 www.slayageonline.com/essays/slayage9/Abbott.htm.
Ackerman, Diane. *A Natural History of the Senses*. New York: Random, 1990.
_____. *A Natural History of Love*. New York: Random, 1994.
"Amount Raised." *Can't Stop the Serenity.com*. 2007. 28 July 2007 www.cantstoptheserenity.com.
Angel. By Joss Whedon, and David Greenwalt. 5 Seasons. 1999–2004. DVD. Twentieth Century–Fox Home Entertainment, 2004.
Aristotle. "Nicomachean Ethics." *Foundations of Western Thought*. Ed. James Gordon Clapp, Morris Philipson and Henry M. Rosenthal. New York: Knopf, 1962.
Austin, Dorothea. *The Name Book*. Minneapolis, MN: Bethany, 1982.
Barclay, William. *The Gospel of Luke*. Philadelphia: Westminster, 1975.
Barnes, Robert. "The Apostle Formerly Known as Saul." *Third Millennium Ministries*. 18 Apr. 2007 http://www.thirdmill.org/answer.asp/file/99746.qna/category/nt/page/questions/site/iiim.
Barnhart, Clarence L., ed. *The New Century Cyclopedia of Names of Names*. Vol. 2. Englewood Cliffs, NJ: Prentice-Hall, 1954.
Bartlett, Wayne and Flavia Idriceanu. *Legends of Blood: The Vampire in History and Myth*. Westport, CT: Praeger, 2006.
Battis, Jes. *Blood Relations: Chosen Families in "Buffy the Vampire Slayer" and "Angel."* Jefferson, NC: McFarland, 2005.
Bauer, Elise. Home page. 21 Jan. 2006. http://www.elise.com/quotes/quotes/faith.htm.
Bergman, Ingmar. Introduction. *Four Screenplays by Ingmar Bergman*. Trans. Lars Malmstrom and David Kushner. New York: Simon, 1960. xiii–xxii.
"Biography for Joss Whedon." *IMDB.com*. Internet Movie Database. 1990–2006. 16 Apr. 2006 http://www.imdb.com/name/nm0923736/bio.

Bloom, Harold. *The American Religion: the Emergence of the Post-Christian Nation.* New York: Simon, 1992.
Bolton, Lesley. *25,001 Best Baby Names.* Naperville, IL: Sourcebooks, 2006.
Bourke, Angela. *The Burning of Bridget Cleary.* New York: Penguin, 2000.
Brown, A. Whitney. *The Big Picture.* New York: Harper, 1991.
Bruggman, Mary Wallace. "The Strawberry in Religious Paintings of the 1400's." In G.M. Darrow, *The Strawberry: History, Breeding and Physiology. United States Department of Agriculture.gov..* 19 June 1998. 3 Aug. 2006 http://nal.usda.gov/pgdic/Strawberry/book/boktwo.htm.
Buckeley, Tim. "Study Notes on Jonah." *Bible.gen.* 2 Feb. 2007. http://bible.gen.nz/jonah/act1.htm.
Buckman, Alyson. Personal Interview. 10 Feb. 2006.
Buffy the Vampire Slayer: The Chosen Collection. Exec. Prod. Joss Whedon. 7 Seasons. 1995–2003. DVD. Twentieth Century–Fox Home Entertainment. 2005.
"*Buffy the Vampire Slayer* Mocks Christian Faith During Holy Week." *Parentstv.org.* Parents Television Council. 17 Apr. 2003. 27 Apr. 2006 http://www.parentstv.org/ptc/publications/release/2003/0417.asp.
Bunson, Matthew. *The Vampire Encyclopedia.* New York: Three Rivers, 1993.
Burtt, E.A., ed. *The Teachings of the Compassionate Buddha.* New York: New American 2000.
"Business Data for *Dogma.*" *Imdb.com.* Internet Movie Database. 26 Mar. 2000. 21 Jan. 2006 http://www.imbd.com/title/tt0120655/business.
"Business Data for *The Passion of the Christ.*" *Imdb.com* Internet Movie Database. 13 Mar. 2005. 21 Jan. 2006 http://www.imdb.com.title/tt0335345.business.
Cabri. "Joss' Dinner Auctions Net More Than $52,000." Online posting. 13 July 2007. *Whedonesque.com.* 28 July 2007 http://whedonesque.com/comments/13711#more.
Campbell, Joseph. "Hero's Journey: Reference." 19 Nov. 1999. Maricopa Center for Learning and Instruction. 10 Aug. 2007 http://www.mcle.dist.maricopa.edu/smc/journey/ref/summary/html.
Campbell, Joseph, and Bill Moyers. *The Power of Myth.* Doubleday: New York, 1988.
Carlyon, Richard. *A Guide to the Gods.* New York: Quill, 1981.
Chesterton, G.K. Frontispiece. *Coraline.* By Neil Gaiman. New York: Harper, 2002.
"Chinese Girl with Bound Feet." The Virtual Museum of the City of San Francisco. 2 July 2006 http://www.sfmuseum.org/chin/foot.html.
Coffin, Wiliam Sloane. *A Passion for the Possible.* Louisville, KY: Westminster/John Knox, 1993.
Colvin, Phil. "*Angel*: Redefinition and Justification through Faith." *Reading Angel.* Ed. Stacey Abbott. London: Tauris, 2005.
"The Confessio of St. Patrick." *Catholic Information Network.* 13 May 2005. 21 Jan. 2006 http://www.cin.org/patrick.html.
Conrad, Roxanne Longstreet. "Mirror/Mirror: A Parody." *Finding Serenity: Anti-Heroes, Lost Shepherds and Space Hookers in Joss Whedon's Firefly.* Ed. Jane Espenson. Dallas: BenBella, 2004.
Coontz, Stephanie. *The Way We Really Are: Coming to Terms with America's Changing Families.* New York: Basic, 1997.
_____. "The Way We Weren't: The Myth and Reality of the 'Traditional' Family." *Selected Readings in Marriage and Family.* Ed. Lorene H. Stone. San Diego, CA: Greenhaven, 1999.
Curry, Dorothy R. "All Saints Day" Sermon. 7 Nov. 2004. 21 Jan 2006. http://www.standrewsepiscopal.org/sermons/11–07–04.htm.
Damrosch, Leopold. *God's Plot and Man's Stories: Studies in the Fictional Imagination from Milton to Fielding.* Chicago: U of Chicago P, 1985.

Davidson, H.R. Ellis. *Scandinavian Mythology*. London: Hamlyn, 1975.
Davis, Wade. *The Serpent and the Rainbow*. New York: Warner, 1985.
Day, William Patrick. *Vampire Legends in Contemporary American Culture*. Lexington, KY: University Press of Kentucky, 2002.
Dillard, Annie. *Holy the Firm*. New York: Harper, 2003.
Donne, John. *The Complete Poetry and Selected Prose of John Donne*. Ed. Charles M. Coffin. New York: Random, 1952.
Doyle.com. 16 July 2001. The Doyle Clan. 3 Feb. 2007 http://www.doyle.com.au/index.htm.
Dundas, Zach. "How Portland Found Serenity." *Williamette Week Online*. 7 June 2006. 28 July 2007 http://www.wweek.com/editorial/3231/7641.
Ebert, Roger. Review of *The Passion of the Christ*, dir. Mel Gibson. *RogerEbert.com*. 24 Feb. 2004. 21 Jan. 2006 http://rogerebert.suntimes.com/apps/pbcs.dll/article?AID=/20040224/REVIEWS/402240301/1023.
Ehrman, Bart D. *Peter, Paul, and Mary Magdalene*. New York: Oxford University Press, 2006.
Engel, Elliot. *Eat, Think, and Be Merry*. Apex, NC: Authors Ink, 2005.
Espenson, Jane., ed. *Finding Serenity: Anti-heroes, Lost Shepherd and Space Hookers in Joss Whedon's Firefly*. Dallas: BenBella, 2004.
"Etymology of First Names." *EnglishWiz.com*. 9 May 2002. 10 July 2007. http://mizian.com.ne.kr/englishwiz/library/names/etymology_of_first_names.htm.
Farmer, David. *The Oxford Dictionary of Saints*. 4th ed. Oxford: Oxford University Press, 1997.
"Female Genital Mutilation." *Encyclopedia of Medicine*. Ed. Jacqueline L. Longe. N.p.: Thomson, 2002. *ENotes.com*. 2006. 2 July 2006. http://health.enotes.com/medicine-encyclopedia.
Firefly: The Complete Series. Created by Joss Whedon. 2002. DVD. Twentieth Century–Fox Home Entertainment, 2003.
Fitzmyer, Joseph A. Introduction, Translation, and Notes. *The Anchor Bible—The Gospel According to Luke (X-XXIV)*. Vol. 28A. New York: Doubleday, 1985.
Forster, E. M. *A Room with a View*. New York: Vintage, 1986.
Forster, Greg. "Faith and Plato: 'You're Nothing! Disgusting, Murderous Bitch!'" *Buffy the Vampire Slayer and Philosophy: Fear and Trembling in Sunnydale*. Ed. James B. South. Chicago: Open Court, 2003.
Frazer, James George. *The Golden Bough*. Abr. ed. New York: MacMillan, 1950.
"Frequently Asked Questions." *Can't Stop the Serenity.com*. 2007. 28 July 2007. http://www.cantstoptheserenity.com.
Funk, Charles E. *Thereby Hangs a Tale*. New York: Harper, 1985.
"Ganga." *Urday.com*. Zed Infocom. 15 May 2006. http://www.urday.com/rivers.htm.
Gaiman, Neil. *Smoke and Mirrors: Short Fictions and Illusions*. New York: Avon, 1998.
Garfield, Ken. "Johnny Cash Was a Man of Great Faith." *Charlotte.com*. 19 Nov. 2005. 5 Dec. 2005. http://www.charlotte.com/mld/charlotte/living/.
"Garth Ennis." *Wikipedia: The Free Encyclopedia*. 21 Jan. 2006. 21 Jan. 2006 http://enwikipedia.org/wiki/Garth_Ennis.
Geisel, Theodor Seuss (Dr. Seuss). *Horton Hatches the Egg*. New York: Random, 1968.
Golden, Christopher, Stephen R. Bissette, and Thomas E. Sniegoski. *Buffy the Vampire Slayer: The Monster Book*. New York: Pocket, 2000.
Goldman, Jane. *The X-Files: Book of the Unexplained*. Vol. 2. New York: Harper, 1997.
Goodbeer, Richard. *Escaping Salem: The Other Witch Hunt of 1692*. New York: Oxford University Press, 2005.
"Great Poems-Poets (on referring to the eyes)." *Canadian Neuro-Optic Research Institute*. 1995–2007. 16 Apr. 2007 http://cnri.edu/.

Grimm, Jacob and Wilhelm. *Grimm's Fairy Tales*. Trans. Mrs. E.V. Lucas, Lucy Crane and Marian Edwardes. New York: Grosset, 1945.
Gross, David C. *1,001 Questions and Answers about Judaism*. Garden City, NY: Doubleday, 1978.
Hagerty, Barbara Bradley. "Mother Teresa Beatified." NPR.org. 14 Oct. 2003. 15 Apr. 2007 http://www.npr.org/templates/story/story.php? storyId=1464889.
Hamilton, Edith. *Mythology*. Boston: Little, 1942.
Havens, Candace. *Joss Whedon: The Genius Behind Buffy*. London: Titan, 2003.
Heins, Marjorie. *Sex, Sin and Blasphemy*. New York: New Press, 1993.
Hobbins, Daniel, trans. *The Trial of Joan of Arc*. Cambridge, MA: Harvard University Press, 2005.
Homer. *The Odyssey*. Trans. Samuel Butler. *The Internet Classics Archive*. Ed. Daniel C. Stevenson. 1994–2000. Web Atomics. 16 Apr. 2007 http://classics.mit.edu/Homer/odyssey.mb.txt.
Horn, Maurice. *Women in Comics*. 3 vols. Philadelphia: Chelsea, 2001.
Hornberger, Jacob G. "Repatriation-The Dark Side of World War II-Part 3." *The Future of Freedom Foundation*. April 1995. 21 Jan. 2006 http://www.fff.org/freedom/0495a.asp.
Howe, Sean. Introduction. *Give Our Regards to the Atomsmashers!* Ed. Sean Howe. New York: Pantheon, 2004.
"I Survived the 20th Century Holocaust." *Holocaust Survivors and Remembrance Network*. 15 Dec. 2002. NatureQuest Publications. 27 Feb. 2007. http://isurvived.org.home.html#Prologue.
"Interview with Joss Whedon About Serenity." 2 Oct. 2005. 21 Jan. 2006. http://www.sffworld.com/mul/130p0.html.
Jackwoski, Karol. *Sister Karol's Book of Spells and Blessings*. New York: Hyperion, 2001.
"Jehovah's Witnesses and Medical Care." *Jehovah's Witnesses*. 2003. Watch Tower Bible and Tract Society of Pennsylvania. 20 May 2007 http://www.jw-media.org/medical/medical_care.htm.
Johnson, Carl. "Agape." *Believe*. n.d. 21 Jan. 2006 http:www.mb-soft.com/believe/txw/agape.htm.
Jong, Erica. *Witches*. New York: Abradale, 1999.
Kaveney, Roz. "A Sense of the Ending: Schrodinger's *Angel*." *Reading Angel: The TV Spin-Off with a Soul*. Ed. Stacy Abbot. New York: Tauris, 2005. 57–72.
_____. "She Saved the World. A Lot." *Reading the Vampire Slayer*. Ed. Roz Kaveney. London: Tauris, 2004.
Kernel, M. "Serenity #1 Translations." 13 July 2005. 21 Jan. 2006. http://kernelm.livejournal.com/137703.html.
Kerr, Jessica. *Shakespeare's Flowers*. New York: Crowell, 1969.
Kolatch, Alfred J. *Dictionary of First Names*. New York: Perigree, 1990.
Korg, Jacob, ed. *The Poetry of Robert Browning*. Indianapolis, IN: Bobbs-Merrill, 1971.
Kramer, Heinrich and James Sprenger. *The Malleus Maleficarum*. Trans. Montague Summers. New York: Dover, 1971.
Kravitz, David. *Who's Who in Greek and Roman Mythology*. New York: Potter, 1978.
Lao-Tzu. *Tao Te Ching*. Trans. Stephen Addiss and Stanley Lombardo. Indianapolis, IN: Hackett, 1993.
Lewis, C.S. "The Problem of Pain." *The Complete C.S. Lewis Signature Classics*. San Francisco: Harper, 2002.
The Living Bible. Wheaton, IL: Tyndale, 1973.
MacKenzie, John, ed. "Masaai or Masai." *People, Nations and Cultures*. London: Weidenfeld, 2005.

Macnair, Trisha. "Human Decomposition After Death." *BBC Health*. Jan. 2007. BBC. 5 July 2007 *http://www.bbc.co.uk/health/ask_the_doctor/decompositionafterdeath.shtml*.
Mascetti, Manuela Dunn. *Vampire: The Complete Guide to the World of the Undead*. New York: Viking, 1992.
Matsuoka, Mitsu. "William Makepeace Thackeray." 13 Jan. 1998. 21 Jan. 2006. http:www.lang.nagoya-u.ac.jp/~matsuoka/Thackeray.html.
"McGuffin." *The Oxford English Dictionary Online*. Mar. 2001. 6 Apr. 2007 http://dictionary.oed.com/cgi/display_header/00303921?case_id=TDr6=OYpj012288.
McGuire, Anne. "Women, Gender, and Gnosis in Gnostic Texts and Traditions." *Women and Christian Origins*. Ed. Ross Shepard Kraemer and Mary Rose D'Angelo. New York: Oxford University Press, 1999.
McLaughlin, Jeff, ed. *Comics as Philosophy*. Jackson, MS: University Press of Mississippi, 2005.
McWilliams, Peter. *Ain't Nobody's Business If You Do: the Absurdity of Consensual Crimes in a Free Society*. Los Angeles: Prelude, 1993.
Mikkelson, Barbara and David P. Mikkelson. "A Star Is Borne." *Urban Legends Reference Pages*. 1995–2005. Snopes.com. 27 Feb. 2007 http:www.snopes.com/history/govern/Denmark.htm.
Money, Mary Alice. "The Undemonization of Supporting Characters in *Buffy*." *Fighting the Forces*. Eds. Rhonda V. Wilcox and David Lavery. Lanham, MD: Rowman, 2002.
Moring, Mike. "Simply Complicated." *ChristianityToday.com*. 25 Aug. 2003. 16 April 2006 http://www.christianitytoday.com/music/interviews/2003/amygrant-0803.html.
"The Motion Picture Production Code of 1930 (Hays Code)." *ArtsReformation.com*. Ed. Matt Bynum. 1 Feb. 2000. 21 Jan. 2006 http://www.artsreformation.com/a001hayscode.html.
Neil, William. *Harper's Bible Commentary*. New York: Harper, 1975.
New Beginnings House of Prayer. "Reflections with Thomas Merton." 2003. 21 Jan. 2006 http://www.geocities.com/newbeginningsprayer/Reflections1.html.
The New Oxford Annotated Bible. Rev. Standard ed. New York: Oxford University Press, 1973.
Niafer, Fenian. "The Tradition of Hospitality." *Ancient Worlds LLC*. 26 Aug. 2005. 25 Feb 2007 http://www.ancientworlds.net/aw/Article/617978.
"Not in Our Town I: The Original Story." *PBS.org*. 1995–2007. PBS. 27 Feb. 2007 http://www.pbs.org/wgbh/pages/frontline/shtetl/righteous/.
Nussbaum, Emily. "Must-See Metaphysics." *New York Times* 22 Sept. 2002, sec. 6: 56+.
O'Donnell, Brian. "Saint John of God Story." *Hospitaller Order of Saint John of God*. 2006. Rossmann Haigh. 16 Apr. 2007 http:www.saintjohnofgod.org/sjog_story/story.php.
"On the Road to Equality: Honoring Men on the Front Lines." *Equalitynow.org*. 16 May 2006. Equality Now. 2 July 2006 http://ww.wbjourdan.com/streep-whedon.mov.
Panati, Charles. *Sacred Origins of Profound Things*. New York: Arkana, 1996.
Pasternak, Boris. *Doctor Zhivago*. New York: Pantheon, 1958.
Pateman, Matthew. *The Aesthetics of Culture in Buffy the Vampire Slayer*. Jefferson, NC: McFarland, 2006.
Peacock, Charlie, and Molly Nicholas. Excerpt. *At the Crossroads: Inside the Past, Present and Future of Contemporary Christian Music*. Rev. ed. N.p.: Shaw, 2004. *RandomHouse.com*. 2006. Random House Inc. 21 Jan. 2006 http://randomhouse.com/waterbrook/catalog/display/pperl?isbn=9780877881285&view.
Pernoud, Regine and Marie Veronique Clin. *Joan of Arc: Her Story*. Trans. Jeremy deQuesnay Adams. New York: St. Martin's, 1998.

Perrault, Charles. *Tales from Perrault.* Trans. Ann Lawrence. Oxford: Oxford University Press, 1996.
Phillips, Berni. "Christian Symbolism in *Buffy the Vampire Slayer.*" *Christian-fandom.org.* July 2003. 14 May 2007 www.christian-fandom.org/ess-buffy.html.
Prasso, Sheridan. *The Asian Mystique: Dragon Ladies, Geisha Girls, and Our Fantasies of the Exotic Orient.* New York: PublicAffairs, 2005.
Pratchett, Terry. *Monstrous Regiment.* New York: Harper, 2003.
Rambo, Elizabeth. "'Nobody Knows ... the Real Me': the Importance of Being Dawn." *Buffy* Conference. UNC-Greensboro. 16 Mar. 2007.
"Religion Tackles Mental Illness." *BBC News* 17 Apr. 1999. BBC Online Network. 18 Apr. 2007. http://news.bbc.co.uk/1/hi/health/321622.stm.
Renard, John. *The Handy Religion Answer Book.* Detroit: Visible Ink, 2002.
Riess, Jana. *What Would Buffy Do? The Vampire Slayer as Spiritual Guide.* San Francisco: Wiley, 2004.
Robbins, Russell H. *The Encyclopedia of Witchcraft and Demonology.* New York: Crown, 1959.
Robinson, George. *Essential Torah: A Complete Guide to the Five Books of Moses.* New York: Schocken, 2006.
Room, Adrian. *Cassell Dictionary of Proper Names.* London: Cassell, 1996.
Sabin, Roger. *Comics, Comix and Graphic Novels.* London: Phaidon, 1996.
Safire, William. *Lend Me Your Ears.* New York: Norton, 2004.
Said, S.F. "From *Buffy* to Blockbuster of the Year." *Telegraph Group Limited.* 1 Oct. 2005. 7 Sep. 2006 http://www.telegraph.co.uk/arts/main.jhtml?xml=arts/2005/10/01/bf buffy01.xml&menuId=564&Sheet=/arts/2005/10/01/ixfilmmain.html.
Schneider, Kirk J. *Horror and the Holy: Wisdom-Teachings of the Monster Tale.* Peru, IL: Open Court, 1993.
Schudt, Karl. "Also Sprach Faith: the Problem of the Happy Rogue Vampire Slayer." *Buffy the Vampire Slayer and Philosophy: Fear and Trembling in Sunnydale.* Ed. James B. South. Chicago: Open Court, 2003.
Serenity. Dir. Joss Whedon. Universal, 2005.
Shakespeare, William. *The Merchant of Venice.* New Haven, CT: Yale University Press, 1957.
_____. *Titus Andronicus.* Ed. A.M. Witherspoon. New Haven: Yale University Press, 1926.
Shaw, George Bernard. *Saint Joan.* New York: Penguin, 1977.
Shenkman, Richard. *Legends, Lies and Cherished Myths of World History.* New York: Harper, 1993.
Simpkins, C. Alexander, and Annellen Simpkins. *Simple Confucianism.* Boston: Tuttle, 2000.
South, James B., ed. *Buffy the Vampire Slayer and Philosophy: Fear and Trembling in Sunnydale.* Chicago: Open Court, 2003.
"St. Patrick's Day: Origins, Symbols, and Traditions." 29 Dec. 2005. 21 Jan. 2006. http://www.fridgedoor.info/spring-celebrations/st-patricks-day.php
Stafford, Diane. *The Ultimate Baby Names Book.* Naperville, IL: Sourcebooks, 2005.
Stedman, Ray C. "Jonah: The Reluctant Ambassador." *Discovery Publishing.* 22 May 1966. Public Broadcasting Company. 2 Feb. 2007 http://www.pbc.org.library/files/html/0232.html.
Strong, James. *Strong's Exhaustive Concordance of the Bible.* Nashville, TN: Abingdon, 1975.
Thompson, James C. "Women in the Ancient World." *Women In the Ancient World.com.* Ed. James C. Thompson. Nov. 2005. 2 July 2006. http://www.womenintheancientworld.com/index.htm.
Tomkins, Stephen. *A Short History of Christianity.* Grand Rapids, MI: Eerdmans, 2005.

Toy Story. Screenplay co-written by Joss Whedon. Disney/Pixar, 1995.
Valea, Ernest, ed. "The Parable of the Prodigal Son in Christianity and Buddhism." *A Comparative Analysis of the Major World Religions from a Christian Perspective.* 1999–2007. 31 May 2007. www.comparitivereligion.com/prodigal.html.
Varnum, Robin and Christina T. Gibbons. Introduction. *The Language of Comics.* Ed. Robin Varnum and Christina T. Gibbons. Jackson, MS: University Press of Mississippi, 2001.
Waimate, Jan. "Liggins Family Tree-New Zealand Connection." *Home Hyper.net.* 10 Apr. 2001. 6 June 2007. http://home hyper.net.nz/Liggins.Family.Tree/names/liggins.htm.
Whedon, Joss. "Faith's Surname." *Whedonesque.com.* 2 Jan. 2005. 6 June 2007. http://whedonesque.com/comments/5682.
_____. *Firefly: The Official Companion.* Vol. 1. London: Titan, 2006.
_____. *Firefly: The Official Companion.* Vol. 2. London: Titan, 2007.
_____. *Fray.* Milwaukie, OR: Dark Horse, 2003.
_____. "Let's Watch a Girl Get Beaten to Death." Online posting. 20 May 2007. *Whedonesque.com.* 28 July 2007 http://whedonesque.com/comments/13271.
_____. *Serenity: The Official Visual Companion.* London: Titan, 2005.
Whedon, Joss and Brett Matthews. *Serenity #1-#3* Art by Will Conrad. Colors by Laura Martin. Milwaukie, OR: Dark Horse, 2005.
Wilcox, Rhonda V. "'Who Died and Made Her the Boss?' Patterns of Mortality in *Buffy.*" *Fighting the Forces.* Eds. Rhonda V. Wilcox and David Lavery. Lanham, MD: Rowman, 2002.
Williamson, Milly. *The Lure of the Vampire.* London: Wallflower, 2005.
Willis, Garry. *What Jesus Meant.* New York: Viking, 2006.
Windling, Terri. Introduction. *Tam Lin.* By Pamela Dean. New York: tor, 1991. ix-x.
Wolverton, Robert E. *An Outline of Classical Mythology.* Totowa, NJ: Littlefield, 1975.
Wright, Lawrence. *Twins and What They Tell Us About Who We Are.* New York: Wiley, 1997.
Wylie, J. A. "St. Patrick: Apostle of Ireland (Chapter 10)." n.d. 21 Jan. 2006 http://www.whatsaiththescripture.com/Voice/St.Patrick.of.Ireland/St.Patrick.of.Ireland.2.html.

Index

Abbott, Stacey 44
Abraham 176
Acceptance as central theme 2, 187, 188; *see also* Whedon, Joss
Ackerman, Diane 43, 111
Actaeon 15
Agassiz 25
Alliance 72, 74, 100, 105, 115, 116, 117, 124, 159, 163; river 150, 151, 160
Angel 9, 26, 85, 139, 143; Angelus, origin of name 32; binary with Spike 27; blood drinking 30; Doyle 86, 88, 89, 96, 97; Faith 137, 140, 141, 142, 144; history 31, 32, 34, 35, 37; negative space 34, 43; origin of name as Liam 30; role of choice 43, 45
Angel 1, 21, 181
Anubis 40
Anya 42
Apollo 55, 56
Arbus, Diane 151
Aristotle 135
Artemis 15, 55
Aswad, Dua Khalil 187, 188, 189
Athena 62
Atlas 106
Aurora (Roman mythology) 15
Aurora (Sleeping Beauty) 15, 16, 18, 19

Barclay, William 142, 143
Battis, Jes 25
Battle of Du-Khang 99
Belief as central theme 2, 187, 188; *see also* Whedon, Joss
Beowulf 151
Bergman, Ingmar 2, 121
Bible as "Good Book" 122, 152; *see also* individual books

Bilhah 176
Billings, Montana 93
Blood as life force 30; *see also* Vampires
Brown, A. Whitney 181
Browncoat 99, 100, 116; as fans 188
Browning, Robert 129
Bubonic plague 29
Buckman, Alyson 160
Buddha (Siddhartha Gautama) 15, 19, 20
Buddhism 20, 22, 72
Buffy Summers 98, 133, 138, 145, 170, 185, 186; Caleb 169, 170, 172, 174, 183; as Christ figure 176, 180; counter stereotype 2; destiny 169; Faith 137, 141, 142, 143, 173; as feminist icon 164, 175; the First 183, 184; home life 135; as protector 177; rejecting authority 179, 181, 182, 184; relationship with Dawn 13, 14, 16, 17, 18, 19, 22, 25, 32
Buffy the Vampire Slayer 1, 2; as course material 186, 187; importance of relationships 135; morally complex characters 3; Parents Television Council 166, 167; scholarly criticism of 5
Bunson, Matthew 29

Cain 80
Caleb 6, 10, 184; as ascetic 172; Buffy 169, 170, 172, 174, 183; desire for knowledge 169, 173, 182; the First 165, 168, 171, 173, 174; free will 169; Gnosticism 170, 173; as human monster 164, 166; misogyny 164, 165, 168, 169, 172, 176, 177, 178, 182, 183; origin of name 167; religion 166, 167, 169, 173, 174, 175, 177; sensuality 173; Shannon 172, 183, 166
Campbell, Joseph 57, 60, 63
Cash, Johnny 102

Cassidy 7
Catholic Church's use of visual arts 5
Chagall, Marc 4
Chase, Cordelia *see* Cordelia Chase
Chesterton, G. K. 3
Choice as central theme 2, 18, 26, 134, 187, 188, 189; *see also* Whedon, Joss
Christian X 93
Christianity
Clement of Alexandria 172
Cobb, Jayne *see* Jayne Cobb
Coffin, William Sloane 79
Coleridge, Samuel Taylor 29, 101
Comic books 50; as home for outsiders 53; women in 52; see also *Fray*; *Preacher*
Communion 30, 33, 66, 78; concept of grace 43; cross 6, 29, 33, 40, 169; *see also* Jesus Christ; Misogyny
Companions 72; *see also* Inara Serra
Coontz, Stephanie 78, 79
Cordelia Chase 90, 94, 95, 138, 141
1 Corinthians 21, 23, 133, 177, 178
Council of Trent 5
Crick, Francis 41

Damrosch, Leopold 173
Darla 31
Davis, Wade 28
Dawn Summers 9, 14, 15, 16, 17, 18, 19, 38; acceptance of purpose 25, 26; first appearance 13; self-discovery 20, 21; use of skills 24; wish to be special 22
Day, William Patrick 134, 136
Demons 4; existence of soul 34; good demons 36, 42, 59; *see also* Doyle; Whistler
Dickens, Charles 7, 185
Dillard, Annie 45, 101
Dr. Seuss 80
Dogma 6
Donne, John 97, 109, 174
Doré, Gustave 6
Doubt 129; *see also* Angel; Operative; Shepherd Book; Whedon, Joss
"Doubting Thomas" 129
Doyle 7, 10, 43, 94, 95, 96, 185; comparison with Jonah 91, 92; as conscience for Angel 86; desire to be normal 95; as example of redemption 85, 90, 97; as Francis 87; as good demon 85; guilt over inaction 87, 88; as hybrid 87; origin of name 86; as outsider 90; painful visions 88, 89, 90, 93
Drusilla 31, 32, 38, 39

Ecclesiastes 26
Edem 170
Ehrman, Bart 177, 178
Eleanor of Aquitaine 66
Elizabeth I 183
Ennis, Garth 6; *see also* Cassidy; *Preacher*

Eos 14, 15
Equality Now 188
Erin 57, 58, 59, 60, 61, 62, 63
Espenson, Jane 37
Esther 128, 130
Eve 109, 171, 176
Exodus 89

Faith (concept) 78, 100; more than single view 179; non-religious 115; rules 107; *see also* individual characters; Whedon, Joss
Faith Lehane 10, 14, 132; attitude toward slaying 134; betrayal of others 136; as Buffy's dark side 134; desire for redemption 140; early history 133; escape to Los Angeles 139; family 145; hubris 136; Nietzsche 135; origin of name 132, 133; as prodigal 137, 138, 139, 140, 141, 142, 143, 144, 145; relationship with Angel 137, 140, 141, 142, 144; relationship with Buffy 134, 135, 137, 138, 141, 142, 143, 173; as sociopath 137
Family: created by shared experiences 78; Dr. Seuss view 80; faith family 79; portrayed on television 78; role of love in creating 79; "traditional" view 78, 79; *see also Firefly*; Whedon, Joss
Faust (Marlowe) 165, 169, 182
Finn, Riley *see* Riley Finn
Firefly 1, 2, 10, 65, 66, 98; common table in 65, 66, 67, 77, 78, 80; family in 67, 98; food in 65, 66, 77, 78; hats in 71; mix of cultures in 120; religion in 120, 152; size of space 110; slavery in 107; society in 72, 73, 74; use of "other" in 160
First Evil 184; and Caleb 165, 168, 171, 173, 174; goals 167; need for others 165, 168
Forgiveness 44; *see also* Redemption
Forster, E. M. 182
Forster, Greg 139
Fray 1, 2, 10
Fray, Melaka (Mel) 50, 54, 55, 185; hero's journey 57–64; origin of name 57; *see also* Twins
Frye, Kaylee *see* Kaylee Frye

Gaiman, Neil 3, 9
Ganges River 150
Garfield, Ken 102
Geisha 72
Genesis 30, 77
Giles, Rupert 17, 23, 31, 34, 139
Gilgamesh 144
Glass, Ron 126
Glory (Glorificus) 16, 18, 19
Gnosticism 123, 170, 171, 175, 179; asceticism in 172; and early Christianity 170, 171, 172; and Sophia 172
The Golden Bough 42, 54
Golden Rule 101, 103
Grace 43, 44; *see also* Prodigal Son

Greenwalt, David 86
Gypsies (Rom) 35

Hansel & Gretel (Brothers Grimm) 132, 133
Harris, Xander *see* Xander Harris
Harth 50, 55, 57, 58, 59, 63
Hebrews 101
Helios 14, 55
Hibbs, Thomas 36
Hinduism 150; concept of grace 43, 44
Horace 29
Howe, Sean 51
Hubris 136, 150
Huckleberry Finn 110

Icarus (*Fray*) 59, 61, 62
Inara Serra 101, 104, 107, 108, 109, 110, 111; and Atherton Wing 107, 108; as Companion 71; faith 72; as mother figure 66, 71; and Nandi 110; origin of name 71, 72; relationship with Shepherd Book 121, 128
Inari 72
Irion, Mary Jean 117

Jacob 176
James 90
Jayne Cobb 3, 76, 77, 103, 104, 105, 106, 107, 108, 161; attitude toward women 71; counter stereotype 70; faith 71; as grown brother figure 70; origin of name 70; relationship with Shepherd Book 121, 122, 127; ties to biological family 71
Jerusalem Council 145
Jesus Christ 19, 80, 145; associating with outcasts 79, 161, 162; baptism of 80, 150; doubt 128; equality between genders 176; on faith 129; as spiritual master 8; tolerance 180; use of parables 79, 169
Joan of Arc (Jeanne d'Arc) 155, 156, 157, 160
Job 87
John 96, 161
1 John 111
Jonah 58, 91, 92, 93
Jong, Erica 158
Joyce Summers 13, 38
Judaism: belief in afterlife 41; charges of witchcraft 155, 156; consumption of blood forbidden 30; Holocaust 156; misogyny in ancient Judaism 175, 176; pigs as unclean animals 138; as roots of Christianity 145, 175; Yom Kippur 90, 91

Kaylee Frye 74, 78, 103, 104, 111, 122, 159, 160; faith 76; as little sister figure 75; as mechanic 75, 76; origin of name 75; relationship with Shepherd Book 121
Key 16, 17, 18, 26; *see also* Dawn Summers
Kierkegaard, Søren 174
King, Stephen 34

Kramer, Heinrich 153
Kyteler, Dame Alice 154, 159

Leah 176, 184
Lee, Harper 113, 117
Lessing, Gotthold 51
Leviticus 30
Lewis, C. S. 44, 90
Lichtenstein, Roy 51
Loo 59, 61, 63
Lord's Prayer, The (Our Father) 80
Love 111, 112, 113, 116, 117, 118
Lovecraft, H. P. 86
Lucas, George 57

Maasai 30
Maclay, Tara *see* Tara Maclay
Madonna 6
Malcolm Reynolds 10, 70, 73, 76, 98, 109, 114, 122; counter stereotype 67; faith 68, 98, 100; as father figure 65; as foil 113; inner conflict 104; isolation 109, 110; as leader 100; loyalty 106; moral code 105, 107, 108, 162; need for crew 112; as older brother figure 68; origin of name 67, 99, 104; personal responsibility 106, 111; "rabbit's foot faith" 101, 117; rejection of belief 114, 115, 117, 118; rejection of faith 101, 102, 103, 162; relationship with River 155, 160, 161; relationship with Shepherd Book 115, 116, 121, 124, 125, 126, 127, 128, 130; use of violence 103, 104; views on slavery 107, 108
Malleus Maleficarum 153, 154, 158
Manichaeism 123, 171
Maricon of Sinope 171
Mascetti, Manuela Dunn 29
Master 28
Matthew 99, 106
Mayor Richard Wilkins 134, 136, 137, 138, 165
McGinley, Phyllis 99
McGuffin 16, 20
McGuire, Anne 170, 171
McWilliams, Peter 161
Merton, Thomas 97, 116
Mickey Mouse 52
Misogyny 172, 180, 183; in ancient Greece 175; in ancient Judaism 175, 176; in ancient Rome 175; in Christianity 171, 175, 178; in modern culture 181, 184; price paid by men 182; represented by body modification 180, 181, 184; *see also* Caleb; Whedon, Joss
Money, Mary Alice 135, 140
Moses 89, 128
Mother Teresa 23, 24
Moyers, Bill 57
Munch, Edvard 29
Mythological figures: Actaeon 15; Anubis 40; Apollo 55, 56; Artemis 15, 55; Athena 62; Atlas 106; Aurora 15; Castor/Pollux 54, 55,

56; Edem 170; Eos 14, 15; Gilgamesh 144; Helios 14, 55; Odin 15; Pandora 102, 116; Prometheus 62; Romulus/Remus 54; Selene 14; Sophia 172; Tithonus 14; Zeus 130, 184

Nahum 92, 93
Names in Whedon's work 7; *see also* individual names
Narcissus 42
Negative space 27, 34, 46
Neil, William 140–141
Neo-Confucianism 21
Neuwirth, Jessica 188
Niemöller, Martin 93, 94
Nietzsche, Friedrich 135, 138, 142
The Night of the Hunter 165
Noah 99, 144
Nosferatu 29

Odin 15
Odyssey 22
O'Keefe, Georgia 4
Operative 108, 112, 113, 114, 116, 117, 118, 124, 127, 130, 159

Panati, Charles 40
Pandora 102, 116
The Passion of the Christ 7
Pateman, Matthew 5
Peer Gynt 45
Pelagius 145
Plato 41, 51, 139
The Powers That Be 87, 89, 92
Pratchett, Terry 161
Preacher 6, 7, 165
Prodigal Son: Buddhist version 144, 145; Christian version 132, 134, 138, 142, 143, 144, 145; Faith as prodigal 137, 138, 139, 140, 141, 142, 143, 144, 145
Prometheus 62
Prophecy 14, 44, 56, 60, 89, 137
Proverbs 40
Pryde, Kitty 50

Rachel 176, 184
Rambo, Elizabeth 24
Reiss, Jana 38, 45
Reynolds, Malcolm *see* Malcolm Reynolds
Rice, Anne 34
"Righteous gentiles" 94
Riley Finn 7, 13
River Jordan 150
River Tam 10, 66, 68, 74, 79, 99, 105, 106, 107, 113, 114, 115, 116, 118, 127, 163; cementing ship's family 70, 161; counter stereotype 69, 149, 150; faith 70, 125; as little sister figure 70; Maidenhead 15; origin of name 150; as "other" 151; past history with Alliance 69; and Patron 154, 155, 157, 160, 161; as psychic 151, 155, 160; relationship with Mal 150, 160, 161; relationship with Shepherd Book 123; relationship with Simon 160, 161; as weapon 159; as witch 152, 154
Robbins, Russell 152, 157
Robertson, Pat 182
Romans 178
Rosenberg, Willow *see* Willow Rosenberg
Rupert Giles *see* Giles

Sabin, Roger 52, 53
Sadism 43
Saffron 71, 78, 108, 109
St. Augustine 123, 145, 171
St. Ignatius of Loyola 123
St. Jerome 8
St. John the Divine 88
St. Patrick 126, 130
St. Paul: contradictions in writings 177, 178; conversion experience 20, 177; and Thecla 178, 179; writings 21, 23, 177, 178
St. Stephen 177
St. Teresa of Avila 165
St. Thomas Becket 123, 127
Sarah 176
Schudt, Karl 142
Scooby Gang (Scoobies) 14, 15, 25, 38
Scourge 88, 95, 96
Scythe 61, 62, 183, 184
Second Council of Nicea 5
Selene 14
Serenity 1, 188; see also *Firefly*
Serenity Valley 99, 102, 107, 109, 118
Serra, Inara *see* Inara Serra
Shakespeare, William 18, 53
Shaw, George Bernard 157
Sheen, Bishop John Fulton 102
Shenkman, Richard 92
Shepherd Book 10, 66, 76, 78, 101, 104, 108, 109, 114, 117; effect of death 127; faith 124; joining ship 121; leaving ship 115, 129; origin of name 121; past history 77, 122, 124; as preacher 76, 120; as spiritual leader 125; redemption 124, 125, 126; relationship with crew 121, 125, 127, 128, 130, 131; self-doubt 77, 119, 127, 128, 130; Shan Yu 122
Simon Tam 66, 65, 74, 79, 102, 103, 104, 105, 107, 110, 114; attitude toward Alliance 75; birthday cake 78; as doctor 74; faith 75; as geeky brother 74; origin of name 75; relationship with River 160, 161; relationship with Shepherd Book 121
Sin 113, 114, 117, 173, 182
Slayage 7, 185
Slayer 58, 59, 60, 168, 172, 184; *see also* Buffy Summers; Faith
Socrates 142
Soul 27, 40, 46, 172; dualist versus reductionist view 41; as moral compass 28; *see also* Angel; Spike

Spee, Friedrich von 158, 159
Spiegelman, Art (*Maus*) 51, 53
Spike 3, 9, 17, 22, 45, 184; binary with Angel 27; blood drinking 30; Cecily 31, 37, 39; Dana 44; emotional hurt 37; history 30, 31, 36; as negative space 35; origin of name 30, 31; regain soul 39, 40; relationship with Buffy 38, 39; relationship with Drusilla 37
Sprenger, Jakob 153
Stearns, Lee 188
Stevenson, Robert Louis 32
Stoker, Bram 27, 28, 29, 30, 33, 34
Summers, Buffy *see* Buffy Summers
Summers, Dawn *see* Dawn Summers; Key
Summers, Joyce *see* Joyce Summers
Superman 52

Tam, River *see* River Tam
Tam, Simon *see* Simon Tam
Tao 150
Tara Maclay 14, 22
Thackeray, William Makepeace 113
Thecla 178, 179
Tillich, Paul 116
1 Timothy 178
Tithonus 14
Tompkins, Stephen 144, 145
Torres, Gina 73
Twins 49; apprehension toward 49; Castor and Pollux (Gemini) 54, 55, 56; compared with doppelgangers 50; fraternal 55; identical 49, 55; identity issues 56; Josef Mengele experiments 49; Romulus and Remus 54; supernatural powers attributed to 54; viewed in society 54, 55

Urkonn 11, 58, 59, 61, 63

Valentinus 171
Vampires 4, 28, 29; reflections 42; as types of demons 34; *see also* Angel; Buffy; Spike
Veronese, Paolo 5, 6, 8

Wash 73, 77, 79, 117, 118, 122, 126, 155; as brother figure 68; faith 69; origin of name 68; as pilot 68
Washburne, Hoban *see* Wash
Washburne, Zoe *see* Zoe Washburne
Watcher (Watchers Council) 58, 168, 184
Wesley Wyndham-Pryce 139, 141, 143
Whedon, Joss: acceptance of others as theme 2, 128, 162, 187, 188; as atheist 2, 4, 8, 102, 119, 145, 167, 171, 174; attached to *Wonder Woman* 52; on *Buffy the Vampire Slayer* 134, 164, 171, 184; on Caleb 167, 171, 174, 175, 177, 178, 181, 183; as comics fan 50, 53; continuing struggle 180; contrasts in characters 108, 109, 110, 119; created family 65, 70, 78, 145; dangers of zealotry 114, 149, 161, 169; as existentialist 180; on faith 102, 106, 116, 129, 139; on Faith 132; family ties 63, 79, 81, 149; feminism 158, 168, 178; First 168; importance of character names 7, 58, 133, 167; on Mal 98, 104; on Mal/Book relationship 121; misogyny 172, 175, 182, 183, 187, 188; on mix of cultures in *Firefly/Serenity* 120, 123; mother as influence 188; name change 8; on relationships 86, 145; religious characters 118; representation of "other" in *Firefly* 160; role of action in redemption 90, 97, 128, 130, 140, 144, 173, 189; role of belief in work 2, 187, 188; role of choice in work 2, 18, 26, 43, 44, 94, 96, 105, 127, 134, 145, 169, 187, 188, 189; role of doubt 129, 130; role of independent thought 117; role of purpose in work 26; role of redemption in work 38, 124; on Shepherd Book 119, 120; as source for course material 186, 187; themes in *Serenity* 113; upset audience expectations 13, 19, 67, 68, 74, 77; use of Christian imagery 33, 34, 186; use of power 159; view of forgiveness 85, 142; views on love 112; youth in popular culture 181
Whistler 36
Wilcox, Rhonda 136, 186
Wilkins, Richard *see* Mayor
Willow Rosenberg 22, 184; as vampire 41, 50
Wilson, Diane 186
Windling, Terri 3
Witch (Witchcraft) 152, 153; charges as means of control 158, 159; Christianity and 152, 153; and Jews 155, 156; *see also* River Tam
Wolfe, Thomas 145
Wonder Woman 52
Wright, Lawrence 54, 56
Wyndham-Pryce, Wesley *see* Wesley Wyndham-Pryce

Xander Harris 15, 23, 25, 174, 183

Zen 130, 184
Zeus 62
Zilpah 176
Zoe Washburne 67, 68, 73, 74, 79, 99, 102, 105, 109, 114; as big sister figure 73; counter to stereotype 73; faith 73; grounding force for Wash 69; origin of name 73; relationship with Shepherd Book 122; warrior qualities 69

www.ingramcontent.com/pod-product-compliance
Ingram Content Group UK Ltd.
Pitfield, Milton Keynes, MK11 3LW, UK
UKHW041944140426
5217IPUK00014B/640